ROTH FAMILY FOUNDATION

*Imprint in Music*

Michael P. Roth
and Sukey Garcetti
have endowed this
imprint to honor the
memory of their parents,
Julia and Harry Roth,
whose deep love of music
they wish to share
with others.

The publisher and the University of California Press Foundation gratefully acknowledge the generous support of the Roth Family Foundation Imprint in Music, established by a major gift from Sukey and Gil Garcetti and Michael P. Roth.

# The Folk

# The Folk

*Music, Modernity, and the Political Imagination*

Ross Cole

UNIVERSITY OF CALIFORNIA PRESS

University of California Press
Oakland, California



Library of Congress Cataloging-in-Publication Data

Names: Cole, Ross, author.
Title: The folk : music, modernity, and the political imagination / Ross Cole.
Description: Oakland, California : University of California Press, [2021] | Includes bibliographical references and index.
Identifiers: LCCN 2021005203 (print) | LCCN 2021005204 (ebook) | ISBN 9780520383739 (cloth) | ISBN 9780520383746 (paperback) | ISBN 9780520383753 (epub)
Subjects: LCSH: Folk Music—Political aspects—History—19th century. | Folk Music—Political aspects—History—20th century. | Folk songs—Political aspects—History—19th century. | Folk songs—Political aspects—History—20th century.
Classification: LCC ML3918.F65 C65 2021 (print) | LCC ML3918.F65 (ebook) | DDC 306.4/8422—dc23
LC record available at https://lccn.loc.gov/2021005203
LC ebook record available at https://lccn.loc.gov/2021005204

Manufactured in the United States of America

30 29 28 27 26 25 24 23 22 21
10 9 8 7 6 5 4 3 2 1

*To my family, past and future*

Your reason and your passion are the rudder and the sails of your seafaring soul.

—KAHLIL GIBRAN, *The Prophet*

# Contents

# Illustrations

# Preface

Henry David Thoreau once complained that books "are for the most part willfully and hastily written, as parts of a system, to supply a want real or imagined."[1] Reader, let me confess. The book you are holding was written in large part during the relative tranquility of summer 2019. Like the majority of first books produced within the academy, it grew out of an overwrought PhD thesis, though little remains now of its shoots and young branches, which have since provided kindling for new ideas. Although bound up with academia, this book seeks to be more than a reply to its cheerless metrics. I hope that it answers some other and more vital need—something that Thoreau both aspired to and struggled with, noting in his journal in October 1853 that meager sales of *A Week on the Concord and Merrimack Rivers* had left him with "a library of nearly nine hundred volumes, over seven hundred of which I wrote myself."[2] For the sake of my shelves, here's hoping I'm spared the same fate.

This book has taken shape against the backdrop of a succession of global upheavals, from Brexit and the renaissance of demagoguery to Extinction Rebellion, Black Lives Matter protests, and (as I type these words) a devastating pandemic. Amid the existential crisis of coronavirus, a book dealing with the poetics of nostalgia has in turn become an object of nostalgia, the relic of a normality ostensibly beyond reach. But if we've learned anything from the recent movements for decolonization, it is that such complacency has all along harbored an uncomfortable inequity drawn along racial lines. This book is an archaeology of such inequities and the ways in which we have invested in ideals of ethnic belonging translated into cultural practice. Above all, it advocates that we should endeavor to hold these ideals lightly. One of its central themes, brought to the fore in the final chapters, is that the act of folkloric remembering offers a powerful tool that can serve the cause of liberation from racialized tyranny just as easily as it can serve as a means to further inscribe such tyranny. The folk, in other words, have bequeathed to us a double-edged sword. We might think of W. E. B. Du Bois's masterful *The Souls of Black Folk* and the fascist politics of *Volksgemeinschaft* as symbols of these polarized extremes.

My aim here is neither to offer an elegiac account of a forgotten world nor to mount an attack on the fallacies of folklore as an emergent discipline. Rather, I wish to trace how and why the folk have been central to our cultural memory in the West. In order to throw light on these questions, the book is limited in time and place, focusing on Britain and the United States between 1870 and 1930, though touching on related eras and nations at points throughout. Dwelling on the age of high imperialism in the wake of Emancipation and the British agricultural depression, it unearths a latent and long-standing critique of globalized modernity—a critique that could, as Du Bois so eloquently demonstrated alongside figures such as William Morris, be recast as a positive force for change. For many sympathizers, this critique rested on the idea that something delicate, deep, and profoundly human was at risk of being destroyed or overlooked by the unrivalled pandemonium of industrial progress. Thoreau anticipated this attitude in his thoughts on Native American culture, suffused, as he saw it, with a wisdom far more subtle and elemental than that of its supposedly civilizing usurpers. For Thoreau, the "steady illumination" of their culture, "dim only because distant, is like the faint but satisfying light of the stars compared with the dazzling but ineffectual and short-lived blaze of candles."[3] In what I shall call the "folkloric imagination," this is the paradigmatic trope: the folk as distant, waning, but eternal, and the modern world as overbearing, insubstantial, and fake. Synonymous with Nature, the folk serve to indicate just how far we have gone astray, seduced by the siren calls of innovation. They are a beacon guiding us home—or, better still, a constellation helping us to navigate a true path through the outer darkness. As Thoreau put it in reference to the fictional Scottish bard Ossian, "behold how [London and Boston] are refreshed by the mere tradition, or the imperfectly transmitted fragrance and flavor of these wild fruits."[4] Whether stars or wild berries, the folk personify something ancient and venerable, a foil to present disarray.

Many wonderful people have contributed to the making of this book, more than I can mention here. Raina Polivka has supported my ideas from the very beginning and offered words of encouragement and wisdom at every step; I simply could not have found a better editor. My deepest thanks also go to Madison Wetzell, Gary J. Hamel, and the two reviewers. My academic mentors, chief among them Nicholas Cook, have been unfailingly selfless in sharing their time and thoughts with me (Nick, indeed, over the past decade). Philip Bohlman was kind enough to examine my thesis back in 2015 and has continued to offer his support. Cambridge has been my home as a young scholar, and I owe an immense debt to colleagues across the University as well as to friends who've left to pursue lives elsewhere. Thanks in particular to the Duck End set, naturally. I have been fortunate enough to be the member of two college communities, King's and Homerton, the latter as a Research Fellow. This fellowship gifted me the time and freedom to write this book; my thanks go to Geoff Ward and the college as a whole for electing me. Some parts of this book first appeared in the journals *Ethnomusicology* and *19th-Century Music*, benefitting from the editorial guidance of Lawrence Kramer and Ellen Koskoff, among others. Beyond this, I've profited enormously from exchanges with Peter Asimov, Vic Gammon, Oskar Cox Jensen, George Lewis, Matthew Pritchard, Friedlind Riedel, Griff Rollefson, and Chris Townsend. Finally, a special thank you to Malcolm Barr-Hamilton at the Vaughan Williams Memorial Library for permission to reproduce a number of Cecil Sharp's photographs. I hardly know how to go about thanking my family—my parents and Grandma for their treasured affection and abiding curiosity, Richard, Liss, and the Khabbazbashis likewise, and most especially Nahal, for all her love and kindness. I'm sad not to have been able to share this project with Alan, Doris, George, and Frieda, but their memory lives on with me every day.

There is no more fitting way to introduce *The Folk* than by quoting Hannah Arendt, writing in the summer of 1950 exactly seventy years before this Preface:

> We can no longer afford to take that which was good in the past and simply call it our heritage, to discard the bad and simply think of it as a dead load which by itself time will bury in oblivion. The subterranean stream of Western history has finally come to the surface and usurped the dignity of our tradition. This is the reality in which we live. And this is why all efforts to

> escape from the grimness of the present into nostalgia for a still intact past, or into the anticipated oblivion of a better future, are vain.[5]

But with one crucial proviso: hope. It is hope, surely, that affords us a precious third way between what Arendt calls "reckless optimism" and "reckless despair."[6] Now more than ever, it is to reasoned hope that we might turn, together.

*Hitchin, Summer 2020*

# Introduction

## *Lost Voices*

Sylvan historian, who canst thus express
A flowery tale more sweetly than our rhyme:
What leaf-fring'd legend haunts about thy shape
Of deities or mortals, or of both,
In Tempe or the dales of Arcady?
What men or gods are these? What maidens loth?
What mad pursuit? What struggle to escape?
What pipes and timbrels? What wild ecstasy?[1]

A copy of the 1963 album *The Freewheelin' Bob Dylan* spins on a turntable. Toward the end of side one, after a short pause, we hear his impish introduction to a track spoken over strummed guitar: "Unlike most of the songs nowadays being written uptown in Tin Pan Alley, that's where most of the folk songs come from nowadays, this is a song, this wasn't written up there, this was written somewhere down in the United States." It was written by a young Dylan, native of Minnesota, in the guise of Woody Guthrie—but it could pass as any relic of the American past, a Lomax-style field recording of an ageless songster drifting through southern sands. As we've since come to expect from Dylan, the message is never straightforward. A lesser songsmith might have prefaced the track with a simple claim on folkloric authenticity ("this is a *real* song, not like one by those Tin Pan Alley *hacks*"), but Dylan's off-the-cuff framing paints Tin Pan Alley—that vilified producer of industrial trash—as a cradle of folk music.[2] On account of his diction, we hear not only "folk song" but also "folks' songs"—that is, songs of the people, popular songs. So, what is the distinction being made, then? It is a claim about authorship: whereas most modern popular music is written by professional songwriters hammering away on weary pianos striving for lucrative reward, *real* songs emerge organically from some nameless *elsewhere*, growing amid the soil of those United States, a product of labor and hinterlands, wild life and community. This is the folkloric polarity Dylan draws even as he applies the term to a paradigm of mass culture: individual vs. commune, untutored artistry vs. commerce, experience vs. cheap imitation, center vs. margins, the present vs. the past.

For Dylan, those Tin Pan Alley songwriters housed like industrious livestock in stalls at the Brill Building "had it down to a science": "the world they knew and the world I knew were totally different."[3] A few subway stops downtown, through Times Square past Bryant Park and the Empire State Building, would take you to 110 MacDougal Street in Greenwich Village and the "citadel of Americana folk music," a focal point of Dylan's world—the Folklore Center owned by Izzy Young.[4] This music "glittered like a mound of gold," testament to a rich and untapped seam running through the nation's bedrock, linking Young's shoe-box-sized chapel and its arcane contents with the people and their history, their inheritance and true worth:

> There were a lot of esoteric folk records, too, all records I wanted to listen to. Extinct song folios of every type—sea shanties, Civil War songs, cowboy songs, songs of lament, church house songs, anti-Jim Crow songs, union songs—archaic books of folk tales, Wobbly journals, propaganda pamphlets about everything from women's rights to the dangers of boozing. . . . A few instruments for sale, dulcimers, five-string banjos, kazoos, pennywhistles, acoustic guitars, mandolins. . . . I listened to as many [records] as I could, even thumbed through a lot of his antediluvian folk scrolls. The madly complicated modern world was something I took little interest in. It had no relevancy, no weight. I wasn't seduced by it.[5]

Song, he implies, is not some kind of industrial science—it's a living art eternally at risk of being lost, killed off by the high tides of modernity. Most of it is already extinct, antediluvian, Edenic. The instruments are acoustic and vernacular; the politics are radical, egalitarian, and opposed to the status quo; the subjects are rugged outlaws, wars, tragedies, hard manual labor, solidarity, loss, religion, and the untamed frontier. Whenever the modern world seems unbearably light, folk music brings us back down to earth, its weight a salvation to those averse to being buoyed up by the madness of time. Seduced by these talismanic folios and traces of the archaic, Dylan was following in the footsteps of an older generation of poets—Romantics and visionaries with minds beguiled by minstrels, peasants, and wandering bards.[6]

~

Poland, 1949. Three figures in a van, in the snow. They carry a microphone and portable tape recorders.[7] We watch them watching others, listening intently as they perform—in the rain, a humble dwelling, a dance, in the cold, on rough-and-ready instruments. These musicians are poor, remnants of a rural way of life that seems of a different century entirely, paradigms of what an enthusiastic Czech musicologist from Milan Kundera's novel *The Joke* describes as "a tunnel beneath history, a tunnel that preserves much of what wars, revolutions, civilizations have long since destroyed aboveground."[8] The three figures listen to a recording in the van. The driver speaks: "You're not afraid it's too crude, too primitive?" The woman answers him, curt but polite, "No, why?" "Where I come from every drunk sings like this." They are looking for folk music in Paweł Pawlikowski's film *Cold War*.

This trio is not just on the hunt for recordings, however; they are collecting people. The camera follows two military transport vehicles heaving with young passengers as they pull up in front of a derelict mansion overrun with livestock. This stately home becomes their new abode—"a world of music, song, and dance," as the driver, now revealed as a figure of authority, puts it. The two fieldworkers look on from a distance, smoking, their mutual reticence palpable as his soapbox address continues. Only the best performers among them will "step onto our nation's stages, and the stages of our brotherly nations" as part of a "fierce and noble struggle"—the struggle for Sovietized communism led by the recently formed *Polska Zjednoczona Partia Robotnicza*, the Polish United Workers' Party.[9] A banner declaring "WE WELCOME TOMORROW" falls down like a slapstick gag while being hung up over the entrance. The film cuts to an inner hallway lined with performers awaiting an audition: "Do we have to be able to read music?" asks a blonde-haired girl, who later emerges as the film's protagonist. The figure to her right shakes his head: no, "they want it peasant-style." This overcrowded mansion is proof, at last, that the peasantry have usurped the aristocracy, even if they're merely playing a part—a ruse involving identical costumes, choreography, arrangement, artifice, and strict discipline. They are performing the state's sanitized vision of the past as a conduit for the future, smiling socialist realism as a tool in the realization of socialism.[10]

As another character from Kundera's novel puts it, what was required under communism was to "purge the everyday musical culture of hit-tune clichés" and "replace them with an original and genuine art of the people"—a national art that would overturn the damage done by capitalism and urban isolation to create a new social collectivity "united by a common interest."[11] It was as if, in the words of his musicologist friend, such figures had "made a secret pact with the future and had thereby acquired the right to act in its name."[12] In Pawlikowski's *Cold War* we find folk song dressed up as Soviet propaganda, orchestrated by experts who watch from the wings to ensure conformity. The ensemble's directors are summoned to official meetings and encouraged to use their platform to educate and embolden the masses—becoming "a living calling card for our Fatherland" that sings about land reform and world peace, incorporating into their repertoire "a strong number about the Leader of the World Proletariat." Soon, an enormous image of Stalin unfurls behind this peasant choir on stage, Orwellian eyes staring out into the audience. The ensemble begins to look more and more like a trained division of the army; the stately home is restored to its former glory; a tour schedule is arranged; and a girl named Janicka is singled out for looking "too dark," failing to resemble the mandatory "folk appearance . . . a pure Polish, Slav look." With events so close in living memory, it is a comment that cuts to the heart of the film's unspoken message: the folk are symptoms of the kind of thinking that underpinned the political terrors of the twentieth century, pawns in a prolonged cold war of ideas stretching back into the Enlightenment.

These two vignettes represent strangely intertwined extremes: folk song as outsider antipathy to the modern world of capitalist industry and political injustice, untutored and with its face turned toward the past like Walter Benjamin's angel of history; folk song as ideological machinery used to envision a new kind of future totalitarian modernity that excludes "impure" ethnic minorities. How can one seemingly coherent concept yield such contradictory outcomes? And why is there still so much common ground between them, both desirous (like Benjamin's angel) of awakening the dead and attempting to "make whole what has been smashed" in the storm of progress?[13] Why are "the folk" themselves similarly absent from Dylan's Greenwich Village underground and Cold War nation-state propaganda?

This book traces such ideas and quandaries back to a pivotal moment when, just as they appeared to be on the verge of disappearing, the folk resurfaced on both sides of the Atlantic as a key indicator of modernity's changing pace—potential saviors, indexes of longing, ciphers of belonging. Although my focus throughout is on England, I follow Paul Gilroy in opposing nationalist or ethnically absolutist approaches to folk material by taking the Atlantic "as one single, complex unit of analysis" in order, as he writes, to produce "an explicitly transnational and intercultural perspective."[14] The tours of the Fisk Jubilee Singers—a pioneering African American vocal ensemble that received international acclaim—are only the most obvious example of what Gilroy refers to as "fractal patterns of cultural and political exchange and transformation."[15] Other instances in this book include cultures and technologies of collecting (Edison's phonograph revolutionizing the capture of sound across oceans), inquiry into non-Western musical practices, the history of the ballad (an enthusiasm shared by British and American scholars alike from Lucy Broadwood to Louise Pound), utopian dreams detailed by novelists such as Edward Bellamy and William Morris, legacies of race thinking and Atlantic slavery, literary modernism, early jazz, Cecil J. Sharp's activities in Somerset and the Appalachian Mountains, and finally the online sphere in its manifestly globalized form.

Woven throughout the chapters that follow is one central claim: that folk music is a lot like shot silk. If you hold this fabric up to the light, its folds reveal a variety of colors depending on the angle and individual point of view. Much like the contrasting warp and weft of *changeant* fabric, folk music has several different and frequently antagonistic threads running through its history—utopianism, fascism, nostalgia, and revolutionary socialism, to name only a few. Unite these discursive strands into a textile and it begins to take on an iridescent appearance, at times impossible to resist. I began this introduction with a fragment of Keats's urn: folk music is another such "sylvan historian," believed to be made by some anonymous figures of the deep past. Somehow it expresses Arcadian truths, leaf-fring'd legends, and florid tales more sweetly than a cultivated art form, its verses infused with all manner of imperfect mortals and strange, otherworldly figures, sounds of forgotten pipes and timbrels, lovers and heroes, wild ecstasies of the imagination. Whereas the Grecian urn, that "foster-child of silence and slow time," is voiceless, however, folk music sings—and yet in singing retains all of its mystery and mute allure.

But such allure has not always been felt by all. Indeed, the central problem facing scholars of folk music has been how to take its appeal seriously while (as good historians and deconstructive critics) revealing its boundless fallacies and fault lines. Charles Keil trailblazed this path in 1978 with a blunt, three-page article in the *Journal of the Folklore Institute* entitled "Who Needs 'The Folk'?" Polemical and ironic, Keil essentially called for an end to this entire field of inquiry:

> Long study of folklore and folklorists has convinced me that there never were any "folk," except in the minds of the bourgeoisie. The entire field is a grim fairy tale. By an act of magical naming, all the peasantries and

> technologically primitive peoples of the world can be turned into "folk." . . . As always, the pros do it better. Sixteen or sixty-four tightly rehearsed whirling couples in matching costumes are certainly a lot more impressive than a bunch of shit-kicking villagers wearing whatever it is that villagers actually wear these days. . . . Unlike "primitive," "folk" has only a positive, friendly meaning. The folk are not the oppressed whose revolution is long overdue, but the Quaint-not-quite-like-us, the Pleasant peasants, the Almost-like-me-and-you, to be consumed at leisure.[16]

Distinctions such as "high art" versus "folk art," he argues, represent "a dialectic that is almost completely contained within bourgeois ideology" itself—one term requiring the other for mutual definition.[17] The folk, in other words, are an invention of the rising middle classes: their "low other," a foil to set against the modern, a token of national character, a well of creative inspiration, a tame pastoral commodity.[18] This argument was later developed into a full-blown Marxist critique of mediation and class expropriation by the British author Dave Harker in his 1985 book *Fakesong: The Manufacture of British "Folksong," 1700 to the Present Day*.[19]

What such a position aimed for was nothing less than to dismantle the folk in favor of a more radical history from below. For Harker, concepts such as "folk song" and "ballad" are "intellectual rubble" blocking the path of a truly materialist account of working-class experience, too compromised for rehabilitation as useful sources, too much the product of "cultural imperialism."[20] Georgina Boyes likewise affirmed that folk song is best seen as an invented tradition sustained by revivalists who enact a "cultural transfer," replacing the folk with performative proxies.[21] Writers arguing from this perspective emphasize, in short, that folk music is yet another example of what the historian E. P. Thompson once described as "the enormous condescension of posterity" (a claim I explore in chapter 2).[22] Although *The Folk* is indebted to such work and the New Left context from which it emerged, it nevertheless seeks to move beyond the well-trodden paths of revivalism and working-class history. I am less interested in attempting to sift the pure from the polluted (as books on folk song often do, even as they mount a critique of this gesture), than in the dynamic affordances of the folk at a crucial moment when the tectonic plates of a global political landscape began shifting into strange new formations. Previous scholars have, to a large extent, either misread or overlooked the politics of folk song during this era, describing it as "a bizarre mixture of radical and reactionary elements" or "an ideological tossed salad."[23] What I demonstrate here is that in spite of this heterogeneous mix, folk's politics are in fact perfectly consonant with what we might call an anti-Enlightenment tradition that finds expression in a tribal, organic vision of identity transcending existing states and nations.[24] "Radical" and "reactionary" in this tradition are not antithetical, but merely two sides of the same coin—signs of what Philip Bohlman characterizes as "a European metaphysics of authenticity" bound up with a distinctive form of pan-nationalism traceable to the work of Johann Gottfried Herder.[25]

It was Herder, of course, who had introduced the term *Volkslied* into German historiography during the 1770s as a way to name salvaged and anthologized songs that ostensibly gave voice to the nation, a collective entity defined by language and origin rooted in the instinctual creativity of a bardic past.[26] Despite Herder's work not being well known in Britain before the early nineteenth century and playing only a relatively minor role in Anglophone conceptions of the folk, British scholars reached strikingly similar conclusions.[27] The English term *folk-lore* first appeared in print in the pages of the London-based journal the *Athenaeum* in late August 1846. Writing under the pseudonym Ambrose Merton, the antiquary William Thoms suggested that what had previously been called "Popular Antiquities" or "Popular Literature" was more "aptly described by a good Saxon compound, Folk-Lore,—*the Lore of the People*."[28] Thoms was self-conscious of having been the first to advance this particular epithet in English, citing Jacob Grimm's *Deutsche Mythologie* (1835) as an inspiration for the preservation of vernacular literature and custom. In 1878 a Folk-Lore Society was set up in London, followed some twenty years later by a dedicated Folk-Song Society—both founded in response to what was perceived as the deleterious effect of the railways, Britain's industrialization, and the advent of mass consumerism.[29]

The term *folk-song*, however, had preceded Thoms's article by some years, appearing in print in 1843 in passing reference to the *Lai*, a medieval French poetic form.[30] Such a casual reference suggests that the term (or at least the concept) was in fairly wide circulation among an educated elite by the 1840s.[31] Although not a major concern of early folklorists, folk music had become a commonplace category by the 1870s, used to describe songs that were felt to be "the 'wild stock' whence the epic and the artistic lyric sprang" and "a vast storehouse of historical evidence of the manners and customs . . . of bygone times."[32] The central period that I focus on in this book stretches roughly from the 1890s to the 1910s—from the activities of the Folk-Song Society and the utopian thought of William Morris to the seminal work of Cecil Sharp and W. E. B. Du Bois. I nevertheless reach back to the theories of Karl Marx and John Ruskin and on to the ideology of the Third Reich (a theme extended up to the present day in the coda). As Stuart Hall points out, this span of time is vital to an understanding of the complex and mercurial nature of the popular.[33] It is an era that wrestled with its own modernity—in the process establishing a powerful and resilient dichotomy between primitive and modern essential to our idea of the folk.

~

In spite of its facetiousness, Keil's short article hints at a number of important points that I want to spend the remainder of this introduction exploring, before finally broaching the thorny issue of modernity. First, that the folk are essentially an artifact of the imagination and are thus notable only by their absence. Indeed, belief in the folk shares much in common with what the distinguished scholar of ancient literature Geza Vermes describes as "man's hopeful and creative religious imagination."[34] Such acts of ingenuity should not be dismissed outright, but read as signs: what might they tell us about those doing the imagining? What ideas did the folk afford at particular historical moments? What new revivalist communities did they help to bring into being?[35] Second, that the existence of the folk stems from "an act of magical naming." And third, that the discourse of folklore was formulated under the influence of colonialist epistemology. Whereas the first of these ideas is familiar within the literature on folk music, the second and third deserve more attention.

The notion of an "act of magical naming" suggests that something's identity subsists in relation to its being named as such, that there exists a circularity between the act of naming something and how we understand it. Slavoj Žižek calls this the "radical contingency of naming."[36] We might ask, however, what it is that links a name to something even when all of its features may have changed. For Žižek, such continuity is predicated on the enigmatic presence of a surplus "something in it more than itself"—the imaginary and unattainable object-cause of desire that we seek in the other.[37] In more simple terms, what he's suggesting is that when a thing is named, its identity is held together by some kind of desire or seductive enjoyment. Applied to the word *folk*, his theory is illuminating. Rather than having any true descriptive currency for music or culture more broadly, it is precisely through an act of magical naming that the term acquires its meaning—a meaning constituted by a nostalgic longing for the unattainable in a (lost) folk other. The term *folk* has a stable meaning in relation to music and song not because it describes historical reality, but because it has been used historically to gather a variety of things together under one simple heading that afford desire or enjoyment beyond the immediate pleasures of melody and harmony: kinship, nature, time, alterity, patrimony, tradition, resistance, nationality, nostalgia. To give an example: Izzy Young's esoteric records, song folios, pamphlets, tales, dulcimers, and mandolins that Bob Dylan encountered in Greenwich Village were united by one word that rendered them all meaningful: *folk*. It is the same word that yokes together the disparate rural performances we see in *Cold War*, giving them substance within the framework of state and nation. Without this concept, these fragments of the past would be just that—mere ruins and remnants.

A simple thought experiment can help to clarify the appeal that tends to lie in this "something in it more than itself." Next time you listen to a performance or recording of folk music, stop to ask yourself what it conjures up. What pleasurable surplus is there beyond the sounds themselves? More often than not, you'll find that folk music carries with it a variety of political subtexts and a congregation of veiled allusions striving to be voiced. Some of these allusions are more pleasant than others. As Keil infers, the folk seem to have some untoward connection with the idea of the primitive—a term freighted with colonialist thinking. European and North American folk others were indeed slotted into a global spectrum of so-called primitives made visible by pseudoscientific theory, the amassing of material culture, and the comparative inclinations of early anthropology. Reflecting the broader value system of colonialism—a worldview determined to uphold a partitioned model of "us" (civilized, modern) versus "them" (primitive, premodern)—the concept of folk song relied on ideals of cultural and racial uniqueness untainted by intrusions of difference. But rather than dwelling on fears of contamination by non-Western alterity, folk song discourse concerns itself above all with aesthetic polarizations of (organic, unsullied) rural music against (contrived, degenerate) urban mass culture, alongside juxtapositions of one nation's "innate" musical character against another. As the contrapuntal perspective adopted by postcolonial theorists has demonstrated, such Manichean thinking is wholly untenable in view of the hybridities arising from globalization and the profoundly porous or interstitial nature of colonial encounter.[38] Likewise, it is impossible to square the emphatic and oft-repeated claims for the unalloyed purity of folk song with a critical genealogy of such material.

One theorist who is particularly helpful in unpacking these convoluted relationships between history, ethnography, and alterity is the French Jesuit scholar Michel de Certeau, whose work has aimed at comprehending the ways in which others have been made to speak from without.[39] For Certeau, the discourses that circumscribe alterity belong inextricably to historians and ethnographers themselves, not the objects of their gaze or praxis.[40] History and anthropology, he suggests, are united by an equivalent "staging of the other in present time."[41] Whereas history confronts and resurrects the dead (as phantasmic other), anthropology orchestrates and aestheticizes the primitive (as exotic other): both approaches force absent bodies to speak through the mediation of written documents, both are "heterologies" or hermeneutics of difference based on knowledge of this unfathomable entity.

All heterologies are unified, he proposes, by the characteristic of "attempting to *write the voice*," which always appears in translation and in the form of a quotation, in view and yet eternally incomplete.[42] Folklore is an archetypal heterology—an attempt, through ethnographic and historiographical writing, to establish knowledge of "the folk." It was in this effort to document the folk, however, that folklorists lost or misread those very customs that motivated their quest. As with prior travel writing on the "savage," Certeau notes, the other "is reciprocally associated with the seduction of speech," a speech that, however ravishing, remains evanescent and impossible to capture save through writing; what remains are mere traces of "irrecoupable, unexploitable moments."[43] Similarly, when nineteenth-century collectors turned their attention to vernacular music via field notes, periodicals, and songbooks, such moments of sonic rapture were inevitably lost—moments that could only be captured later via mechanical sound recording, which failed in turn to record the multitude of ways in which songs were woven into people's everyday lives. What "cannot be uprooted" from such environments, Certeau attests, "remains by definition outside the field of research."[44] The drawback of such methodologies is therefore the very condition of their success. In order to gather, analyze, and classify folk material, it first had to be reified (made into a collectable thing) and extracted from its surrounding ecology, effacing intricate patterns of meaning and memory. Collectors, furthermore, were only ever interested in recovering one facet of singers' repertoires, rearticulating this material in the service of new and unfamiliar aims.

In consequence, I want to suggest that we think of folklorists' work as representing the voice *sous rature*, or "under erasure" (to borrow a term from Jacques Derrida).[45] This can be written as a neat formula: folk culture = ~~vernacular culture~~. In musical terms, this pairing indicates that transcribed songs, field recordings, songbooks, and settings were only ever partial reflections of the culture from which they were taken as representative samples. Much was lost in this process of translation from vernacular into folk—most of all the agency of "the folk" themselves, those singers from whom such material was selected and reclaimed. In this semi-erased form that Certeau calls a "fable," traces of the folk presuppose scholarly exegesis, positioning a specialist (the collector or folklorist) as an interpretive spokesperson for a seemingly unconscious, childlike, or ignorant subject (the singer). The fable, he argues, typifies "speech that 'does not know'": analysis is hence required to bring out its meaning, legitimating the role of scholarly expertise.[46] Folk song, in other words, would not have existed without the discipline of folklore. Certeau characterizes this process as "folklorization"—a purifying operation in which a less powerful milieu is reduced by an external authority to a series of fragments constructed "like a diorama in *trompe l'oeil* perspective."[47] There could be no better way of describing folk culture than this inspired simile, encapsulating as it does the static, staged quality of collected material organized as a cunning trick of the eye to make its miniature recreations appear real. Offering up vistas ripe for the imagination, folklorists were meticulous model makers forever looking down upon a culture frozen in time and two dimensions. Captive to such illusory and distorting situations, the folk in turn offered up a tantalizing vision of that enticing but inscrutable signifier "the people."

With all this in mind, we can begin to nuance Keil's claims. First, it was not simply that the folk only ever existed in the minds of the bourgeoisie, but rather that they appeared via the imagination of those with the power and agency to foreclose, transcribe, and repurpose them. By crafting folk culture from a highly selective and politically charged engagement with the vernacular sphere through technologies of writing, nineteenth-century folklorists brought something to life that had never existed before: folk-song. This newly invented category was one among many similar English-language constructs circulating at the time—from "folk-life" and "folk-lore" to "folk-beliefs," "folk-passions," "folk-traditions," "folk-customs," "folk-sayings," "folk-music," and "folk-poesy."[48] These were all miniature heterologies that relied upon acts of reification and external reclassification indulged in with unconcealed contempt for an emerging mass culture. Second, such objects had consistency not because of any innate quality that we can identify, but rather on account of an act of magical naming that assured their meaning and coherence—a gesture that used the concept of "folk" as a way to bind together disparate practices, signs, and material things with cabalistic ribbons of *jouissance* and desire. Naming, we should remember, is the very signature of authority. Adam names livestock, birds, and wild animals, and in so doing establishes dominion over them, just as empires name territories and parents name children. A name attests to the ascendency of the namer and tells us far more about the capacity *to* name than the identity of what is named. Several years after the foundation of London's Folk-Lore Society, members were still unsure what exactly it was they were supposed to be investigating—G. L. Gomme, for one, pointing out in 1884 that his fellow collectors had not yet "satisfactorily settled the proper meaning of the term 'Folk-lore.'"[49] Similar issues would plague the Folk-Song Society and linger on well into the twentieth century until the International Folk Music Council elected to rename itself the International Council for Traditional Music in 1981.[50]

And finally, when we peel away the positive or friendly veneer of the term, *folk* reveals its kinship with less estimable concepts such as "savage" and "primitive" embedded in colonialist thought and given credence by comparative anthropology. As Johannes Fabian points out in his classic text *Time and the Other*, anthropological discourse "contributed above all to the intellectual justification of the colonial enterprise" by offering up a fantasy of evolutionary unfolding in which "not only past cultures, but all living societies were irrevocably placed on a temporal slope, a stream of Time."[51] It was only through such discourse that folk music could be classified as the product of "primitive" or "premodern" culture. Indeed, folk song was brought into being on the back of four mutually reinforcing concepts that, as Certeau notes, organized the field of anthropological inquiry from its origins in the eighteenth century: *orality* ("communication within a primitive, savage, or traditional society"), *spatiality* ("the synchronic picture of a system" that appears timeless), *alterity* ("the difference which a cultural break puts forward"'), and *unconsciousness* ("the status of collective phenomena, referring to a significance foreign to them").[52] It was precisely this intellectual landscape that offered up the possibility of locating folk tradition as one of the deepest wellsprings of European or even Aryan musical heritage and thus as a potentially restorative force. Just as anthropology observed, studied, and thought "*in terms* of the primitive," so folk collectors—rather than studying a thing identifiable as "the folk"—saw past and present culture only ever *in terms* of their own vocabulary and worldview.[53] They discovered the folk simply because they named them as such; the traditions they encountered never existed as "folk" outside the discursive bounds of folklore and revivalism. Through such modes of observation, collectors effectively constituted the objects of their own investigation.

Such music always seems to presuppose a temporal schism, a loss. Although Dylan, much like generations of antiquarians and fieldworkers before him, situates folk material as the antithesis of the "madly complicated modern world," the folk are in truth coextensive with this labyrinthine modernity. A number of scholars have pointed out that although folkloric ideals were rhetorically envisioned as a bulwark against technological progress or an antidote to the modern, "premodern" folk culture is constitutively tied up in the characteristic fears and desires of a society in the throes of modernization.[54] Folklore, as Robin Kelley argues, is an example of *bricolage*, "a cutting, pasting, and incorporating of various cultural forms that"—as we shall see later on in this book—"become categorized in a racially or ethnically coded aesthetic hierarchy" and employed for particular ends.[55] At its most basic, the concept of folk culture is a *symptom* of modernity, a sign that things are changing more quickly than desired, shifting gears and propelling humanity down the dark road to ruin. Folk songs are thus always elegies—laments for a first fine careless rapture never to be recaptured, home-thoughts from a different era. As Julian Johnson puts it in relation to the nineteenth-century *Lied*, folk music was "a vehicle of nostalgia"—a form of "musical re-membering, defined by a peculiarly modern quality of temporal dissonance."[56] Often called upon during periods of upheaval, this Golden Age chimera resurfaces like the transpositions of a ritornello throughout modern history. It is, to borrow Raymond Williams's wonderful phrase, "a myth functioning as a memory."[57]

What is particularly useful about the "ethnological rectangle" that we encountered above (consisting of *orality*, *spatiality*, *alterity*, and *unconsciousness*) is that, when inverted, it supplies a diagram of the modern condition: *writing*, *temporality*, *identity*, and *consciousness*.[58] The primitive and the modern, in other words, are effectively mirror images of one another, brought into existence through a similar logic as dialectical pairs. Where the modern historian or ethnographer (read: folklorist or collector) defines the other's world as an oral culture, this orality is the corollary of a modern obsession with writing, print, and documentation; where the historian or ethnographer sees the other in a synchronic or timeless state, this timelessness is the outcome of modern conceptions of evolutionary Time and nostalgic dissonance; where the historian or ethnographer finds alterity, this alterity becomes both a foil to modern, Western notions of self and a means to restore a lost communal or tribal identity; where the historian or ethnographer believes a society to be unconscious or unaware of its own ability to bring forth art, this naive artlessness becomes a corrective to self-awareness and decadent individualism.

Modernity has most often been viewed in this way as a convergence of interlaced factors wedded to technological change. This is the position that Martin Heidegger takes in a major public address written toward the end of the period under discussion here, but later revised in order to erase his sympathies with Nazi resistance to Cartesian philosophy—a tradition seen to epitomize inauthentic rationality at the expense of *völkisch* spirit.[59] Heidegger states that modernity can be identified by a confluence of scientific research, machine technology, "the process of art's moving into the purview of aesthetics," the fact that "human action is understood and practiced as culture" (i.e., that it is *cultivated* as a higher good), and a "loss of the gods," better defined as "the condition of indecision about God and the gods" brought about by Christianity whereby belief is "transformed into religious experience."[60] What he wishes to define in this essay, however, is "the essence of modernity," something he locates above all in the codification and institutionalization of scientific knowledge—a process in which "the scholar disappears and is replaced by the researcher engaged in research programs" pressing ever forward "into the sphere occupied by the figure of . . . the technologist."[61] This shift from scholarship to research is characteristic of the late Victorian age, where antiquarian and literary pursuits were brought increasingly under the rubric of science (as I discuss in chapter 1). Imitating such a method, Heidegger is interested in discovering through this particular facet a truth about modern thinking in general—a truth revolving around representation.

The decisive feature of modernity, Heidegger claims, is that "the essence of humanity altogether transforms itself in that man becomes the subject . . . that which, as ground, gathers everything onto itself."[62] Humankind thereby "becomes the referential center of beings as such," inaugurating the possibility of a "world grasped as picture."[63] In this sense, a premodern world picture could never have existed:

> Now for the first time there exists such a thing as the "position" of man. Man makes depend on himself the way he is to stand to beings as the objective. What begins is that mode of human being which occupies the realm of human capacity as the domain of measuring and execution for the purpose of the mastery of beings as a whole. The age that is determined by this event is not only new in retrospective comparison with what had preceded it. It is new, rather, in that it explicitly sets itself up as the new.[64]

Modernity, in short, is characterized by a novel approach to the natural world defined by research, technology, reification, and acts of re-presentation (*Vor-stellen*). Indebted to empirical mastery that transforms the world into an object to be used and observed, it is a phenomenon synonymous with humanity's "self-establishment in the world."[65] Related symptoms of the modern condition can be detected "in humanity's freeing itself from the bonds of the Middle Ages" and in a new prestige accorded to "the non-individual, in the shape of the collective."[66] Folk music would seem both to confirm and to complicate this argument. On the one hand (as I demonstrate in chapter 3), the folkloric imagination remains transfixed by aspects of the medieval world, particularly with regard to visions of unalienated or artisanal labor; yet on the other, such thinking is evidence of a modern desire to envisage the collective in a fundamentally new way—as a people or nation defined by blood and soil. Folk culture, moreover, resulted from modern processes of scrutiny and objectification indebted to the scientific method and new technologies of representation.

Folkloric thinking might well represent what Heidegger sees as a misguided attempt to negate the age—a "flight into tradition" that "achieves, in itself, nothing, is merely a closing the eyes and blindness towards the historical moment."[67] But this would be to put things too crudely. Instead, we should see this form of negation itself as being inherently modern. The folk epitomized a nostalgic or utopian longing that appeared very much in response to specific historical moments being faced head on. In an African American context, for instance (as we'll see in chapter 4), a conception of the rural folk was central to the ways in which a new and cathartic form of Black modernity was theorized in the wake of emancipation, laying the groundwork for the Harlem Renaissance. As I shall argue, the folk emerged in the modern imaginary as a constituent of the world-grasped-as-picture—of mankind as a historical subject in the narratives of Industrialism-as-Fall and

Time-as-Loss. Folk and modern cannot simply be mapped onto brave progress versus blind reaction; rather, they are twin or chiralic elements, chirality being the condition of similitude in mirror image, like our hands or certain ions and molecules in chemistry. As Frankfurt School theorists would remind us, myth and enlightenment are better seen as an entangled pair—modern rationality being necessary for social freedom yet containing within itself a dangerously "recidivist element," the seed of its reversal, a descent into myth, irrationality, and instrumentalized horror.[68] Folklore exhibits a corresponding revival of mythology in the modern era. Folk song offers up tools of democratization and resistance, yet in so doing cannot escape a dark recidivism at its heart heralding and validating the ascendance of fascist ideology, as I demonstrate in chapter 5 and the coda.

But perhaps we're being led up the wrong path. What if we have never actually been modern? For Bruno Latour, the problem with Heidegger is that he believes too much in the project of modernity to see that it has been deceiving us all along.[69] Latour advises that rather than giving credence to modernity we should look closely at what he calls the modern "Constitution," a system of beliefs and claims founded on a disingenuous logic. This mode of thinking entails an acknowledgment of hybrids but then spends an inordinate amount of critical energy dividing the world into humans and nonhumans, nature and culture, science and pseudoscience, modern and premodern, us and them. "Simply applying the modern Constitution," he argues, "was enough to create, by contrast, a 'yesteryear' absolutely different from today"—just as, we might say, the project of colonialism worked to demarcate the other.[70] Modernity, in this sense, is the very *idea* of a radical temporal or conceptual break where one does not in fact exist. The folkloric imagination is a typical example of such modern mythology, forever dividing pure from impure, the present from the past, nature from culture, and nation from nation in spite of long-standing hybridities and admixtures.[71] Latour's point is that we have never quite existed as this conceptual framework implies: folk song has never been pure, folk traditions are never as ancient as we would like to believe, "the folk" were never the voice of unalloyed Nature ranged against mass culture, nations are never as clear-cut as nationalists assume, and so on. Modernity, in other words, is a modernist misreading of the past. Even though folk music collectors opposed this vision, they did so on the Constitution's very own terms—this "antimodern reaction," Latour points out, accepting the notion of a temporal arrow that "annuls the entire past in its wake."[72] Tradition and folk culture are rendered inaccessible—and thus longed for—precisely "because these great immobile domains are the inverted image of the earth that is no longer promised to us today: progress, permanent revolution, modernization, forward flight."[73]

Discourse on the folk creates the ground of its own possibility. The modern constitution establishes the temporal dissonance and momentum that is required for loss and nostalgia to be felt in the first place. The folk are necessarily modern, the artifact of an imagination conditioned to think always in terms of a stream of Time forever running into the unknown. They not only offer up a critique of modernity from its margins in the name of spirit and being, but also help to generate the idea of modernity itself. A profoundly political set of relations masquerading as an apolitical universal, folklore is ultimately a mirage—but only insofar as the purifying binaries of the modern world are also seductive illusions. This book is the incomplete ethnography of a people who existed only as a symptom of the modern political imagination, an imagination defined by dreams of transcendence and tribal patrimony, national solidarity and racial belonging.[74] It is also, therefore, an excavation of the terrain that continues to direct flows of populism around the globe to this day.

The chapters that follow are adventures in what Zygmunt Bauman has dubbed "retrotopia"—examples of a ubiquitous turn to the past as a halcyon elsewhere, signs of "abandoned but undead" things being dug up and selectively recuperated, "in particular, rehabilitation of the tribal model of community, return to the concept of a primordial/pristine self predetermined by non-cultural and culture-immune factors, and all in all retreat from the . . . presumably non-negotiable and *sine qua non* features of the 'civilized order.'"[75] The enduring motivation behind the work of folklorists and song collectors, however, was less to bury collective heads in the sands of time in order to escape the present than to remedy the disasters and disenchantments of the present by recovering forgotten treasures of the unfathomed past—treasures revived on alien terms as blueprints for an alternative, even revolutionary future.

CHAPTER 1

# Collecting Culture

## *Science, Technology, & Reification*

If you were interested in collecting during the late nineteenth century, there were plenty of things that might have caught your eye, and plenty of advice on offer. One volume of the American periodical *The Art Amateur* from June 1880, for instance, contained articles on a wide range of options from butterflies' wings and ferns to prints from the British Museum—with one feature reminding its readers that along with the immediate "pleasure in collecting rare books, fine paintings, old coins, and other treasures" there were often lucrative rewards in the long run that might save your family from financial ruin.[1] Other handbooks or gazettes offered instructions on taxidermy or how to collect birds' nests and eggs, china, fossil plants, shells, orchids, insects, hunting specimens, and fleshy fungi. The late Victorian era, of course, was also the era of the great public museums—the Smithsonian Institution (founded in 1846 but expanded in the 1880s), London's Natural History Museum (opened in 1881), the South Kensington Museum (opened in 1857 and renamed the Victoria and Albert Museum in 1899), and Oxford's extraordinary Pitt Rivers Museum (founded in 1884).[2] Both these civic and individual modes of collecting attest to the process that Jean Baudrillard characterizes as an "*abstractive operation*" in which an object is "*divested of its function and made relative to a subject*."[3] Collecting, in short, is about a particular kind of possession or "abstract mastery" in which things are drawn into a relationship not only with subjectivity but also narrative and meaning.[4]

This chapter delves into the world of collecting around the fin de siècle, looking in detail at a defining feature of the folk revivalist project that has often escaped due attention: the compulsion to own, accumulate, and display. Collecting, as we shall see, was not unique to the folk revivalist mentality but was a phenomenon manifest across society and tied up in complex ways with cultural memory, scientific inquiry, and newly emergent technologies. Two of the most intriguing developments in this regard were the phonograph and the mass-produced camera—both were used to document and collect folk materials alongside the more familiar field notebook, leaving us with wax recordings of performances and (through the work of Cecil Sharp) photographs of singers themselves. A decade after his book *English Folk-Song: Some Conclusions*, Sharp was still insisting—to an audience in New York City—about "the importance of collecting songs & dances before it was too late."[5] This sense of urgency pervades the folkloric imagination. At whatever moment it occurs, collecting always seems to come too late, providing a glimpse of something on the brink of extinction. Such eternal belatedness was the primary reason for the folk's allure—a people only ever observed in their final days, fading and receding into the obscurity of history perhaps to be forgotten entirely. This was the feeling that animated the revivalist imagination, spurring enthusiasts on to collect before the shifting tides of modernity washed away the past and with it the nation's memory of a more noble time. We can see these cultures of collecting along a line from Orhan Pamuk's *Museum of Innocence*, with its lovingly framed "totems of obsession," to the more disturbing extremes of abduction and control explored by John Fowles in *The Collector*—attempts to restrict and suffocate the objects of adoration.[6]

In the introduction to *English Folk-Song* in 1907, Sharp describes his initial forays into collecting, noting that this valuable work, "on any comprehensive scale, has only just begun," largely as a result of his own personal endeavors:

> It is eight years ago since I began, at first desultorily, to note down and collect English traditional music. During the last half of that period I have spent every available moment of my leisure in country lanes, fields and villages, in the quest of folk-singers and folk-dancers. Chance, in the first instance, guided my footsteps into Somerset, to which county my labours for the past four years have been almost exclusively confined. I have, so far, deliberately

> resisted the temptation to stray farther afield, because I believe that by concentrating my energies upon a limited area, instead of spreading them out over a wider one, I shall acquire information of especial value, and thus, perhaps, gain a deeper insight into the subject.[7]

There are notable resonances in this passage with what was referred to at the time as the "romance of book collecting"—the "book-hunter" (or "book-fancier," in a less intrepid appellation) setting off on their quest for "lucky discoveries . . . to be met with casually, and by the merest of accidents."[8] These figures, J. H. Slater notes, were "naturally anxious to obtain the credit and still more the solid advantages of a startling discovery" to such an extent that "charity in matters that relate to their pursuit is dead."[9] Sharp likewise portrays his work as the "unexpected discovery of an immense mass of melody" that he alone was able to locate, with many "great surprises" surely in store if collecting were to be extended further.[10] Tellingly, Sharp makes use of the term *hunting* to describe his explorations of Exmoor, where he had collected a number of "exquisite melodies" from a certain "old man, eighty-six years of age."[11] We can feel in his excitement what Percy Fitzgerald described as a "romantic interest" in "the rare old edition, the old printer . . . and the stray survivor of a whole edition, by some miracle preserved to our time."[12] The collecting of these old tomes, Fitzgerald notes, had seen a revival in the decades before Sharp began his work.

This particular trip served to remind Sharp that folk collecting was a vital pursuit given the apparently dire state of popular culture in England:

> In the evening of the same day, my peace was rudely disturbed by the raucous notes of coarse music-hall songs, shouted out, at the tops of their voices, by the young men of the village, who were spending the evening in the bar of my hotel. The contrast between the old-fashioned songs and kindly manners of my friend the old parish clerk, who lived hard by, and the songs and uncouth behaviour of the present occupants of the bar, struck me very forcibly, and threw into strong relief the deplorable deterioration that, in the last 30 years or so, has taken place in the manners and amusements of the country villagers.[13]

As we shall explore more fully in the next chapter, Sharp is here referring to the dramatic expansion of the commercial music hall at the turn of the century, a business that had developed into a rationalized and highly profitable enterprise spanning the country.[14] For Sharp, "noxious weeds" such as music-hall songs that "flourish so luxuriantly" in the modern world would not have been able to grow in the first place if the country had managed to hold onto its native folk traditions.[15] In his attempts to salvage every last remnant of folk material he could lay his hands on in the service of resisting this dreadful deterioration, Sharp shows himself to have been a special kind of collector symptomatic of the folkloric mentality. Such collectors, John Elsner and Roger Cardinal argue, are akin to the biblical figure of Noah, the "ur-collector" imperiled by a flood and desperate to salvage that which would otherwise be lost forever.[16] Noah's vocation, much like the folklorist's, was "in the service of a higher cause"—a calling that takes the form of "collection as salvation."[17]

Like Noah, Sharp seems to have been overcome by what Elsner and Cardinal term the "pathology of completeness" in his crusade to preserve what was left of a more venerable people's culture—describing his anticipation of an "exhaustive treatise" that would eventually be produced when "every scrap of the existing material has been recovered."[18] Tellingly and typically for the collector, it is *material* that is to be recovered and preserved, not culture, practice, or individual experience. As objects to be amassed, folk songs were like handsome rare books waiting to be unearthed in the country's villages and fields, hidden away invisible to the untrained eye in the mouths and minds of the folk. Out there, it appeared, was an entire library of precious heritage at risk of passing away undiscovered, succumbing to the blight of time if not rescued and properly conserved—an invaluable bastion of virtue set against the marauding hoards of a volatile popular mass. Here we find the distinctive mode of nostalgic, Manichean thinking at the core of every new moral panic.

Hence, what is saved through the folkloric process, we should remember, is not living custom, but tokens, written texts, and fragments brought together as a well-ordered collection. The mania of the collector is a mania of cohesion and authority, of command over the material traces of the past. The excitement of collecting is in discovering and gathering this material—once obscured and dispersed, secreted or neglected—into a coherent whole. This hunt is undertaken only ever on the terms of the collector and routinely at odds with the milieux from which they collect. It is the collector who holds the power to establish relationships between these precious, isolated things, deciding what is collectable and what is not, what survives and what should be left to rot. According to Francis James Child, for instance, certain old ballads were truly "popular" (i.e., of the people, here a synonym for the folk), whereas others represented something else entirely. Discussing the enormous collections of Broadside ballads amassed by Samuel Pepys and John Ker, Duke of Roxburghe, he remarks in a notorious letter to the Danish scholar Svend Grundtvig that they "doubtless contain some ballads which we should at once declare to possess the popular character" and yet on the whole are "veritable dung-hills, in which, only after a great deal of sickening grubbing, one finds a very moderate jewel."[19] For the collector, this scavenging is the price one pays for jewels—their allure all the more exhilarating on account of a stark contrast between treasured object and worthless waste. Prior ballad enthusiasts such as Joseph Ritson and Thomas Percy, Bishop of Dromore, relished this challenge of slumming through the slurry and stench of popular culture to stumble upon the relics of ancient English poetry.

Indeed, generations of British antiquarians had preceded Sharp's amateur ethnography of Somerset. In 1891, Frank Kidson subtitled his volume of *Traditional Tunes* "a collection of ballad airs." The book, he writes demurely in the third person, was "the outcome of much pleasant labour" driven by a similar impulse to Sharp:

> The compiler's wish has been to at least temporarily rescue from oblivion some few of the old airs, which, passing from mouth to mouth for generations, are fast disappearing before the modern effusions of the music hall and concert room. He believes that many of the airs here noted down are excellent specimens of melody, and as such, are worthy of preservation; that they have a peculiar quaintness, a sweetness, and a tenderness of expression, absent in the music of the present day, which it is impossible to successfully imitate. . . . They are now seldom or never sung, but rather *remembered*, by old people.[20]

Without the collector, this fragile mausoleum of melodies would have been buried under the ever-changing vistas of modernity. Setting these songs down "with utmost fidelity," he notes, was essential to securing "the antiquarian value of the whole."[21] Here was a "collection" of pleasing tunes—a scrupulously edited compendium attained through scholarly investigation. These were songs that had "made history," songs of solace no longer passed down like heirlooms from older to younger rural inhabitants, who, owing to "cheap trips to the larger towns," were now able "to compete with the town's boys in his knowledge of popular musical favourites."[22] Although "popular" is the same term Child employed with such veneration, here it is loaded with its opposite meaning—a Jekyll and Hyde expression that could, in different contexts, resound paradoxically with positive (as in folk, democracy, resistance) or negative (as in mass, industry, sedition) overtones.[23]

We can find, for instance, William Chappell using the term in direct contrast to Kidson, titling his 1855 magnum opus *The Ballad Literature and Popular Music of the Olden Time*. Ordering this material chronologically, Chappell was at pains to stress that his first volume "may be considered as a *collection*," whereas "the number of airs extant of later date is so much larger than of the earlier period, that the second volume can be viewed only in the light of a *selection*."[24] This is a crucial distinction, and yet one that can easily be made to dissolve. Selection, of course, can come after collection, yet it is also fundamental to the initial process of collecting; the two are interlinked. Chappell thus directs us toward an important insight: when we look at a collection, what we see are the results of a long and complex series of decisions—careful selections from an impossible totality constrained by the limitations of media, space, finance, time, availability, sanity, and so on. "Choice," as Susan Pearce notes, "is at the heart of the collecting process"—a process predicated on "the allotment of value."[25] A collection is always already itself a selection, but a selection that masquerades as a whole. Calling something a selection draws attention to the limitations that collection inevitably runs up against, but in so doing seems to undermine the mythos of collecting itself, the struggle it stages and strives to win against the inevitable tendency of things to disperse, multiply, disappear, and decay. The collection of folk music necessarily involved acts of selection. What antiquarians and field collectors were interested in preserving was not the totality of a prior musical culture, but gems amid the dirt and debris of the past. Figures such as Chappell, Child, Sharp, and Kidson selected only "folk," "traditional," or "popular" material to collect, abstracting this from the shifting and diverse abundance of stuff they encountered. Consciously unrepresentative selections of vernacular musical practice, collections of songs served a higher purpose: to be quixotic barricades not only against the spread of mass culture but also against the deluge of time.

What set Sharp apart from this long antiquarian tradition of ballad collecting, however, was his distinctive way of operating. Sharp was not interested in hunting for rare printed texts or ballad sheets; rather, his efforts attest to a new facet of collecting culture during the nineteenth century. We find a hint of this attitude in Kidson's reference to preserving "specimens of melody." As Sharp wrote in 1907, "the work is now being done in the right spirit, scientifically, accurately, and above all with a scrupulous honesty and conscientiousness."[26] The responsibility of the collector, he emphasizes, was to record "the people's music" as truthfully as possible:

> Only those, perhaps, who have been brought into close contact with the old folk-singers of to-day, can fully realize how intimately folk-singing and folk-dancing have, in the past, been bound up with the social life of the English village. It becomes, therefore, a matter of the highest importance that not only the songs, but that all things that relate to the art of folk-singing, should be accurately recorded while there is yet the time and opportunity. . . . In the present volume I have recorded many of the characteristics of the folk-singer, his manner of singing, peculiarities of intonation, his attitude towards tradition and so forth, all of which have come under my own observation.[27]

He places great emphasis on the importance of accurate *observation* in the field and the fact that his ideas had been "logically deduced from actual experience" or "tested and verified by experiment."[28] Sharp, in short, was interested in turning folk culture into something empirical that could be collected, preserved, and analyzed, providing a basis for understanding the hidden workings of natural history.

It was in this self-professed role as a folk scientist that Sharp "enunciated certain theories concerning the origin and nature of the folk-song" that were "deduced from these observations, and to which they seem to lead"—theories that, he adds, "perhaps, in the fullness of time and in the light of wider research, may have to be modified."[29] We'll look more closely at these theories and their attendant politics in chapter 5. For now, I'm interested in Sharp as a collector—a specimen gatherer and musical naturalist within a burgeoning world of scientific inquiry. Sharp's project was characterized by a focus on empiricism and a distinctive form of inductive reasoning (his use of the word *deduction* possibly stemming from his training in mathematics, and employed inexactly). Above all, Sharp was intent on using his collected samples to arrive at generalizable theories of cultural change. He was following in hallowed footsteps, to borrow a definition from the polymath and philosopher William Whewell, Master of Trinity College shortly before Sharp came up to Cambridge: "The *Sciences* to which the name is most commonly and unhesitatingly given, are those which are concerned about the material world. . . . In all these Sciences it is familiarly understood and assumed, that their doctrines are obtained by a common process of collecting general truths from particular observed facts, which process is termed *Induction*. It is further assumed that both in these and in other provinces of knowledge, so long as this process is duly and legitimately performed, the results will be real and substantial truth."[30] Sharp plainly saw his endeavors as belonging to this pageant of intellectual progress, sure that, as Whewell argues, "on one subject of human speculation after another, man's knowledge assumes that exact and substantial character which leads us to term it *Science*."[31] His folkloric research was to be no mere antiquarian leafing through libraries and timeworn collections, but rather a means of getting to grips with fundamental truths about the human condition—one among many cases "whether inert matter or living bodies, whether permanent relations or successive occurrences" that could be used to "point out certain universal characters" and "general laws."[32]

This version of the scientific method helps to explain the curious focus Sharp directed upon one particular county in his collecting. He even preempts this reproach, noting that "the critic may object that the title *English Folk-Song* is misleading, in that the book deals with the folk-songs of Somerset rather than with those of England."[33] This objection, however, was "more apparent than real" as "the distribution of folk-songs throughout the kingdom is, to a large extent, independent of locality": "this," he writes, "is the general conclusion at which I myself have arrived after examining and comparing with my own, the material gathered by others."[34] Somerset, in other words, functioned just as Whewell describes, providing Sharp with the particular observed facts (the raw data collected together in his notebooks) that afforded speculation about general truths, laws, and universal characters. But it was a very different kind of truth to that offered by collectors such as Frank Kidson. Although Kidson noted the presence of melodies passed down via oral tradition in "places so widely apart as the South of Scotland, and the North and West Ridings of Yorkshire, and in Berkshire and Oxfordshire," he knew (unlike Sharp, it seems) that these melodies had originally been carried as far as forty miles per day "from place to place by pedlars and by journeymen who travelled to ply their trade."[35] Kidson and Sharp thus present two ostensibly similar yet radically different epistemologies or ways of thinking. Whereas Kidson saw complex patterns of trade, cheap print, local memory, and vernacular improvisation, Sharp saw a homogeneous rural population expressing itself organically with one voice detectable via the particular instantiations he found. Science and antiquarianism led these two folk song collectors in two opposing directions: one toward particularity, the other toward general laws.

Sharp's desire to offer universals and generalizable truths culminated in a Darwinian theory of cultural evolution expressed as *continuity* ("accuracy of oral transmission"), *variation* ("melodic alterations unintentional and intuitive"), and *selection* ("communal taste—racial characteristics").[36] It was this scientific mind-set that allowed him to turn his back so easily on history in favor of a more pure and simple hypothetical truth: folk song had nothing to do with the convoluted cultural byways of the past, but was instead the natural indication of a deep-rooted reflex found amid the nation's true inhabitants—an outpouring of spontaneous communal creativity offering a window onto prehistoric society. Unlike art music, he concludes, folk song is both "communal in authorship, and communal in that it reflects the mind of the community": it is "the product of a race."[37] In Sharp's collecting, therefore, the individual songs and melodies themselves have relatively little importance in comparison with the grand system they seemed to uncover—an entire mechanism for explaining folk music's growth from simple origins through difference and variation to its final existing state of tribal uniqueness and aesthetic supremacy. As a good scientist, Sharp saw his specimens as symptoms of some larger process. Given that, in his view, folk songs had been "unconsciously produced" by the people, they were valuable principally insofar as they were able to throw new light on "the essential and basic qualities of the human mind" and the "fundamental laws and principles of music."[38] Folk music, he insists, is "scientific music."[39] At work behind the humble charm of folk song, in other words, was a universal process of unfolding that revealed the relative "cultivation" of mind across "the several nations of the world"—a cultivation that Sharp was intent on confirming the English race possessed.[40]

Sharp's scientistic mode of thought also encouraged a fixation on taxonomy and classification. He points out, for instance, that when a collector compares variants of a particular song, "he will usually find that they will readily submit to some simple scheme of classification, and that he can easily place each of them into one or other of quite a small number of categories."[41] This enthusiasm extended well beyond the categorization of song variants into classifications of mode, melodic patterns, technical features, and a rending of folk music from art and mass-cultural spheres. In the folkloric imagination, such classification is fundamental to the practice of collection and saturated with a value system in which instinctual or collective creativity is prized above individual and industrial realms. As Sharp puts it, "Folk-music is as distinct from art-music as is the wild flower of nature from the gorgeous blooms of the cultivated garden."[42] Cultivating song—whether through popular commerce or professional artistry—destroys and corrupts its rough, simple beauty. We find a similar outlook in Thoreau, where natural wilderness is always better than the best of human cultivation: "In the wildest nature," he writes, "there is not only the material of the most cultivated life, and a sort of anticipation of the last result, but a greater refinement already than is ever attained by man."[43] Where Thoreau and Sharp diverge, however, is in their respective attitudes toward understanding nature's great gifts, its wild vigor and freedom. "There is a chasm," Thoreau maintains, "between knowledge and ignorance which the arches of science can never span."[44] These impassive arches were unfit for the appreciation of poetry and art, which are "the mysticism of mankind"—things as strange and untamable as nature herself that neither empirical analysis nor scholarship could ever comprehend fully.[45]

Although appearing to be sound and logical conclusions drawn from the data he gathered, Sharp's theories were chiefly his own invention and, as such, betrayed a basic weakness running through the inductive approach, as Whewell points out:

> [Through induction] the particular facts are not merely brought together, but there is a New Element added to the combination by the very act of thought by which they are combined. There is a Conception of the mind introduced in the general proposition, which did not exist in any of the observed facts. . . . The facts are known, but they are insulated and unconnected, till the discoverer supplied from his own stores a Principle of Connexion. The pearls are there, but they will not hang together till some one provides the String. . . . Thus in each inference made by Induction, there is introduced some General Conception, which is given, not by the phenomena, but by the mind.[46]

The conclusion, in short, "is not contained in the premises," but necessitates traveling beyond immediate examples to some form of "Ideal Case in which the relations are complete and intelligible"; "we take a Standard," Whewell reasons, "and measure the facts by it," but this Standard "is constructed by us, not offered by Nature."[47] This is precisely what Sharp did when he sought out and subsequently brought together hundreds of "folk" songs in his collection: he was not simply arranging them, but adding a new element that emerged from his own a priori ideas rather than from the songs themselves. His elaborate theory of musical evolution is the perfect example of this "principle of connexion," arrived at as a means to string together pearls of gathered data along a string of intelligibility. By combining songs and compiling them *as* folk songs, collectors were always working with and within a particular "conception" imposed upon such material. The idea of folk song was not to be found lying dormant in collected melodies and words but was in truth introduced by folklorists themselves. In anthropological language, this problem is referred to as the clash of the emic and the etic—the view from within the culture being observed versus the view of the external observer. The risk of a scientific approach is that even this distinction disappears, transmuted into what Thomas Nagel refers to as "the view from nowhere," the impossible standpoint of innocent objectivity.[48]

We should see Sharp as a key figure in the history of folk song not because of the sheer amount of material he accumulated, but for his aspiration to shift the practice of collecting from something romantic and questing to something empirical and scientific. The word *antiquarian* appears on only a couple of occasions in his book and always as a slur, the sign of an outmoded or inadequate approach: "recorded on no written or printed document," he proclaims, "all the antiquarians in the world are incapable of reviving [folk song]."[49] If this rebuke wasn't enough, he goes on: "Those who regard the collector as an amiable archaeologist, and ascribe to his recoveries an antiquarian value only, altogether mistake the nature of the folk-song."[50] The word *scientific*, in contrast, appears far more frequently, signaling his wish for folk song to be given a "scientific meaning," his interest in its construction upon "scientific principles," and the necessity of collecting melodies with "scientific accuracy."[51] He hopes, furthermore, "scientific use will be made of the material now being amassed by collectors" and reminds his readers that as folk songs "throw a searching light upon the character of the peasant," they "possess great scientific value" and must be examined only by "those who will not misunderstand them."[52]

The closest parallel to this undertaking in the scientific world would have been botanical inquiry. We can think of Sharp as a kind of musical botanist interested in candid, genuine, and unconscious oral products of the native folk—figures that he compares to acorns having fallen from an oak tree in perpetual autumn with "its roots in the past."[53] To quote from a contemporaneous book on the subject by Brown professor William Whitman Bailey, Sharp was devoted to a scientific pursuit that "trains the observing and reasoning faculties" and "leads to close inspection, to accurate comparison, to terse and forcible forms of expression, to the habit of correct delineation."[54] Much like botanical field collecting, folk song collecting necessitated only curiosity and "inexpensive apparatus"—the kind that one could easily carry around the countryside in search of specimens, given that

> materials lie abundantly about us at all seasons and in every climate. Winter yields us her lichens and mosses on rocks and trees; her algae in salt or fresh water; her mushrooms and toadstools in meadows and woods; her smaller fungi as blights and moulds on leaves, etc. Spring and summer overwhelm us with abundant floral treasures, and autumn offers us her harvest of fruit. Let

> the traveller proceed to the utmost north, and still he will find plants. The dry Sahara presents its oases verdant with palms and grasses; the steppes of Asia or the barren heights of Arizona bristle with cacti; the Alpine summits of the Andes or the Himalaya bloom with brilliant flowers.[55]

Folk collectors likewise saw their material as being tied to the seasons, ecologies, and geographic locals from which it arose—producing, in Sharp's words, a "rich harvest" in the English countryside for the collector to gather.[56] From careful observation, Bailey notes, "the student rises by gradual steps to complex conceptions, profound generalizations, philosophic discussion, which will require his most mature thought."[57] Botanizing, he writes, demands the ability not only to look at the "infinite variations" of natural forms and relate them to one another, but also an appreciation of the "aesthetic aspects" of nature.[58] Sharp shared both this enthusiasm for the beauty of the natural world and for evolutionary theorizing predicated upon meticulous habits of selection and taxonomy. His vision of folk song was predicated upon a systematic approach to conservation that could, one day, be used to reestablish living musical practices via a curated herbarium of treasured specimens. This, we might say, is the very definition of revivalism—the reinstatement of culture through collection.

One area in particular that Sharp thought scientific accuracy could be usefully extended was in the recording of pitch variation and intonation. Given that "the attention of the collector is ordinarily occupied with other matters" while noting down melodies in the field, he argues, these subtleties "can best be noted and studied on the phonograph."[59] This machine looked set to revolutionize the practice of song collecting—promising, as it did, to capture every nuance of individual performance and allow exact repetition in a way impossible before mechanical sound recording.

As Walter Benjamin famously remarked, such technology facilitated two dramatic transformations. First, to take the example of photography, "reproduction can bring out those aspects of the original that are unattainable to the naked eye" and "capture images which escape natural vision," and second, "reproduction can put the copy of the original into situations which would be out of reach for the original itself" enabling it "to meet the beholder halfway, be it in the form of a photograph or a phonograph record."[60] In the case of song collecting, a

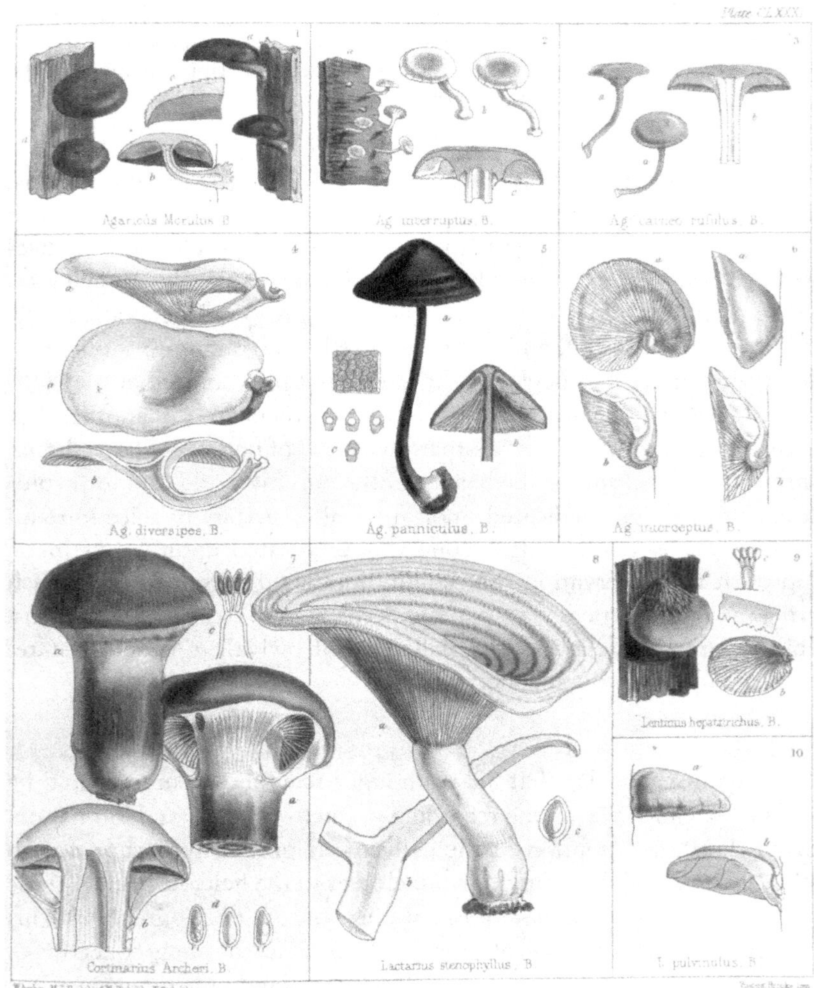


FIGURE 1. Plate CLXXXI from Joseph Dalton Hooker, *The Botany of The Antarctic Voyage of H. M. Discovery Ships* Erebus *and* Terror, *in the Years 1839–1843: Part III, Flora Tasmaniæ; Volume II, Monocotyledones and Acotyledones* (London: Lovell Reeve, 1860). Books such as this serve as a reminder of the intimate connections between botany and empire building.

sound recording could indeed bring out those aspects of a performance difficult to detect on first hearing with the naked ear, and it could also carry a performance into strange new contexts—the city, the folklorist's office, the drawing room, the record company, meetings of the Folk-Song Society, the internet, and so on. These two novelties relied on a yet more fundamental transformation brought about by this mediating technology: reification, that is, the conversion of a single performance from a unique, evanescent event (suffused with "aura") into a repeatable *thing*, an object to be collected, analyzed, and replayed. Reification would have a profound effect on the folk revivalist project and those musicians caught up in its wake. The uniqueness of art, Benjamin argues in folkloric spirit, "is inseparable from its being imbedded in the fabric of tradition"; what reproduction achieves, conversely, is detachment, plurality, and "a tremendous shattering of tradition" that "reactivates" its object.[61] This peculiar reactivation of tradition and the emergence of mechanical reproduction from sound to cinema are, for Benjamin, decisive indications of modernity—signs of a society moving undeniably toward a condition of mass being, its assemblies and wars constituting "a form of human behaviour which particularly favours mechanical equipment."[62]

The phonograph became a focal point for debate amid the Folk-Song Society. Principal of the Guildhall School of Music W. H. Cummings proposed in March 1905 that collectors must notate "precisely what they hear": if "a landscape looks different when seen through glasses of different colours," he contends, "it is quite possible that the folk-songs may be very materially changed by the medium through which they pass before they come to us."[63] J. A. Fuller Maitland thought Cummings's suggestion of using a phonograph to counter this issue "excellent," noting that "if the Folk-Song Society were rich enough we would buy one at once."[64] The benefits and drawbacks of using such a device became clear at the next year's annual meeting:

> The machine on the present occasion did not work well, but members were able to appreciate the advantages of the phonograph. . . . [It] gave an exact imitation of the peculiarities of the singer—staccato effects, grace notes introduced, and so on. An irregular rhythm would be carried right through a song, *e.g.*, a bar of 5-8 time would be heard in every verse of a song in 3-4 time. Singers were apt to vary the major and minor third, also the seventh, the singers following their emotional impulse. Inaccuracies could often be detected by comparison. . . . The effect of the songs was enhanced by the dialect, and this could be enjoyed through the phonograph. The collector could repeat the record until he was clear as to the notation.[65]

The new technology nevertheless brought with it a new set of complications: one song tended to fill three or four wax cylinders—such that pauses had to be introduced in both recording and listening—and the machine had a propensity to introduce significant errors of intonation. One singer, moreover, described the experience of facing its imposing brass horn as "singing with a muzzle on."[66] Perhaps unsurprisingly, the majority of Folk-Song Society members were uninterested in or adamantly against the intrusion of such modern technology into their field—one member worrying that this "awful instrument" would surely "eliminate all the poetry and romance of song collecting."[67]

Undeterred by such qualms, the Australian-born composer Percy Grainger had pioneered phonograph collecting in Lincolnshire during the summer of 1906 using a standard Edison-Bell machine. He presented this material at the annual meeting in December described above and wrote at length on the subject in the Society's *Journal*, taking up an entire issue with the material he had recorded and painstakingly transcribed. Grainger's description of how wax cylinders aided the collector is a precise analogue of what Benjamin would later write about photography: "It is possible to note down from the machine difficult and very fast tunes with far greater accuracy if the speed-screw be screwed down until the record is running much below its original pitch and speed. Baffling intervals, short hurried notes, the component notes of twiddles and ornaments, etc., that are impossible to make out at the original speed, become, by this means, comparatively clear and distinguishable. . . . Enticing points became as it were enlarged and graspable where before they had been tantalizingly fleeting and puzzling."[68] To achieve this level of detail and precision, Grainger slowed records down so that they sounded an octave below their original pitch, at half their original tempo.[69] Here was an entirely new perspective on the folk mediated by the technology of mechanical reproduction: the voices of singers were not only being captured and collected in strange new ways, but were also being stretched out, slowed down, and made to divulge their secrets and obscurities under a scientific gaze. Such technology, in addition, made these socially marginal performances newly mobile, able to meet folk enthusiasts "halfway"—in London's Royal Academy of Music, for instance, where the 1906 meeting was held.

Grainger was not alone in using such technology to understand the bewildering complexities of musical difference. In his paper, he mentions being directed by Sharp himself to recent research on musical ethnology by the Cambridge psychologist and anthropologist Charles Samuel

FIGURE 2. Percy Grainger (right) at a player piano, 1916.

Myers. Shortly before Grainger began his collecting work, Myers had visited Borneo to record and examine what he describes as "some exceptionally complicated methods of gong-beating which are in vogue among the Sarawak Malays."[70] The ways in which he set out to understand the rhythmic structures of this music foreshadow Grainger's approach:

> I endeavoured to investigate the peculiar methods of sounding the *tawak* [a large gong of about sixty centimetres in diameter] . . . by allowing a Malay to tap upon a Morse key just as if he were beating the *tawak*, while the other instruments were being played as usual. . . . In this way I was able to obtain a record of the number of tenths of seconds which elapsed between successive beats of the *tawak*. I hoped that a leisured visual study of these intervals would lead to an understanding of this curious performance which to the European ear appeared so completely devoid of system, defying every attempt at rhythmization.[71]

What we find is an attempt to comprehend an alien musical culture by subjecting those "peculiar" and defiant things apparently "devoid of system" to a rationalizing methodology underwritten by clock time. Through this experiment Myers created a kind of sound graph—an object abstracted from its original setting and used to pin down rhythms that failed to make sense within a Western musical framework. Although motivated by a desire for scholarly understanding, such practices are inextricable from the dynamics of colonial encounter—domination and scientific investigation of the other being simply two sides of the same coin.[72] "There can be no doubt," Myers confesses, that the performer in this experiment was "disconcerted by the substitution of a Morse key for his accustomed instrument."[73]

What is particularly telling about Myers's research in relation to Grainger's collecting is that they both direct their focus upon rhythm. This was no accident. As the comparative musicologist Richard Wallaschek noted in his 1893 book subtitled *An Inquiry into the Origin and Development of Music, Songs, Instruments, Dances, and Pantomimes of Savage Races*, rhythm was the defining feature of "primitive music." "A general view of primitive music," he writes "shows us that in the most primitive state the main constituent of music has always been rhythm, while melody has remained an accessory. . . . Primitive music is not at all an abstract art, but (taken in connection with dance and pantomime) is a part of the necessaries of life (war and hunting), for which it seems to prepare."[74] "The origin of music," Wallaschek asserts, "must be sought in a rhythmical impulse in man."[75] In this teleological scheme, non-Western practices seemed to offer profound insights into the musical past reaching back into the very dawn of human civilization. It is a clear example of the "allochronic" inclination Johannes Fabian identifies in early ethnographic literature—a "persistent and systematic tendency to place the referent(s) of anthropology in a Time other than the present of the producer of anthropological discourse."[76] Locating global others in prior states of evolutionary development, this thought process spawned the very idea of primitive culture, supposing that perplexing rites and customs were something like fossils or insects trapped in amber.

Following in Wallaschek's footsteps, Myers placed special emphasis on the relative importance of rhythm among what he calls "less advanced peoples"—a habit of mind that would go on to provide the reception context for ragtime and early jazz in Britain, their distinctive syncopations heard as beacons of racial alterity.[77] As signals of musical difference, rhythmic complexity and irregularity were used to distinguish a spectrum of subaltern traditions. In his paper, for instance, Myers makes passing reference to musical practices from India, Japan, Thailand, Turkey, and Indonesia, as well as among Native American tribes and the Kwakiutl people of the Pacific Northwest. He links these examples, furthermore, to "the rhythms of the Ancient Greeks and of the Arabs."[78] The typical features of this so-called "primitive music," he suggests, are as follows: "a delight in change and in opposition of rhythm, and a demand that relatively long periods filled with measures of diverse length be apprehended as an organic whole or 'phrase.'"[79] Whereas sophistication in harmony and melodic contour (and, by inference, abstraction, intellect, text, and reason) characterized Western music, non-Western music was identified in this enduring colonial schema above all with rhythm—and thus with the body, the collective, movement, trance, exertion, performance, and ritual.[80] Folk music fell within this imaginative rift. In "early medieval music and among the existing folk-songs of many parts of Europe," Myers writes, "curious irregularities or even defects of rhythm are met with."[81] The rhythmic eccentricities of folk music thereby identified it as a form of antique, aboriginal expression at a similar state of development to non-Western music—traces of an exotic primitive culture secreted within Europe itself.[82]

Grainger, however, was more sensitive than Myers in many respects—less interested in uncovering psychological truths than the individual idiosyncrasies of the environment in which he was working. Phonograph records, Grainger felt, were able to offer something that collecting with a paper and pencil could never achieve:

> To my mind the very greatest boon of the gramophone and phonograph is that they record not merely the tunes and words of fine folk-songs, but give an enduring picture of the live art and *traditions* of peasant and sailor singing and fiddling; together with a record of the dialects of different districts, and of such entertaining accessories as the vocal quality, singing-habits, and other personal characteristics of singers. . . . Much of the attractiveness of the live art lies in the execution as well as in the contents of the songs.[83]

Quite simply, the phonograph gave folk song enthusiasts much more to collect and examine: unique performances, vocal timbres, ornamentation, and a living tradition. It widened the horizons of the collector, opening up possibilities far beyond volumes of dusty broadside ballads. Here was romance once more revived—this time, however, not the romance of antiquarianism, but the romance of ethnography, the unearthing and collection of a whole way of life. As Grainger writes in another essay, the phonograph opened access to the "impress of personality in traditional singing"—at its best striving to generate "a representative picture" of a singer's "complete art and artistic culture" by collating the specifics of a gifted individual's repertoire.[84] These singers were not carrying some shared racial urtext (as Sharp supposed), but rather manifesting individual "artistic creativeness and versatility" in execution—their irregularities "not mere careless or momentary deviations from a normal, regular form, but radical points of enrichment, inventiveness, and individualism."[85]

Yet however democratic and progressive the phonograph appeared to be, mechanical recording was still a tool in the project of song collecting. Grainger made it abundantly clear that he was interested in the "host of details . . . fascinating, interesting, or instructive" that could be "extracted" from his wax cylinders.[86] It is "of the utmost importance," he emphasizes, "that such records be handed over for their translation into musical notation to none but collectors and musicians highly versed in the wide possibilities of musical notation" with experience of "the vast realms of irregular rhythm."[87] In the process, these songs afforded what Robert Cantwell refers to as "ethnomimesis," exemplified by Grainger's own performances of some of his collected songs in dialect and with accompaniment at the 1906 Folk-Song Society annual meeting—renderings, a report in the *Musical Herald* noted, "enjoyed much more than those which were machined."[88] At its most basic, collecting is this very endeavor to represent—literally, to re-present—material in a new context, reframed and reclaimed by those with access to the material means of reproduction. Whether the re-performance of a song by a collector or the playing of a phonograph recording, folk music's meaning emerged from within these "noetic vacuums" of mimicry.[89]

We should always ask, in such circumstances, who holds the power to represent and on whose terms such representations are playing out. In the world of folk revivalism we have been exploring here, this power remained in the hands of revivalists themselves—figures with the means to institutionalize their vision of folk culture over and above the opinions held by individual singers. Consider, for instance, how Grainger portrays one of these singers in the Society's *Journal*:

MR. GEORGE GOULDTHORPE

> Was born at Barrow-on-Humber, North Lincolnshire. His age is sixty-eight. He was a lime-burner. His personality, looks, and art are a curious blend of sweetness and grim pathos. Though his face and figure are gaunt and sharp cornered, and his singing voice somewhat grating, he yet contrives to breathe a spirit of almost caressing tenderness into all he does, says, or sings; even if

> a hint of tragic undercurrent be ever present also. A life of drudgery, ending, in old age, in want and hardship, has not shorn his manners of a degree of humble nobility and dignity, exceptional even among English peasants; nor can any situation rob him of his refreshing (unconscious) Lincolnshire independence. His child-like mind, and his unworldly nature, seemingly void of all bitterness, singularly fit him to voice the purity and sweetness of folk-art. He gives out his tunes in all possible gauntness and barrenness, for the most part in broad, even notes; eschewing the rhythmic contrasts, ornaments, twiddles, slides, and added syllables that most North Lincolnshire singers revel in. His charm lies in the simplicity of his versions, and the richness of his dialect, which he does not eliminate from his songs to the extent that most singers do, while in his every-day speech it might be hard to beat.[90]

In this portrait, we hear only Grainger's voice portraying Gouldthorpe as a "peasant" with a "child-like mind"—a perfect vessel for "the purity and sweetness of folk-art." It's hard not to read such passages as another form of collecting: not of songs, but of people and representations, images and archetypes. As collectors amassed such material, they strengthened their imaginative hold on the folk.

This description almost feels like a photograph, the result of an asymmetrical encounter in which Gouldthorpe is made relative to Grainger—the singer becoming a passive object and the collector an active, observing subject. Indeed, the phonograph was not the only novel and readily available technology of inscription that could be used in this regard. Photography likewise transformed human subjects into mute objects through observation, offering an ideal way to collect and represent difference.[91] Sharp, we know, was a keen amateur photographer for whom folk song collecting and photography were entwined aspects of field collecting practice. Although he theorized in the abstract about national folk song and dance, Sharp paid great attention to individual singers and dancers to the extent that they illustrated and provided the evidence for his scientific thesis. He took a large number of monochrome photos of his informants in both southwest England and the Appalachian Mountains, leaving well over three hundred in his archive today—aside from more tourist-like snapshots, such as those he describes of a particularly captivating sunset in Asheville, North Carolina (hard to imagine in black and white).[92] Negatives of these photographs, he notes in a personal diary, were neatly "filed away and indexed" and the best of them professionally copied and made into "lantern slides" (to be used in conjunction with an early projecting device called a magic lantern) shown as illustrations during his talks and demonstrations.[93] These slides were clearly prized possessions and are mentioned frequently in his diaries in relation to lectures. Printed photos were also given away to singers themselves, and Sharp's own copies kept in an album—that classic repository of the collected artifact.[94]

Although taken during the first two decades of the twentieth century, Sharp's photographs have an air of social realism about them. As such, they anticipate the thousands of Farm Security Administration (FSA) photographs taken in the 1930s during the Great Depression, epitomized by Dorothea Lange's iconic *Migrant Mother, Nipomo, California* of 1936.[95] But whereas these FSA photographs sought to document rural hardship and suffering as part of President Franklin D. Roosevelt's New Deal initiatives, Sharp's work functioned more as a kind of conservation photography—striving to conserve in print a way of life he saw rapidly disappearing, calling attention to traditions threatened by urbanization, industrialization, universal education, progress, and mass entertainment. As with those collectors who opted to use a phonograph to document folk music, Sharp's use of a pocket vest camera held a certain irony in that he was using modern technology to document those very customs such technology appeared to be destroying. These devices, according to folklorists, were accelerating the "corruption and decay of traditional ways of life" yet, as Erika Brady points out, were also chosen as the tools with which to preserve and revitalize these cultures.[96] As one book on collecting noted at the time, photography not only enabled excellent forgeries to be made, but had also "killed the woodcut" and the art of wood engraving across the globe.[97] Modern technology cut both ways—on the one hand undermining or obsolescing tradition, and on the other offering a variety of new ways in which it could be preserved and collected, reified and scrutinized.

Much like the FSA's photographs, Sharp's pictures not only functioned as documentary artifacts but also contained a significant degree of personal and political expression. A book of hobbies published shortly after Sharp's voyages to the United States describes two kinds of photography, "record photography" and "interpretative photography." The purpose of record photography, the authors write, was "solely to make records of places and events" for the traveler "as a pleasant reminder of his travels and adventures."[98] This was the kind of photography commonly encouraged by advertising—such as that by the Eastman Kodak company, which had introduced the first mass-market camera in 1888—intended to capture fleeting moments that would otherwise have passed the observer by unrecorded, the forerunner of today's off-the-cuff smartphone shots. But another approach to photography existed:

> Interpretative photography is the recording of emotions or abstract ideas suggested by or seen through something tangible. There may be a friend who arouses in us certain ideas, let us say the idea of nobility. It is possible, by means of photography to express this idea. . . . We are not photographing our friend, but rather the abstract quality of nobility. We must prepare to do this with the same care that an artist would use. . . . It often becomes necessary to depart from physical verity in the developing or printing of the picture in order to express more clearly something abstract.[99]

Sharp pursued a distinctive fusion of these two approaches to photography—mixing the documentary immediacy of record photography with an interpretative desire to express emotions and abstract ideas through his chosen subjects. The singers and families he photographed were never merely pleasant reminders of his travels, but rather means to express and consolidate his particular conception of the folk.

The faces that stare out at us from his photographs stare not only from a different era, but also from the margins of society—in anachronistic clothing, with an archetypal gaze, as emblems of what is being lost to commerce and globalization, machine technology and urban sprawl. They are strangely solitary in the frame of the picture, alone and lost metonymically in the contemporary world, seemingly surprised they are worthy of the picturesque. We see beards and rustic waistcoats, flat caps and gingham skirts, a sunken-ribbed horse, dogs, violins, an old couple holding hands, log cabins, walking sticks, a tent, a mule, shawls, crooked windows, a haystack, hedgerows, thatched roofs, front porches, workers and wives, poverty, modesty, resilience, strength, age, innocence, and integrity. Sharp's figures haunt the present of these photographs, carrying with them the last remnants of a life lived out in the open air, in small communities, in rural landscapes unmarked by mechanization. Every now and then, there is a "punctum," something unintentional that leaps out at us from the photograph with its own mysteries—the folds of a white pinafore, the styling of a beard, the rough lines of a face—but mostly we see Sharp's attempt at the "studium," at making these images stand in for his vision of the folk: pastoral, elderly, artisanal, dignified, homespun.[100] There is a hint of John Ruskin's melancholia running through these photographs, a sense that, as he writes, "the life of a nation is usually, like the flow of a lava stream, first bright and fierce, then languid and covered, at last advancing only by the tumbling over and over of its frozen blocks."[101] We can see in these extraordinary portraits the romance of age, but a romance imbued with nostalgia for childhood—something, Ruskin argues, "full of promise and of interest . . . full of

FIGURE 3 (top left). William Bayliss, an agricultural laborer, Gloucestershire, England. Photograph by Cecil Sharp, 1909. Reproduced by kind permission of the English Folk Dance and Song Society.

FIGURE 4 (top right). William Henry Sparks, a blacksmith, Somerset, England. Photograph by Cecil Sharp, 1904. Reproduced by kind permission of the English Folk Dance and Song Society.

FIGURE 5 (bottom left). Susan Williams, a weaver, Somerset, England. Photograph by Cecil Sharp, 1905. Reproduced by kind permission of the English Folk Dance and Song Society.

FIGURE 6 (bottom right). Mrs. Townsley, Bell County, Kentucky, United States. Photograph by Cecil Sharp, 1917. Reproduced by kind permission of the English Folk Dance and Song Society.

energy and continuity" always at risk of being lost.[102] Sharp's figures are indeed symbols of waning and loss, of an unrecoverable past where folk culture once thrived, its uncertain future now left in the hands of revivalists like Sharp himself. As with all photographs, his prints and lantern slides are mechanical repetitions, as Roland Barthes would remind us, of "what could never be repeated existentially."[103]

One of the primary motivations behind these forms of collecting in the early twentieth century was an interest in what the archaeologist Walter Johnson referred to at the time as "folk-memory"—the "conscious or unconscious remembrance, by a people collectively, of ideas connected with the retention of rites and superstitions, habits, and occupations."[104] By the time Sharp began his fieldwork, it appeared that this precious chain (tied up with what Johnson refers to as "racial continuity") was becoming increasingly "dim and fugitive, almost to the point of extinction."[105] Collecting these survivals held in oral circulation was an urgent matter given the risk that an older generation might take an entire nation's memory to their graves. The best place to look for such material characteristic of "the genius of the multitude," Johnson suggests, was in the countryside: "the persons who furnish the inquirer with the choicest material are the peasantry, whose recollections must be submitted to every possible test."[106] As with folk music, it fell to the "savage" or childlike "rural labourer" to safeguard the nation's cultural heritage.[107] But this was not because they had superior faculties of retention, but rather because they exhibited something like a "latent" or "unconscious memory."[108] This is precisely how Sharp saw folk song—the latent, unconscious musical emanations of a race that needed to be "scrupulously examined" by an expert.[109] And here, moreover, is the reason why folk enthusiasts were so adamantly opposed to the spread of mass culture. "Arts and crafts and customs," Johnson claims, "may utterly perish when they have ceased to be of immediate practical use. . . . Leave the age of stone for that of metal and recollections of the past begin to fly away like sparks from a crackling fire of sticks."[110]

Collecting was thus a battle against time in defense of a nation's cultural and ethnic memory, a means to provide fuel for the glowing embers of tradition before they became a mere handful of ash. We find this trope appearing wherever the folkloric imagination reigns free—not just in Britain, but across the Atlantic, where folk song offered a gossamer thread uniting Old and New Worlds. Prefaced with a handwritten letter from none other than former president Theodore Roosevelt, John Lomax's 1910 book *Cowboy Songs and Other Frontier Ballads* is an archetype of this way of thinking. Roosevelt congratulates Lomax on an undertaking "emphatically worth doing" as it revealed "the reproduction here on this new continent of essentially the conditions of ballad-growth which obtained in medieval England"—the outlaw Robin Hood, for instance, morphing into Jesse James.[111] Collecting these songs, he writes, was "of vital importance" given that under "modern conditions . . . the native ballad is speedily killed by competition with the music hall."[112] In their guise as frontiersmen and cowboys, the folk offered a national identity grounded in a disappearing past—a vision partaking in the ethos of Reconstruction resistant to what some saw as the feminization of American life.[113] Having "fought back the Indians" and "played his part in winning the great slice of territory that the United States took away from Mexico," the cowboy offered a way to envisage a spirit of national autonomy—a man "always on the skirmish line of civilization . . . fearless, chivalric, elemental."[114] Steeped in theories of communal and thus anonymous authorship, Lomax insisted that these songs had "sprung up as had the grass on the plains," revealing "the ballad instinct of the race, temporarily thrown back to primitive conditions"—never mind that authors existed and were willing to file lawsuits.[115] Such facts mattered little to Lomax, who was far less concerned with historical or ethnographic accuracy than the imaginative connections that could be drawn between song collecting and the fading folk-memory of virile frontier independence.

Why do we collect? Perhaps as a way to arrest, however briefly, the insistent flow of time; to adjust ourselves to the death of loved objects; perhaps not simply to halt time, but to revise and rewrite the past, to reconcile ourselves to some form of exile, imaginative or real; perhaps as a means to dwell in a different time altogether (in childhood, alongside lost love, within a lost home, another epoch, another land, amid other possibilities). Collectors believe in Gatsby's green light; they build boats to row against the current, and in so doing are "borne back ceaselessly into the past."[116] Collecting is a kind of daydreaming, a wistful escape from the present. And yet it is also about control—refusing to give up control, whether to time or to other people. The collector becomes the authority, the author of the meanings of those things they have collected. But time always wins in this perpetual struggle for stasis. Even if collections are housed neatly in drawers or albums, away from light and other hindrances to longevity, they eventually succumb to change, whether materially or as a result of vagaries and changes in the minds of collectors themselves. As Barthes writes, the function of drawers and cupboards is often "to ease, to acclimate the death of objects by causing them to pass through a sort of pious site, a dusty chapel where, in the guise of keeping them alive, we allow them a decent interval of dim agony."[117] Whereas aspects of the vernacular recovered new life as a result of collectors' actions, the collected material itself tended to follow this course, acclimating revivalists to the demise of the folk as they were slowly rendered mute in the dusty caskets of an archive. Something can only be revived, after all, if it is already dead.

As we've seen, such acts of remembrance are also projects of salvation, of recovery and rescue that create alternative prospects. This is certainly the case for Orhan Pamuk, whose Museum of Innocence in Istanbul presents us with a lyrical history of everyday life in a way intimately bound up with narrative and the novelistic form. As Pamuk stresses, when things are brought together in such a collection and framed in new ways, it is as if they begin to speak, gaining a voice of their own:

> What I found most enthralling was the way in which objects removed from the kitchens, bedrooms, and dinner tables where they had once been utilized would come together to form a new texture, an unintentionally striking web of relationships. . . . The more I looked at the objects on my desk next to my notebook—rusty keys, candy boxes, pliers, and lighters—the more I felt as if they were communicating with one another. Their ending up in this place after being uprooted from the places they used to belong to and separated from the people whose lives they were once part of—their loneliness, in a word—aroused in me the shamanic belief that objects too have spirits.[118]

What Pamuk is drawing attention to here is the close bond between collecting and the imagination. Collecting is not only predicated on a certain kind of imaginative work, but also gives rise to new imaginative connections and possibilities. Individual objects (songs, recordings, transcriptions, photographs, written descriptions) are removed or uprooted, but in the process become woven into a textile of new relationships with a greater significance than they originally possessed. Once lonely and solitary things, they begin to take on the character of spirits whispering to each other, suggesting new ideas and associations. Just like the historian and the scientist, then, the collector salvages meaning from chaos, stringing these disparate pearls together—to return to Whewell's apt metaphor—to make sense out of them.

But unlike Pamuk's modest museum housed in a residential street in the Çukurcuma neighborhood of Istanbul, folk collecting is typically constructed on the political cornerstones of nation, state, race, and empire. "Large national museums such as the Louvre and the Hermitage," Pamuk points out in his Manifesto for Museums, "took shape and turned into essential tourist destinations alongside the opening of royal and imperial palaces to the public"; as official institutions, they "present the story of the nation—history, in a word—as being far more important than the stories of individuals."[119] They are essentially tribal and divisive, narrating the nation's identity in epic and monumental form, assembling galleries of alterity as a corollary to the colonial project. Sharp's vision of folk song shares much in common with such institutions. It strives to present the history of English music (and by extension the English people) as an epic process over and above the stories of the individual singers who make up this narrative. As I shall argue throughout this book, folk song is a figurative museum in which the primitive beginnings of a race or nation are narrated so that deep connections emerge between a people and a locality, insider and outsider, blood and soil. The antidote to such proto-fascist thinking, as Pamuk suggests, is to be found in a new kind of microhistory—a museum that instead of dwelling on the nation could "re-create the world of single human beings."[120]

Folk song collectors around the turn of the twentieth century were never simply hoarders, but strove to exercise mastery over their material, abstracting it from its original environments, controlling its representation, and ultimately drawing it into a relationship with new subjects. In the process, choices were made, and value judgments cemented concerning what was profitable to collect and what was not. Collecting is inherently selective, and all the more suspect when this selectivity is underplayed or rebuffed. The title of this chapter contains a deliberate double meaning: song collectors were both attempting to collect a specific culture (that of the imperiled folk) and one aspect of a broader culture of collecting inextricable from a scientific epistemology characterizing Western modernity. Folk revivalist culture, in short, was a culture of collecting—a culture that strove to collect, analyze, and represent another culture through song. This culture of collecting involved amassing things other than songs, notably singers cast as metonyms for a way of life in desperate need of salvage. Frequently, it seemed as if collectors wished to collect these very figures—in Sharp's case, transmuting them into silent lantern slides or photographic prints; in Grainger's case, translating them into descriptive prose printed in the pages of a learned society's journal. In all such cases, these gestures turned a living culture into something that could be displayed and deciphered.

Armed with notebooks, phonographs, and cameras—those material symbols of asymmetry and observation—folk song collectors were at once setting the terms for a scholarly discipline that would become known as ethnomusicology and disciplining the objects or traditions that fell under their gaze. The camera (and here we could substitute phonograph or field notebook), as Susan Sontag writes, "is the ideal arm of consciousness in its acquisitive mood."[121] Attesting to a desire at once insatiable, elegiac, and aggressive, these technologies of inscription were devices for appropriation—things able to turn "people into objects that can be symbolically possessed."[122] Sontag could equally well be describing folk song collecting, a practice that turned a variety of rural people into an object called "the folk" that could then be symbolically possessed through books, images, performances, transcriptions, dances, and recordings. In such contexts power over the other and knowledge of the other are interwoven.[123] Folk music is embroiled in this Möbius-like power-knowledge interface—scientific or antiquarian knowledge of the folk constituting a form of power over them, and this power in turn bringing forth new kinds of information in the form of folklore as a scholarly endeavor. Collecting, in short, epitomizes what Michel Foucault calls a "will to knowledge," to observe and analyze.[124] Although never the initial locus of such power, he points out, institutions tend to be "the terminal forms power takes"—a power that became vested in institutions such as the Folk-Song Society and its later incarnation under Sharp's leadership, as well as the Library of Congress as it turned Lomax's collecting into national heritage.[125]

If Lomax's cowboy anthology represents the more benign aspects of folkloric romanticism, his subsequent work on African American music in the southern United States reveals the authoritarian undercurrents of collecting practice. We have seen how British collectors documented both songs and people, but it was Lomax who staged the most striking attempt to collect what he describes as a "folk artist"—the songster Huddie Ledbetter, better known by his sobriquet Lead Belly.[126] Collecting, in this sense, did not merely involve cultural memory, but trading human freedom for the spoils of authenticity. In the next chapter, we shall look more closely at the idea that collecting folk music involved a fundamental imbalance of power by focusing on the Folk-Song Society, an institution founded in London in 1898 that played a crucial role in propagating a vision of the folk squarely at odds with vernacular custom.

CHAPTER 2

# A Geography of the Forgotten

## *Vernacular Music & Modernity's Discontents*

Let's imagine you're attending a meeting of the Folk-lore Society in London in 1893, at the heart of the imperial metropolis. You're most probably a Londoner of some means, perhaps involved with the Pitt Rivers Museum, and either a supporter of an older "Thomsian" tradition of national salvage-oriented antiquarianism or a new "anthropological" school interested in a comparative global approach indebted to the natural sciences.[1] In any case, you are part of a world in which folklore, anthropology, archaeology, and philology set the terms for understanding both "peasant" and "primitive." The folklorist and eminent Jewish historian Joseph Jacobs steps up to read a paper as a stopgap. It's an essay he's simply titled "The Folk." He begins:

> During the discussions which took place some years ago in the Folk-lore Society as to the nature of folk-lore, there was one curious omission. Much was said about what the Folk believed, what the Folk did, and how these sayings and doings of the Folk should be arranged and classified. But very little indeed was said as to what the Folk was that said and did these things, and nothing at all was said as to how they said and did them, and especially as to how they began to say and do them. In short, in dealing with Folk-lore, much was said of the Lore, almost nothing was said of the Folk.[2]

Tearing down distinctions between folklore, literature, and the music hall, Jacobs declared that "the Folk is simply a name for our ignorance . . . a publishing syndicate that exploits the productions of that voluminous author, Anon."[3] Reminding the audience that this "mysterious entity" was in truth hybrid, mediated, and "many-minded," he states and restates an uncompromising claim: "When we come to realize what we mean by saying a custom, a tale, a myth arose from the Folk, I fear we must come to the conclusion that the said Folk is a fraud, a delusion, a myth."[4]

A remarkable exception to folkloric thinking during this decade, Jacobs's paper nevertheless hit the proverbial nail on the head, apparently sealing the coffin on the very idea of folk music. Throughout the intense disputes surrounding folk song over the years, such views—despite or rather due to their critical aptitude—have most often been silenced, drowned out, or simply ignored. Indeed, the mythos of the folk turned out to be hardier than anticipated, harder to kill off, and Jacobs's opinions did not stop a landmark institution being set up in the capital five years later with the express purpose of collecting, publicizing, and speculating about the music this native folk allegedly produced—the Folk-Song Society. This chapter unfolds, in response, as an unequal counterpoint. On one hand, we'll trace the practices and attitudes of the nascent Folk-Song Society at the fin de siècle; and, on the other, what Michel de Certeau would describe as a "geography of the forgotten," the experiences of vernacular singers unwittingly identified and written into our cultural memory as the folk.[5] While retracing the contours of this discourse, we should pay attention to what I term the "folkloric imagination"—a distinctive habit of thought in which the past is falsified and mythologized and subsequently envisaged as the fountainhead for an alternative future.[6] Folk song collectors were far less interested in traditional forms of music making during the nineteenth century than they were in preserving the beguilingly antique "survivals" they unearthed and the ways these might then be used as a means to reform society in their image. Rather than describing something, folklore is thus in essence a trope, a strategy for refining the opacities of vernacular culture as a bastion against an era's intellectual concerns: in this case, racial degeneration, the rise of suburbia, and anxieties surrounding rapidly proliferating mass culture.

In late January 1898 a gathering chaired by Alfred Nutt, president of the Folk-Lore Society, convened in the rooms of the Irish Literary Society in central London. The purpose of this meeting, as reported by the *Manchester Guardian*, was "to discuss the formation of a Folk-Song Society, having for its object the preservation of the traditional songs of the United Kingdom."[7] This report continued as follows:

> In spite of the efforts of many enthusiastic collectors, there are still in outlying districts many melodies unknown to musicians but familiar to the peasant or the miner. As musical culture advances these old tunes naturally recede more and more, and are forgotten, or, what is worse from the point of view of the student, they are adapted to the supposed requirements of "form" and modernised in every way. It was soon evident from the tenour of the speeches made that this was the crux of the matter. Should songs be taken down precisely as heard, or should they be "restored"?[8]

Here, in familiar folkloric fashion, peasants and miners from various marginal areas are juxtaposed nostalgically with metropolitan musicians and a culture that advances to the detriment of authentic, timeworn modes of expression. In what is undoubtedly an allusion to William Morris's architectural ideals exemplified by his Society for the Protection of Ancient Buildings, these old tunes were to be preserved in their original, historic form rather than irresponsibly "restored"—or, in Morris's phrase, barbarically "destroyed" when they ought instead to be protected as "sacred monuments of the nation's growth and hope."[9] Another way of putting this, as a report made clear in the *Musical News* echoing themes we encountered in the previous chapter, was that the new Society was dedicated to the task of musical conservation—to "collecting and preserving specimens of folk-song."[10]

The Folk-Song Society was officially constituted in June and by early 1899 boasted a membership of over one hundred, funds of over forty pounds, and four vice presidents including the principal of the Royal Academy of Music, the director of the Royal College of Music, and professors of music from the Universities of Oxford and Cambridge.[11] Recognized in her obituary as "the virtual founder" of this Society, the professional contralto Kate Lee had been elected honorary secretary and soon became known for delivering amusing lectures on her own rather audacious collecting work.[12] An embodiment of fin-de-siècle feminism, Lee not only spoke at the Society's inaugural conversazione but also at the 1899 International Congress of Women, where she gave an account of her experiences.[13] Described by the *Musical Herald* as "a lady of winning personality" who could "equally well get to the heart of an old longshoreman or of an aristocratic audience at the West End," Lee sought out songs in rural and urban areas alike, noting that folk material still existed in towns and cities among "those who have left their homes" and were less suspicious of outsiders.[14] One of her most humorous anecdotes, for instance, involved "a very old lady living in the East of London" whom she characterizes as "a veritable storehouse of folk-songs": "I had qualms when she first threatened to come and sing to me; I thought she might be a burglar in disguise, so when she arrived I took down songs with one eye on the umbrellas and the other on the paper, but she did not take anything, although she left, I think, a good deal. She said that she hadn't ever visited a real lady before, but 'that I wasn't the least bit like one.' This was, of course, a sort of back-handed compliment, at least I took it to be so."[15] This woman (identified as Mrs. Mainwaring Bodell of Lloyd's Square, Clerkenwell), Lee notes, had remembered material originally "sung as a girl, about fifty years ago, in Prees Green" in rural Shropshire—songs such as "The Bonnie Irish Boy" and "The Cottage by the Wood." These songs were reproduced in the first issue of the Society's *Journal* in the form of strophic melodies followed by stanzas of printed text.

Lee had begun collecting such material in "a little seaport town in the north of Norfolk, not patronised by tourists, and with no special attraction of any sort, except fresh air and level roads" suitable for her bicycle, named Wells-next-the-Sea.[16] One morning as she wandered along the Quay, Lee had plucked up the courage to confront four elderly fishermen whose faces had become familiar on her promenades:

> Finally they told me I had better find "Tom C——," whose aunt, they thought, "sang old songs, but was dead," but that, no doubt, Tom himself could sing them if I liked to hear them. So Tom was sent for and told to call on me in the evening, and he came, dressed up in his best, and shaking with fright. He said he thought he could sing, but when he began he was so frightfully nervous that not a note could he utter, and he gave way to groans, interspersed with whistling when he got anywhere near the air, and I almost gave up the idea as hopeless after hearing him, although I took down one tune which was fairly good, which, as I afterwards found from Mr. Frank Kidson, was not traditional.[17]

A more fruitful occasion for collecting was afforded by the now celebrated Copper brothers of Rottingdean, a picturesque village near Brighton on the south coast:

> I shall never forget the delight of hearing the two Mr. Coppers. . . . They were so proud of their Sussex songs, and sang them with an enthusiasm grand to hear, and when I questioned them as to how many they thought they could sing, they said they thought about "half a hundred." You had only to start either of them on the subject of the song and they commenced at once. "Oh, Mr. Copper, can you sing me a love song, a sea song, or a plough song?" It did not matter what it was, they looked at each other significantly, and with perfectly grave faces off they would go. Mr. Thomas Copper's voice was as flexible as a bird's. He always sang the under part of the song like a sort of obbligato, impossible, at first hearing, to put down.[18]

Lee notes that in transcribing this material for the Society's *Journal* "I simply tired out the two Mr. Coppers after three evenings' hard work."[19] If such tunes were "left to take care of themselves in the villages," she remarks, "how soon will they die and be heard no more"—it was thus the responsibility of members to "find their way down to the piers and quays before the old fishermen have gone out with the tide."[20]

These fleeting sketches are the only insight Lee gives us into the complex social world of vernacular singing at the turn of the century—a world largely inaccessible to her on account of her gender and class. Few sources give us a picture from the reverse angle of this outsider's viewpoint. One rare exception is Bob Copper's retrospective account of Lee's meeting with the two Copper brothers:

> Mrs Kate Lee came to the village to stay at Sir Edward Carson's house up at Bazehill. She had heard of James and Tom singing their old songs down in the Black Horse and, wishing to learn more about them, invited them up to the big house one evening. They put on their Sunday clothes and went along. Any embarrassment they might have felt at being asked to sing in front of a lady in an elegantly furnished drawing-room instead of at home in the cottage or in the tap room of the "Black 'un" was soon dispelled by generous helpings from a full bottle of whisky standing in the middle of the table with two cut-glass tumblers and a decanter of water. They sang, they drank and sang again and all the time Mrs Lee was noting down the words and music of their efforts. They kept this up all evening and were not allowed to leave until the bottle on the table was empty and the book on Mrs Lee's lap was full. After several more evenings, proceeding on the same lines as before only with different songs, she returned to London with what was later referred to as a "copper-ful" of songs.[21]

Along with his elder brother James "Brasser" Copper, Thomas had worked as a farm laborer in rural Sussex for most of his life, although by the time of Lee's visit in 1898 had become landlord of a local public house called the Black Horse.[22]

What emerges between the lines of these two accounts is that Lee was drawn to James and Thomas not because of how they enjoyed singing in their homes and the Black Horse, but as repositories of material that could be carried in written form from the countryside to the city as tokens of folklore. In doing this, Lee was effectively extending the Folk-Lore Society's original remit into song, an institution that had "for its object the preservation and publication of Popular Traditions."[23] What concerned collectors at the time was neither the lived experience nor the social world of these singers, but rather the songs themselves. Lee, in other words, viewed the Coppers much like Bishop Thomas Percy had once viewed his apocryphal folio of ballads—as something to be salvaged from the ravages of time for the precious content they conveyed.[24] Reading Lee's and the Coppers' versions of events against each other exposes a telling disjunction, as if we were privy to the photographic negative of Lee's portrait (the only perspective, of course, that appeared in print at the time). Uprooted from pub and cottage and held captive in a country house by an unfamiliar woman of higher status, the Coppers sang in a manner foreign to their quotidian experience, wearing clothes ordinarily reserved for churchgoing. Although bottles of whisky were plainly an indispensable provision, moreover, Lee tactfully omits to mention them. This peculiar environment played a decisive role in James and Thomas's choice concerning which songs to sing. As fellow collector Lucy Broadwood admitted, self-censorship regarding impropriety "makes it hard for a woman to collect" because "the singer is far too kind to offend her ears, but is almost always unable to hum or whistle an air apart from its words."[25]

Lee's vignettes, in other words, are depictions of a collision between two spheres, one of which was denied its own voice and refused control over how it was to be represented. Formulated without consultation with singers, Lee's judgments held the power to determine what constituted a national tradition and what did not. Removing material from the province of everyday life, as we saw in the last chapter, collectors reclaimed selected songs as ciphers of the past rather than aspects of the present. Their collections offered up small points of illumination that, strung together, seemed to form a constellation enabling the outlines of a story to be told—a story always narrated according to the desires of folklorists themselves. Collectors were doing something very similar to historians when they abstracted material from the field in this way. In the writing of history, as Michel de Certeau notes, "everything begins with the gesture of *setting aside*" objects of investigation—a gesture that more accurately involves "*producing* such documents by dint of copying, transcribing, or photographing these objects, simultaneously changing their locus and their status."[26] Folk song collectors did precisely this, setting aside particular songs by transcribing them, changing both their locus (from country to city) and their status (from songs to *folk* songs). Whereas some material was conserved, the rest was ignored and hence rendered invisible. We might think of collecting, therefore, not as the discovery, but as the *manufacture* of culture—just as history is a surrogate for the past.[27]

Members of the Folk-Song Society were not only interested in publishing collected specimens, but also in composing refined arrangements for performances in the very social setting that made Tom C. and the Coppers so evidently uncomfortable. Held at 7 Chesterfield Gardens in London's Mayfair—the lavish residence of Rachel Beer, born in India to the merchant Sassoon dynasty and later editor (as well as owner with her husband Frederick) of both the *Observer* and the *Sunday Times*—the first general meeting of the Society in February 1899 had featured Lee singing a number of the Copper brothers' songs accompanied on piano by J. A. Fuller Maitland.[28] After "continuous laughter" occasioned by what the *Musical Standard* describes as her "very solid and useful" paper, Lee's performance of a song titled "The Claudy Banks" (presented as a duet with the baritone Charles Phillips) was the "most applauded" performance of this "very successful" evening's entertainment.[29] London audiences were hence granted access to the Copper brothers only through a chain of mediations in which their songs were first classified, notated, arranged, and then restaged by metropolitan folk song enthusiasts. Performing in the place of an absent folk, these figures were bringing to life a strange simulacrum of the vernacular on their own terms, shorn of its ecology and imbued with new meanings. Although aspiring to be a genuine reflection of folk culture, the music presented by the Society on such occasions is better viewed as the basis of a new revivalist community—a community drawn together by affinity and a shared enchantment with descent filtered through what Kay Kaufman Shelemay describes as "creative transformation."[30]

What is particularly noteworthy is that those very singers identified as bearers or creators of folk song never seemed to use or identify with the term *folk* itself. "The traditional singer," as Maud Karpeles later confessed, "does not distinguish between folk songs and other songs in his repertory."[31] One of the most moving examples of this forgotten social world is provided by Henry Burstow, "celebrated bellringer and song-singer" of West Sussex, in his 1911 book *Reminiscences of Horsham*. Then in his mid-eighties, he describes an especially poignant recollection:

> I remember, when quite a boy, buying for my mother of a pedlar, as he sang in the street, the old ballad "Just Before the Battle, Mother." This was her favourite song because, I think, her mother's favourite boy, after having fought in many battles, had deserted and fled and was never more heard of. I have sung this song to her many times, never without bringing tears to her eyes; her last request to me as she lay on her death bed (she died 14th March, 1857) was to sing it to her again. It was this occasion—the occasion that comes but once in a lifetime—in which my prospective loss was measured by the depth of a mother's requited love, that I proved most fully the resources of my natural hobby as an outlet for expressions of the tenderest sentiments.

> I feel as sure as that I am myself awaited by death, that as she lay there, her hand in mine, with this her favourite song in her ear, nothing I could say or do, nor that anyone else could say or do could have better pleased or satisfied her last moments.[32]

The son of humble clay tobacco-pipe makers, Burstow had grown up in poverty but come to earn his living as an artisan shoemaker. In old age he had narrowly escaped the workhouse through a charitable pension provided by local donations.[33] A mildly eccentric character dedicated to model making, painting, and local history, Burstow was also known for his vociferous anti-clericalism and commitment to Darwin's theory of evolution. The twin pastimes of bellringing and singing had nevertheless proved to be his two greatest pleasures—the latter, as he describes it, "my chief mental delight, a delight that has been my companion day after day in my journey from infancy through every stage of life to my now extreme old age."[34]

His passing at the age of ninety was announced with sadness in the *Musical Herald* and accompanied by another touching anecdote: "A few years ago he promised to sing to his wife all the songs he knew, and it took him six weeks, singing ten songs a day . . . all from memory."[35] Burstow portrays the scene as follows:

> Some few times I have sung the list of 420 songs right through, every song from beginning to end; the last time I did so I sang them to my wife, commencing on the 4th April, 1906, the 78th anniversary of her birthday. I sang about ten on 41 consecutive evenings, and as we sat, evening after evening, one on either side of the fire, as happy as a king and queen, I singing my best, she listening and occasionally herself singing one of the fifty songs I had taught her, the old songs seemed as fresh and as pretty as they did when I first sang them fifty, sixty, perhaps seventy years or more ago.[36]

By this point, Burstow had become a local celebrity—one correspondent for the *Musical Herald* dubbing him Horsham's "grand old songster" after his performance at a public band concert at the ripe age of eighty-two.[37] His customary surroundings, however, tended to be rural pubs, "where song singing was always regularly indulged in during the evenings" throughout the year.[38] There was "not a village Inn for miles around," he remarks, "where I have not sung" and been asked to return.[39]

He had acquired this vast repertoire from a number of people in a variety of different ways. These sources are recorded in detail: his father, mother, and brother-in-law; local laborers and craftsmen; a sailor, a tailor, and an ex-soldier; the parish clerk; encounters in "taprooms and parlours of public houses in the Towns and Villages round . . . where the words of many songs have been taught and learnt, exchanged or sold, for perhaps a pint of beer"; and, finally, "ballad sheets I bought as they were being hawked about at the fairs, and at other times from other printed matter."[40] New songs, he notes, had also been composed to mark specific occasions or stemmed from the creative flair of his friend Jim Manvell, a Horsham bricklayer.[41] In Burstow's catalog we thus find a typically eclectic assortment of music including broadside ballads, minstrel songs, Victorian sentimental airs, and other material by a variety of professional songwriters such as Henry Russell, Charles Dibdin, Henry Clay Work, Frederic Weatherly, M. G. Lewis (author of the Gothic novel *The Monk*), and the American composer Stephen Foster.[42] The vast majority of his repertoire could be found in printers' catalogs across the country.[43] Ironically, republication of songs by folk collectors thereby obscured the very materiality of the environments from which these songs had been collected. Whereas Burstow saw little reason to segregate such material according to its antiquarian or scientific value, folk song enthusiasts were interested above all in sifting what they saw as examples of folklore from Burstow's list—ignoring his diverse and heterogeneous tastes along with the ways in which music had come to be woven throughout his long life.

Although he neither portrayed himself as a folk singer nor identified his repertoire as folk song, Burstow was cast as an epitome of the folk following an encounter with one of the foremost collectors of the late nineteenth century:

> In 1892–3 I lent my list of songs to Miss Lucy E. Broadwood (later Hon. Secretary and Editor to the Folk Song Society), and sang to her a large number of them, which she noted. . . . I am glad to know that in these ways have been preserved the words and tunes of nearly all those songs of mine that come within the objects of the Society, viz.: those that are "traditional survivals of songs expressive of the thoughts and emotions of untaught people passing between mind and mind from more or less remote periods to the present time." Some of them have been published, with the tunes harmonized, by Miss Broadwood, and can now be bought in cheap book form.[44]

The quotation—noted in what appears to be an editorial codicil as a definition meeting "with the approval of the Hon. Secretary of the Folk Song Society"—strikes as an awkward intrusion into Burstow's otherwise lyrical narrative.[45] Only those songs falling "within the objects of the Society" warranted attention as exemplars of anonymous material having survived the passage of time by moving among the rural population through some kind of unspecified osmotic process. In this definition, folk songs even appear to have more agency than the old laborers who sing them—untaught people who, it seems, could not be trusted with the classification or preservation of their own culture. This idea that folk song was a paradigm of organic, unsullied orality downplayed not only Burstow's evident literacy and personal experience, but also the convoluted intertextual byways of the musical past.[46]

Elected as honorary secretary in 1904 after Kate Lee was forced to resign owing to serious ill health, Broadwood had been a central figure in the world of folk music before the Folk-Song Society was founded.[47] She had published a collection entitled *English County Songs* in 1893 in collaboration with Fuller Maitland, remarking in the preface that elderly singers were "not unnaturally pleased to see their old songs appreciated by anybody in these degenerate days"—a topic to which we shall return.[48] These songs were harmonized and arranged for voice and piano, uprooted from the field and conveyed as objects to the middle-class drawing room. As Broadwood and Fuller Maitland confess, "while to give the tunes without accompaniment is doubtless the most scientific method of preserving the songs, it has the disadvantage of rendering them practically useless to educated singers."[49] The chosen idiom, furthermore, consciously aligned these tunes with the European art song tradition. In several cases, they note, where melodies showed "remarkable affinity with a song of Schubert's, the accompaniment has been treated in more or less his style."[50] Indeed, much like Lee, Broadwood was far less interested in preserving the culture that Burstow epitomized than in safeguarding one particular facet of his repertoire. The same year, she had written to the *Magazine of Music* with an appeal described as being of interest to "students of the science called folklore."[51] Although figures such as Frank Kidson and Sabine Baring-Gould had rescued traditional tunes, her letter notes, "We want these wild-flowers of minstrelsy to be systematically and accurately arranged and classified, and, if possible, their inner meaning extracted."[52]

Central to this project was the widespread belief at the fin de siècle that contemporaneous culture contained and occasionally reproduced remnants of a prior epoch. These ancient remnants were referred to at the time as "survivals"—rare "phenomena of our present civilization," as the anthropologist E. B. Tylor put it, traceable "from more primitive states of culture."[53] In their present form as folklore, these intriguing elements of a "savage" past could shed light on the present:

> The more we study civilization, the more clearly we shall see that the civilization of any age is not a new creation to meet the wants of that age, but that it is a result of past times, modified to meet new conditions of life and knowledge, yet showing in its cases of survival clear vestiges of the course of its development. . . . It is needful that the student should gain the most thorough comprehension not only of barbarian, but also of savage life, in order that he may be able to trace up, from as primitive a state as possible, the phenomena of civilization, whether they have become greater and stronger in their after-development, or have lingered as obscure survivals.[54]

Savage life, he adds, "has been written, as it were, on Sibylline books," once little cared for but now in their state of scarcity and impending disappearance "read with eager eyes."[55] This belief system underpinned the extraordinary emphasis that folklorists and folk song collectors placed on the distinction between folk material and inauthentic products of the modern world: only *some* kinds of song held the mystical inscription of the primitive and were thus able to act as pointers to "the origin and development and meaning of our own life."[56] Rural songsters, when viewed through this archaeological lens, appeared to be what Tylor portrays as "modern representatives of pre-historic man"—not important in themselves, but in their role as bearers of heritage attesting to the deep and unrecorded past.[57]

Broadwood was familiar with such ideas, having participated in discussions at the Folk-Lore Society—one, in particular, during which the antiquarian T. F. Ordish presented a paper arguing that Mumming plays "place us in contact with the pagan beliefs and rites of our northern and Teutonic forefathers."[58] Broadwood's colleague Baring-Gould, moreover, had published a book-length study of the subject that offered interpretations of curious mores from architecture and riddles to dolls, ovens, umbrellas, beds, and the gallows. Relying on the idea that survivals provided a link "to a period when all men were children" and equally to "savage races" with a "low mental condition" (the example, in habitually racist fashion, being sub-Saharan Africans), the patient research "of the comparative mythologist and ethnologist," Baring-Gould insists, enabled European customs to be deciphered and traced to their roots.[59] This precious heritage, he believed, was at risk of slipping away, with ballads becoming "extinct as the Mammoth and the Dodo, only to be found in the libraries of collectors."[60] Such statements demonstrate the extent to which the outlook of folk song collectors was suffused with colonialist thought filtered through anthropological theory. Whether guardians or inventors of primitive song, the folk were trapped in this childlike state of purity, representative of humanity before it had attained the full powers—and experienced the most unfavorable consequences—of Enlightenment rationality. Although folklorists were attempting to survey the culture of these native noble savages, they were in fact shrouding it further in mystery. Projecting ideas onto the milieu they aimed to document in lieu of embracing its own values, folk collectors were generating a taxonomy utterly at odds with their field of inquiry.

The increased attention shown to folkloric materials during this period testifies not merely to genteel curiosity, but also to a seam of anxiety and social dissent peculiar to the fin de siècle. We can observe these fears most clearly by turning to look at the Inaugural Address Hubert Parry gives as vice president of the Folk-Song Society in 1899: "Ladies and Gentlemen.—I think I may premise that this Society is engaged upon a wholesome and seasonable enterprise. For, in these days of high pressure and commercialism, when a little smattering of knowledge of the science of heredity impels people to think it is hopeless to contend against their bad impulses because they are bound to inherit the bad qualities of countless shoals of ancestors, there is a tendency with some of us to become cynical."[61] The "best remedy available," Parry claims, is to "revive a belief in, and love of our fellow-creatures" through the study of folk music—as in "true folk-songs" there is nothing "common or unclean . . . no sham, no got-up glitter, and no vulgarity."[62] These "treasures of humanity" were nevertheless becoming ever more rare, "written in characters the most evanescent you can imagine, upon the sensitive brain fibres of those who learn them and have but little idea of their value," the folk themselves.[63] The Folk-Song Society existed to rescue this music from degeneration, just as folk song itself might rejuvenate a culture edging ever closer to the brink of ruin.

For Parry, the chief agent of decay in this profligate world of commercialism was urban popular music—a symptom of the exponential growth in retail, leisure, and mass entertainment industries during the late nineteenth century. Driven by a small but significant rise in working-class real wages, this growth encompassed everything from music hall variety theater to cheap sensationalist newspapers, penny novels, soccer, and gambling. Parry's contempt for this domain was unequivocal:

> There is an enemy at the doors of folk-music which is driving it out, namely, the common popular songs of the day; and this enemy is one of the most repulsive and most insidious. If one thinks of the outer circumference of our

> terribly overgrown towns where the jerry-builder holds sway; where one sees all around the tawdriness of sham jewellery and shoddy clothes, pawnshops and flaming gin-palaces; where stale fish and the miserable piles of Covent Garden refuse which pass for vegetables are offered for food—all such things suggest to one's mind the boundless regions of sham. It is for the people who live in these unhealthy regions—people who, for the most part, have the most false ideals, or none at all—who are always struggling for existence, who think that the commonest rowdyism is the highest expression of human emotion; it is for them that the modern popular music is made, and it is made with a commercial intention out of snippets of musical slang.[64]

In his view, mass culture spread like a virus, infecting the enfeebled and unhealthy population with the disease of industrialized modernity. The unrefined conduct and counterfeit commodities of "the seething towns," in other words, appeared to herald the disintegration of society.[65] By contrast, Parry expounded, "folk-music is among the purest products of the human mind," as it "grew in the hearts of the people before they devoted themselves so assiduously to the making of quick returns."[66] Artisanal, spontaneous, and self-sufficient, folk song was an outgrowth of the natural world that afforded imaginative opposition—something, as we'll explore in the next chapter, that flourished in Edenic innocence before capitalism brought on the fall, and with it the veil of social alienation.

Folk music, Parry stresses, is "characteristic of the race, of the quiet reticence of our country folk, courageous and content," and should be cherished "as a faithful reflection of ourselves."[67] Foreshadowing Cecil Sharp's evolutionary theory, he suggests that such music supplied "the ultimate solution of the problem of characteristic national art" in that it stemmed from "crowds of fellow-workers, who sift, and try, and try again, till they have found the thing that suits their native taste."[68] As a product of communal choice over time, folk song seemed to offer up the possibility of cutting across class divisions to unite the nation as a harmonious whole. As such, it could be the great social—or even socialist—leveler. Indeed, Parry makes an overt connection between folkloric material and what he sees as the Society's broader political ambition: "To comfort ourselves by the hope that at bottom, our puzzling friend, Democracy, has permanent qualities hidden away somewhere, which may yet bring it out of the slough which the scramble after false ideals, the strife between the heads that organise and the workmen who execute, and the sordid vulgarity of our great city-populations, seem in our pessimistic moments to indicate as its inevitable destiny."[69] Providing

FIGURE 7. Arts and Crafts illustration accompanying Hubert Parry's "Inaugural Address" published in the first issue of the *Journal of the Folk-Song Society* (1899), page 1.

joy through "the simple beauty of primitive thought," folk song was an aesthetic panacea laying bare the bedrock of humanity via "emotions which are common to all men alike."[70] Hidden away under its surface was the source of economic parity, brotherhood, and an intimation of radical change.

It is easy to forget, given Parry's disdain for the popular and his nationalist sympathies, that the folkloric imagination intersects with the politics of fin-de-siècle radicalism.[71] Parry's address, for instance, reiterated Oscar Wilde's conviction that society could be restored to full health by "substituting cooperation for competition" and liberating art from the tyrannizing "vulgarity and stupidity" of popular taste.[72] Parry's daughter Dorothea was at pains to stress that even though he epitomized a life of privilege, Parry was in fact "naturally unconventional . . . a Radical, with a very strong bias against Conservatism" who counted both William Morris and Edward Burne-Jones among his close friends.[73] The influence of these two figureheads of the Arts and Crafts Movement (some fifteen years older than Parry himself) was evident not only in a small decorative print depicting entwined lilies adorning the published text of his address, but also in his elevation of organicism, communal tradition, equality, and integrity over laissez faire economics and an apparent deterioration of public culture. Parry's hope for folkloric redemption echoed Morris's vision of a utopian society, as we shall see, "in which there should be neither rich nor poor, neither master nor master's man, neither idle nor overworked."[74] For Morris, Victorian society was a "sordid, aimless, ugly confusion"—a harbinger of future evils that would be brought about "by sweeping away the last survivals of the days before the dull squalor of civilization had settled down on the world."[75]

Rereading Parry's address in this light reveals his indebtedness to literary Romanticism. The idea of reviving "love and well-thinking of our fellow-creatures" through an embrace of rural life recalls the title Wordsworth gives to Book Eight of *The Prelude*: "Retrospect.—Love of Nature Leading to Love of Mankind."[76] It is almost as if Parry were consciously paraphrasing the opening of the Book's second stanza, during which the poet reflects on his unhappy sojourn in London:

> With deep devotion, Nature, did I feel
> In that great City what I owed to thee,
> High thoughts of God and Man, and love of Man,
> Triumphant over all those loathsome sights
> Of wretchedness and vice; a watchful eye,
> Which with the outside of our human life
> Not satisfied, must read the inner mind.
> For I already had been taught to love
> My Fellow-beings, to such habits trained
> Among the woods and mountains, where I found
> In thee a gracious Guide, to lead me forth
> Beyond the bosom of my Family,
> My Friends and youthful playmates. 'Twas thy power
> That raised the first complacency in me,
> And noticeable kindliness of heart,
> Love human to the Creature in himself
> As he appeared, a Stranger in my path,
> Before my eyes a Brother of this world;
> Thou first didst with those motions of delight
> Inspire me.[77]

Here, Nature is the wise instructor, the gracious guide offering not only a foil to the unhappiness and immorality of the sprawling capital, but also a pathway to social cohesion and tranquility (Wordsworth's meaning of the word *complacency*).

Parry was a great admirer of Walt Whitman, and his address also betrays the influence of another celebrated poetic work of the era—*Leaves of Grass*.[78] His folkloric imagination resounds Whitman's ecstatic paean to egalitarianism: "Faith is the antiseptic of the soul . . . it pervades the common people and preserves them . . . they never give up believing and expecting and trusting. There is that indescribable freshness and unconsciousness about an illiterate person that humbles and mocks the power of the noblest expressive genius. The poet sees for a certainty how one not a great artist may be just as sacred and perfect as the greatest artist."[79] This freshness and unconsciousness was precisely what Parry and his fellow folk song enthusiasts found most appealing and redemptive about the native folk—an outdoor people who represent a humble art that mocks commerce and expressive genius, born of "the passionate tenacity of hunters, woodmen, early risers, cultivators of gardens and orchards and fields, the love of healthy women for the manly form, seafaring persons, drivers of horses, the passion for light and the open air."[80] The beauty of folk song was not to be found in its "rhyme or uniformity or abstract addresses to things," but in its mirroring of the spirit and the inscrutable movements of nature.[81] Parry might even be providing his own gloss on Whitman's lyrical injunctions—to "Love the earth and sun and the animals, despise riches . . . hate tyrants, argue not concerning God, have patience and indulgence toward the people . . . go freely with powerful uneducated persons . . . [and] dismiss whatever insults your own soul."[82]

Reverberating through the writings of the Transcendentalists, the legacy of Romantic thought afforded the folk song movement many of its key philosophical tenets. In *Walden*, Thoreau laments that as a result of the market "the laboring man . . . has no time to be anything but a machine" in the service of capital—a situation antithetical to "the finest qualities of our nature," which, "like the bloom on fruits, can be preserved only by the most delicate handling."[83] For Parry, folk song was precisely this tantalizing bloom, an organic manifestation of humanity's finest qualities threatened by materialism and the entrenchment of Victorian industry. Much like the Transcendentalists, folk song collectors united in a crusade against the social ills of nineteenth-century capitalism by elevating nature into a crucible of signs pointing toward a higher state of being. The resulting discourse goes some way toward explaining why the childlike or innocent qualities of folk song were so greatly prized by revivalists. As Emerson writes, "The lover of nature is he whose inward and outward senses are still truly adjusted to each other; who has retained the spirit of infancy even into the era of manhood."[84] Folk song represented this delight in primitive natural forms as a restorative balm that would in turn inspire the production of art. For Emerson, art is "nature passed through the alembic of man"—a domain suffering corruption "when simplicity of character and the sovereignty of ideas" is disturbed by "the desire of riches, of pleasure, of power, and of praise."[85]

Yet despite sharing in what Morris portrays as this "love of the earth and the life on it" inspired by a "passion for the history of the past of mankind" and a hostility toward capitalism, Parry's vision of democracy rests on a paradoxical foundation.[86] Unlike Whitman, he chooses to single out the masses for disapproval, revealing an overriding concern not with politics per se, but with aesthetics. A decade before delivering his inaugural address to the Folk-Song Society, Parry had lamented "the present condition of English song-writing" in a short article for *The Century Guild Hobby Horse*, a publication devoted to rendering "all branches of Art the sphere, no longer of the tradesman, but of the artist."[87] For Parry, song functioned as "a sort of barometer for the state of public taste in its widest sense"—either revealing a healthy taste and a high "musical intelligence," or the opposite.[88] The outlook for England was unfortunately poor. The public, he writes, had been cursed by a music industry intent on feeding it with "a perfect flood of insipid and commonplace concoctions, which have been consumed by the gallon, with the most pernicious effects to art."[89] The writers of hit songs were the primary culprit, "helpless dullards whose sentiment is sodden with vulgarity and commonness, whose artistic insight is a long way below zero."[90] Parry's ire, however, was directed equivocally both at these purveyors of the popular and the audience for their wares. There is a fundamental ambivalence in his argument (common at the time) between a disparagement of popular *material* and a condemnation of popular *sensibility*, of which popular material is somehow both a disturbing symptom and the unwanted cause. Lurking in his rhetoric is not simply a condemnation of mass culture, but of those who consume it—the masses.[91]

This hierarchy of taste found its way into Parry's influential book *The Evolution of the Art of Music*, which translated aesthetics into historical unfolding on a global scale with the help of a teleological theory of cultural development.[92] In the book, Parry argues that music progresses "parallel to the general development of capacities of all kinds in the human race."[93] As a pure, aboriginal, and autonomous outpouring of collective expression one step beyond a "savage" phase of humanity, folk songs were "the spontaneous utterances of the musical impulse of the people," something diametrically opposed to the "vulgarised and weakened portions of the music of the leisured classes."[94] It is in this guise that the folk become the vicarious mouthpiece of a fearful establishment—conduits of a pastoral, unsullied, and restorative populist sensibility to counter the false and disconcerting populism of treacherous metropolitan masses. Working within this framework derived from evolutionary philosophy and permeated with a colonialist mentality, folk theorists were able to establish a vision of humanity containing within itself demonstrable traces of its own progression from barbarism to modern civilization. Revivalism relied upon this postulate to stage a dialectical return, employing traces of primitive folk culture as a redemptive antidote to the ills of fin-de-siècle modernity.

As we have already seen on several occasions, the music hall was central to such denunciations of mass culture and a concomitant embrace of the folk. In 1878, the logician and political economist W. Stanley Jevons wrote at length on what he felt was "a tendency in England at least, to the progressive degradation of popular amusements": when "our English masses try to amuse themselves," he claims, "they do it in such a clumsy and vulgar way as to disgust one with the very name of amusement."[95] For Jevons, there was only one place to look for such errancy: "What can be worse than the common run of London music-halls, where we have a nightly exhibition of all that is degraded in taste? Would that these halls were really music-halls! but the sacred name of music is defiled in its application to them. It passes the art of language to describe the mixture of inane songs, of senseless burlesques, and of sensational acrobatic tricks, which make the staple of a music-hall entertainment. Under the present state of things, the most vulgar and vicious lead the taste, and the conductors of such establishments passively follow."[96] Rather than laying blame at the feet of the lower classes, however, Jevons impugns an elite that has refused to cultivate civilizing forms of leisure. In his opinion as a passionate social reformer there appeared to be little provision for wholesome recreation, leaving the doors open for shrewd caterers to vice and coarseness—"no necessary characteristics of hard hands and short purses," but instead symptoms of "the way in which for so long popular education and popular recreation have been discountenanced."[97]

For writers concerned with social change, the music hall attracted violent criticism not only for its incoherent mishmash of popular variety entertainment and "musical slang" but also because, as J. Spencer Curwen put it, "the sole object of the proprietors is to sell their beer and spirits."[98] Intellectuals writing at the turn of the century were particularly attuned to this vision of the popular as a dangerous and disorderly realm defined by the intersection of free market capitalism and a demand for frivolous amusement. As Wilde put it, popular authority was "a thing blind, deaf, hideous, grotesque, tragic, amusing, serious and obscene."[99] When interpreted in relation to Francis Galton's ideas of heritability, moreover, the music hall seemed to signal a one-way road to cultural decline. If certain faculties such as the perception of color were not fittingly used or cultivated, this view suggested, they would atrophy over time and eventually disappear completely.[100] Heralding an analogous deterioration of listening habits and aesthetic sensitivity, the music hall posed a danger to the nation's ability to

FIGURE 8. "Bird's-Eye Views of Society, No. IX: A Popular Entertainment" (detail), *Cornhill Magazine* 4/24 (1861), foldout image adjacent to page 713.

understand and benefit from "good" music, whether classical masterworks or traditional song. It was the task of the reformer to stop the population being lured with alcohol away from edifying pursuits and led astray by commercial interests—replacing their infatuation with the music hall with more healthy activities that would amount to a true re-creation of society. Folk song, as Parry depicts it, was one of these reformist proxies—music that the people had once loved in their bucolic now past rescued by an anxious elite and fed back to errant masses as a remedy for urban depravity and flourishing consumerism. "Once the prerogative and the pride of the people," he writes, folk songs had given way to a "hideous inanity" that suggests the masses "do not know that what they are wallowing in is degrading."[101] This conviction was typical of a highbrow elite hostile to new lowbrow entertainment. The denial of humanity to the so-called masses and even a eugenic thirst for their extermination afforded what John Carey calls "an imaginative refuge" for writers including D. H. Lawrence, W. B. Yeats, and Virginia Woolf.[102]

Rather than hunger for practical activism or a demonstrable change in position for the working class, Parry's address reveals a social reformist vision in which romanticized aspects of the rural folk are positioned as an antidote to what one of the foremost evolutionary philosophers of the day, Herbert Spencer, characterized as "miserable drawing-room ballads and vulgar music-hall songs"—those things consumed by the working and lower-middle classes.[103] Parry lays his cards on the table in a later book titled *Style in Musical Art*, arguing that an "emancipated democracy" taking pleasure in low entertainment "has brought about a phase of music . . . which has no parallel for hollowness, blatancy, and reckless levity in any previous period of art's history."[104] Again, blame lies equivocally with both the masses and the capitalist culture that feeds them—distinguished from "sincere and spontaneous folk-songs" and a minority's high art that "subsists in defiance of the most familiar principles of political economy."[105] An enigmatic politics therefore lay dormant under the surface of the Folk-Song Society's ideals: a socialism mistrustful of democracy and its reflection in the flourishing consumerism of what Parry cannot help but call an "unregenerate public."[106] The community these figures wished to see involved a peaceable unification of intellectuals and docile country dwellers in place of the liberal economics spawning wealthy industrialists and the "workmen who execute"——cast in another light, the potentially threatening forces of organized labor epitomized by violent clashes between protestors and police on 13 November 1887 in London's Trafalgar Square.[107] The folk revivalist project held this political ambiguity at its heart, preferring to stage a flight away from any socioeconomic antagonism within the body politic—the "strife" Parry depicts between head and hands—in the service of securing a mythical and classless national identity increasingly articulated in racial terms. In chapters 3 and 5, we shall explore the limits of these jarring affordances in greater depth. Folk revivalism is shot through with such incongruities, its political vision always at once radical and reactionary—elevating (as "folk") and demonizing (as "mass") different facets of the working-class population.

~

Underpinning these anxieties regarding mass culture, unchecked capitalism, and dubious popular taste was the fallout of rural depopulation and an attendant trepidation over inner-city destitution, congestion, crime, and sanitation. As Sidney J. Low remarked in the *Contemporary Review* in 1891 after decades of agricultural depression brought about by cheap grain imported from the United States, "depletion of the rural districts is a fact which is not to be disputed. . . . [England's] life-blood is being drained from the surrounding country-side" into mining and manufacturing districts and also into the maelstrom of Greater London.[108] To many people, he continues, this "revolution has seemed one which has nothing to relieve its disaster and gloom":

> We have thought of the agricultural labourer converted into a town-dweller, the yokel torn from his hamlet to live in the sweltering black slums of the East-end of a great city. The limbs that were "made in England"—on its healthy ploughlands and fresh meadows—must stunt and dwindle in narrow courts and filthy alleys; the children, who should have pulled the honeysuckle in the lanes and hunted for birds' nests in the hedges, will tumble in the gutter outside the public-house. As the process continues, almost the whole population will be jammed into some score of monster towns, of which London will be the greatest and worst; and tens of millions will be exposed to the physical and mental blight of the "submerged" slum-dweller.[109]

This is the dread that spurred on an interest in folk song at this moment in time—its nostalgic vision a means to restore the hamlet and resist the slums, to celebrate the plowman and rejuvenate the factory worker, to rejoice in the hedgerow and oppose the drunken hordes of a monstrous conurbation blighted by prostitution and figures such as Jack the Ripper stalking the caliginous alleyways of Whitechapel.

Yet what was occurring during the 1890s was a further stage in this social revolution—an unprecedented movement away from the metropolis into the suburbs. Indeed, this new demographic trend was the primary impetus behind Parry's concern with urban degeneracy, and it reveals the Folk-Song Society's concern to be less with rural England than London itself. Drawing on the recently published Census Report, Low notes that inner city slum dwellers "are obeying the great law of centrifugal attraction, and quitting the inner recesses of the metropolis to find new homes in the outskirts."[110] The suburbs, he notes, represent the future of the city across the developed world as segments of the working-class and lower-middle-class population colonize new areas of overflow within commutable distance of their employment. The country's lifeblood was thus in truth "pouring into the long arms of brick and mortar and cheap stucco that are feeling their way out to the Surrey moors, and the Essex flats, and the Hertfordshire copses"; not one, Low

FIGURE 9. "London Life at the East End—Sack-Making by the Light of a Street Lamp," *The Graphic*, 3 April 1875, page 321.

predicted, "but a dozen Croydons will form a circle of detached forts round the central stronghold" of the capital.[111]

Whereas Low believed such resettlement would mitigate any unease caused by the "great exodus from the fields," folk song devotees saw a very different picture.[112] A review of the Society's inaugural meeting in the *Manchester Guardian* singled out Parry's likening of "the latest abomination from the music-halls" to a "jerry-built slum suburb" for special praise, extending this metaphor by suggesting that folk song was unquestionably "a noble memorial of the past" in need of conservation.[113] A similar piece in the *Musical Standard* praised Parry's "eloquent and forcible comparison," adding that his address "was naturally much applauded."[114] Refusing to be reconciled with the realities of a thoroughly urbanized population, folklorists appeared to be what Low calls "nervous and impressionable persons" who tormented themselves with pessimistic dreams, regarding this relinquishment of the native soil as "unnatural," and querying with dismay "where the strength and stamina of the race will go": "Pondering over the lessening vitality, the bowed and stunted frames, the white faces, which are so often the inheritance of the men and women who have been reared close to the hard heart of London, we may have asked ourselves what the lot will be of those who will be doomed to live and toil and die in some dim nest of streets, yet further by many miles from the places where you may see the green of open meadows and hear the rustle of leaves and the music of running brooks."[115] Yet Low was clear that such visions, however persuasive and haunting, were just that—fantasies of gloom and despair impossible to square with data that showed the population moving slowly away from London's dark heart. Parry refused to share in such optimism, his argument projecting what had previously been associated only with noxious inner-city environments onto the cheap stucco of its new outskirts—now also branded as slums and unwholesome wastelands of mass cultural junk.

He was not alone in harboring these suspicions. Betraying pervasive fears surrounding poverty, housing, and morality crystallized in the work of Charles Booth, (then pioneering the large-scale mapping of London's social fabric for reformist ends), slums were a major concern of Victorian life.[116] Such fears tended to revolve around degeneration—one of the foremost obsessions among European intellectuals at the time, exemplified by Max Nordau's *Entartung*, a book attempting to identify the pathological aspects of contemporary art, urbanization, and social decadence, and their baleful effects on the human body.[117] An 1892 article in the *National Observer* entitled "Degeneracy," for instance, bemoaned the "plain," "under-sized," and "ill-made" figures of London's working class, observing by contrast that their forebears "were ruddy, upright peasants" living a village life that had afforded mankind its "highest development"—a life that folk song enthusiasts lamented and desperately struggled to revive.[118] In this view, popular culture was routinely cast as the primary instigator of mental and moral degeneration. A prison physician by the name of Isabel Foard, for instance, asserted that the country risked encouraging "a mechanical mind" signaling a descent into atavism as a result of "the slight sketchy novel, without plot, appealing merely to the senses," "variety entertainment," and "numberless magazines . . . of a light nature, with no attempt at literary effort or style, turned out for the reading of the million."[119] This debilitating culture of "rapidity" and a "growing inability to concentrate ideas," she notes, was also due (as Parry had implied) to "the influence of alcohol."[120] The journalist Robert Donald similarly noted that under the clamor of reporting on the Boer War "the needless waste of life in the struggle for existence in the slums of our large cities goes on, silently and unseen": diseases spread, children "die by the thousand before they know how to suffer," and "degeneracy—moral and physical—poisons an ever-widening circle."[121] "Unless the workmen's colonies in the suburbs are built under better conditions," he stresses, "we will be simply manufacturing more slums for the future."[122]

Parry's remedy for such terminal malaise was the restorative power of folk song. Understood as an instantiation of the rural more broadly, folk song offered a means to revitalize the deteriorating cultural life of the nation just as influxes of rural laborers themselves might regenerate the ailing and enervated racial stock of slum conurbations. The folk, in short, would rejuvenate both the physical and moral life of the nation. As Low emphasized, in an epoch of "urban supremacy, the greatness of the towns has been made less by townsmen than by immigrants from the country." "What will become of the feeble anaemic urban population," he inquires, "when there can be no more immigration from the villages to repair its exhausted vitality?"[123] Replenishing the metropolis and delivering men "with the stalwart frames, the well-chiselled features, the straight limbs of the descendants of the Norse and Saxon tribes that settled on the soil," rural inhabitants—and, by analogy, the songs they conveyed from the depths of time—were prospective redeemers of national character, cures for both the East End slum and the burgeoning cultural wilderness of suburbia.[124]

Set up as an antidote to the pitfalls of industrialized capitalism, the envisioned corpus of the folk proved to be the ideal blank slate upon which the historiographical, social, and geopolitical fantasies of the fin de siècle could be inscribed. Although this folk never existed, they were in effect conjured up through acts of writing and collecting that claimed

FIGURE 10. "Map Descriptive of London Poverty 1898–9, Sheet 5: East Central District" by Charles Booth. The darkest areas were marked as "Lowest class. Vicious, semi-criminal." Note in particular the light-colored area in Shoreditch toward the top left known as the Boundary Estate, which resulted from a clearance of the Old Nichol slum during the 1890s. This was the East End location fictionalized in Arthur Morrison's 1896 novel *A Child of the Jago*.

merely to describe them—a process in which women were respected as collectors, though largely eclipsed when it came to theorizing about the perils of mass culture, which itself was caught up in a gendered schism with the authentic. Consumerism and mass culture were, during this era, progressively bound up with a femininity figuratively coded as inferiority or inauthenticity, marking it as modernism's low other while literally excluding women from the institutions of high culture.[125] We can catch a vivid glimpse of this particular trope in Parry's characterization of popular taste as "lazy and slatternly."[126] Envisaged as a bulwark against this domain and an instrument of social metamorphosis, folk song animated the folk from the purified and reforged residues of vernacular culture—a domain that first needed to be transcribed, categorized, and sanitized in order to count as folklore. Collectors affiliated with the Folk-Song Society thus acted as channels through which folk culture had to pass in order to be understood *as such*. Tellingly, the rural folk they sought out were required to only ever be artisanal producers or bearers of an endangered tradition, never alienated consumers of commercial entertainment—the very opposite of new identities developing within urban mass society.

Although claiming to be a window onto the vernacular and the marginal, folk song was in fact employed to combat the very thing it is most often taken to embody: popular culture. This popular voice, as Richard Middleton reminds us, is forever "plural, hybrid, compromised"—and, we should add, *imagined*.[127] The folk appear to give us access to an unalloyed popular spirit, untroubled by the perversions of the marketplace and the bewildering hybridities of a postcolonial world. They speak with one voice; they compose or sift as one homogeneous, classless body; they channel nature, granting access to the primitive origins of musical culture. And yet we've seen that folk traditions actually emerge from a series of asymmetrical encounters with individuals such as Henry Burstow and the Copper brothers—singers whose material attests not to the clarity of nature, but to the long and murky history of commercial cheap print.[128] Suitably reframed, these figures become entrapped in a twofold synecdoche in which a singer is made to stand in for "the folk," and "the folk" in turn are made to stand in for the imagined community of the nation. Predicated upon a quixotic pursuit of origins, Certeau points out, the vocabulary of folklore defines "less the content of a popular culture than the historian's gaze itself."[129] It is the historian, the folklorist, and the collector who are able to name and neglect, select and reconfigure traces of the past; it is their history we confront in the folk.

Twenty years after Joseph Jacobs's paper at the Folk-Lore Society that we encountered at the opening of this chapter, an extraordinary yet largely overlooked scholar on the other side of the Atlantic by the name of Louise Pound echoed his critique.[130] Much like Jacobs, her incursions on folkloric consensus were sidelined in favor of the seductive essentialism of more publicly prominent (though far less qualified) figures such as John Lomax—one of Pound's early targets for reproach.[131] Pound was convinced that a number of central assumptions needed to be abandoned: belief in communal authorship and ownership, disbelief in primitive artistry, reference to ballads "as the earliest and most universal poetic form," belief in a link between narrative song and festal dance, belief in "the emergence of traditional ballads from the illiterate," belief in the "special powers of folk-improvisation," and finally belief that such culture was dead.[132] After reading her monograph, one instructor wrote to Harvard professor George Lyman Kittredge lamenting that he was unable to refute its tenets: "I felt much as if I had bade adieu to all my lares and penates. . . . She seemed not to have left even one minor god free from attack."[133] The impulsive generation of songs by a homogeneous community, she declares, is a "fatuously speculative" hypothesis detrimental to the field.[134] The fact "that songs have been preserved in remote districts and among the humble," she points out, "is no proof that they were composed in such places and by such people": these songs were better seen, in an inversion of the familiar dictum, as "literature 'for' not 'by' the people."[135]

Given that many collectors focused their salvage on the prestigious Child ballads, Pound argues, they were liable to ignore "many related types of song of equal or greater currency among the folk."[136] Writing in *PMLA*, she summed up her position by charting how Romantic efforts to conceive of humanity en masse had led toward "the bizarre belief in a collective soul which is not to be found in the nature of the souls of the individuals which compose the social group, but which in some mystic sense enwraps the individuals in its all-obscuring fog."[137] Folk song is just this—a history of collective souls, not of individuals, of nations over and above the practice of everyday life. The songs amassed by the Folk-Song Society were valued not in relation to the memories impressed within them by long patterns of use, but as artifacts and signs, treasures and cryptograms, survivals of a time that held the possibility of a cultural rebirth for the coming century. Pound's great insight was to identify a distinction between two irreconcilable approaches to such material, one the province of make-believe, the other of understanding:

"Where the primitivist seeks to replace human thought by dancing puppets, the critic of the tradition endeavors to single out, from the midst of puppetdom, creative human intelligences."[138]

The institutionalization of folk song as an object of intrigue at the fin de siècle exhibits precisely the failing that Pound diagnosed—a cultural dramaturgy in which vernacular singing is replaced by shadow play. Her perspective offers a useful way to begin rethinking the history of the popular by resisting romantic visions of the working class and transforming (to borrow a phrase from Certeau) "what was represented as a matrix-force of history into a mobile infinity of tactics."[139] In so doing, we might in time rescue the forgotten histories of the vernacular from the conceptual shackles of folk song. By detaching this field of inquiry, as Mary Ellen Brown writes, "from the fanciful and intriguing imagined past" we might resuscitate popular singing "as a fluid, dynamic practice more nearly reflecting its lived reality."[140] Folkloric thinking has repeatedly downplayed this lived reality in favor of an Arcadian vision in which songs emerge from a lost, communal state of being. The next chapter asks why this persistent "communal prepossession" that Pound identified among folklorists exerts such a powerful hold on the political imagination.[141]

CHAPTER 3

# Utopian Community

## *Nostalgia from Marx to Morris*

William Morris famously notes in his 1894 essay "How I Became a Socialist" that he had "suffered agonies of confusion of the brain" while grappling with the economic aspects of Marx's *Capital*.[1] He is certainly not alone here. What did appeal to Morris, however, was the historiographical architecture of "that great work."[2] We can find this idea outlined in embryonic form in Marx and Engels's early manuscript *The German Ideology*. In a section on Individuals, Class, and Community, they argue that a class "achieves an independent existence over against the individuals, so that the latter find their conditions of existence predestined, and hence have their position in life and their personal development assigned to them by their class, become subsumed under it."[3] It is "the same phenomenon," they affirm, "as the subjection of the separate individuals to the division of labour and can only be removed by the abolition of private property and of labour itself."[4] We can imagine Morris reading this passage with verve and elation: in it, we find the seeds of his utopian philosophy.

This chapter explores the political impulses and imaginaries of folk song in greater depth. In particular, I argue that folk revivalism manifests a special kind of utopian thinking both in its commitment to more radically egalitarian forms of collective existence and in its envisioning of alternative places or futures for human flourishing. In a folkloric worldview, these possibilities involve the imaginative creation of different social spaces grounded in pastoral or premodern tropes, yet ones that are not simply nostalgic attempts at recreation or restoration, but rather aim at establishing new communities and ways of being. In order to understand this visionary or utopian aspect of the folkloric mentality shared by figures well beyond the folk revival itself, I want to turn to Marx, Morris, and John Ruskin, opening onto their writings and folk music more broadly what Lawrence Kramer once termed a "hermeneutic window"—an aperture "through which our interpretation can pass."[5] Such openings are "a means of recognizing performativity in action" and "responding to it in kind."[6] We will come to see that the discourse of folk song drew upon and evoked a much wider history of antipathy toward industrialized modernity during the nineteenth century expressed by figures with an explicit political agenda: to create a communal society impelled by a distinctive blend of hope and remembering.

In 1886 London's *Pall Mall Gazette* ran a column titled "The Best Hundred Books by the Best Hundred Judges," a forerunner of today's proliferating "must-read" lists. Inspired by a collection of texts drawn up by John Lubbock, the paper had sought to produce its own series by prominent men and women from different walks of life in order to guide the public through "the bewildering labyrinth" of available books and ultimately to help them choose their reading material "more wisely."[7] Along with respondents including William Gladstone and Emilia Dilke was the indefatigable William Morris. The editor framed Morris's offering by noting that it was "one of the freshest and most interesting of all the lists which have been sent to us."[8] Declining to reach the target number of one hundred, Morris instead proposes fifty-four titles beginning with the Hebrew Bible and ending with Jacob Grimm's *Deutsche Mythologie* (1835), published in English translation as *Teutonic Mythology* between 1880 and 1888. It is significant that Morris includes Grimm's book among what he chooses to call "works of art." In a short addendum he reasons that although *Teutonic Mythology* functions more as a "tool" or valuable source of information, "it is so crammed with the material for imagination, and has in itself such a flavour of imagination, that I felt bound to put it down."[9] Indeed, imagination appears to be the defining criteria for inclusion in Morris's list. Although celebrated novelists such as Scott and Dickens and poets such as Coleridge and Keats appear as expected, they are overshadowed by what Morris describes as "Medieval story-books" and "Medieval poetry" ranging from "Danish and Scotch-English Border ballads" to *The Thousand and One Nights*.

At the top of Morris's list are works that he describes as "Bibles"—books that, he confesses, "cannot always be measured by a literary standard, but to me are far more important than any literature," as "they are in no sense the work of individuals, but have grown up from the very hearts of the *people*."[10] As we shall come to see, this is the folkloric imagination at its most clear-cut: the belief that the best art is not the product of individual creative artifice but rather the instinctive expression of the populace, the humble and uncorrupted folk, the collective, the race, the homeland. Morris is far less interested in upholding ideals of nationalism, however, than in texts that are somehow more organic and mystical than others—ones that show the imagination more fully at play. They include works that Grimm portrays as containing "the evident deposit from god-myths," survivals "found to this day in various folk-tales, nursery-tales, games, saws, curses, ill-understood names of days and months, and idiomatic phrases."[11] This fascination with ancient legends and mythical heroes was bound up with Morris's affection for imagined worlds, timeless epics, and the exotic—an aesthetic inclination that went hand in hand with his distinctive form of fin-de-siècle radicalism.[12]

Also included in Morris's list is Thomas More's *Utopia*, a work that he reproduced in an elaborately decorated edition for the Kelmscott Press in 1893. Morris offered a foreword to this edition, in which he notes that the book seemed to offer up "a prediction of a state of society" almost like "a Socialist tract" newly resonant with a nineteenth-century political mindset.[13] More's book, he insists, "is a necessary part of a Socialist's library" as it condemns "the injustice and cruelty of the revolution which destroyed the peasant life of England, and turned it into a grazing farm for the moneyed gentry"—something built on the backs of propertyless wage earners.[14] Moderating or perhaps unconcerned with the satirical virtuosity of *Utopia* (the report of a man named Hythloday or "purveyor of nonsense" about a place called "no-place" in which the governor's title is "people-less"), Morris finds in More a kindred spirit longing for communism and equally repulsed by "the ugly brutality of the earliest period of Commercialism," that "new-born capitalistic society."[15] Such opinions on mass culture and urbanization, as we saw in the previous chapter, are another hallmark of the folkloric imagination. By replacing feudalism, in this view, capitalism abolishes the peasant life of England with its ancient communal rites and introduces alienating urban squalor, individualism, and unscrupulous market conditions in which the lowest forms of art multiply just like the masses who heedlessly consume them. What we have, in other words, is the blueprint for an Adornian antipathy toward commodity culture as the ruthless commercial debasement of creative expression.[16]

What had spurred Morris on to pen his own utopian romance in 1890, however, was the appearance and unprecedented popularity of a contemporary utopian novel entitled *Looking Backward: 2000–1887* by the American author Edward Bellamy. Despite being appreciative of the spur it had given to socialist discussion across the Atlantic, Morris was deeply skeptical of Bellamy's premise. His criticism revolved around the question of just how radical and disruptive a socialist upheaval would be—a question vital to understanding the convoluted ways in which aspects of socialism laid the groundwork for fascist ideology (something I address in chapter 5). For Morris, what Bellamy offers up in his novel is a "dangerous hope": "It follows naturally from the author's satisfaction with the best part of modern life that he conceives of the change to Socialism as taking place without any breakdowns of that life, or indeed disturbance of it, by means of the final development of the great private monopolies which are such a noteworthy feature of the present day. He supposes that these must necessarily be absorbed into one great monopoly which will include the whole people and be worked for its benefit by the whole people."[17] With history and hindsight on our side, it's clear that Morris's concerns about a robust state and bureaucratic centralization—"the mere *machinery* of life," as he puts it—were entirely justified.[18] Indeed, Bellamy's book easily and unintentionally shades into the dystopian landscapes drawn so vividly by Huxley and Orwell.[19]

Reading his review, it is hard not to pick out phrases that signpost an unwitting descent into totalitarianism: "organization of life," "State Communism," "the very extreme of national centralization," "a huge standing army, tightly drilled."[20] But above all, according to Morris, Bellamy's problem was a deficiency of creative imagination—a failure to push beyond the most obvious and comfortable middle-class answers to deep-rooted problems of social harmony. If a nationalistic monopoly was indeed the solution, it had been arrived at through the very means (competition, privilege, and profit) that Morris found so wasteful and objectionable in the first place. In many ways, Bellamy's utopia was thus simply an intensification or nightmarish expansion of the commercial mindset—the exact opposite of Morris's revolutionary socialist ambition to overthrow Victorian economic organization and its supposed prosperity. Though all the citizens appear to have their every need and caprice satisfied, Morris indicates that this may not be the best definition of concord and happiness. Instead, he notes, it points toward Bellamy's obsession with cogs and systems over and above questions of mind, aesthetics, and being. The resultant picture is too limited, too stratified, and far too urbanized ("such aggregations of population," Morris feels, "afford the worst possible form of dwelling-place").[21] In short, what we have is a kind of futurism *avant la lettre*—"a machine-life" orchestrated by ever evolving labor-saving technologies and innovations.[22] The result, Morris wonders? More and more machines with precious little gains in time, energy, or freedom.

The penultimate paragraph of his review ends with a rough draught of the kind of society that Morris would attempt to create in his own idiosyncratic utopia:

> It will be necessary for the unit of administration to be small enough for every citizen to feel himself responsible for its details, and be interested in them; that individual men cannot shuffle off the business of life on to the shoulders of an abstraction called the State, but must deal with it in conscious association with each other: that variety of life is as much an aim of a true Communism as equality of condition, and that nothing but an union of these two will bring about real freedom: that modern nationalities are mere artificial devices for the commercial war that we seek to put an end to, and will disappear with it. And, finally, that art, using that word in its widest and due signification, is not a mere adjunct of life which free and happy men can do without, but the necessary expression and indispensable instrument of human happiness.[23]

From this succinct outline we can see just how different Morris's utopian vision is from Bellamy's patriotic, meritocratic, and coldly rationalized ideal—the result of a quasi-Fabian "process of industrial evolution" organized and staffed by a vast "industrial army."[24] For Morris, art was not simply the raw material for recreation and social reform, but something much more profound: the flower or foliage of a healthy society, the efflorescence of human nature under conditions of true liberation.

So what would this society look like? A rather unsympathetic *New York Times* review of Morris's novella *News from Nowhere; or, An Epoch of Rest* suggested that his utopian idyll resembled something familiar to Oxford undergraduates—"one long water party on the Thames."[25] It was, this review noted, "the aesthetic or sentimental side of future socialism" that had entranced Morris in a book filled with strangely courteous and picturesque characters dressed in medieval garb "hitting right and left at what the conservative Englishman deems sacred."[26] New York opinion seems to have been ranged against Morris. A similar article in *The Critic* asserted that although utopias had become "the fashion of the day" owing to a widespread desire to escape unsatisfactory aspects of the present by taking "refuge in ideal systems and societies of the future," Morris's book read more like a "burlesque" of the genre.[27] British attitudes at times echoed this view. An amusing article in *The Speaker* pointed to the fact that Morris had somehow managed to reform England's weather in the process of reorganizing its society. Crime, aggression, and exasperation, furthermore, had entirely disappeared in this dreamland "so cultivating is the influence of oak bridges on the mind, so ennobling is the atmosphere beneath a gabled roof."[28]

But other readers were somewhat more taken with Morris's bucolic vision. Comparing *News from Nowhere* favorably with *Looking Backward* ("a nightmare spectacle of machinery dominating the world" that "deserved the bonfire"), the poet Lionel Johnson found much to be grateful for—above all, those "virile and pleasant pages . . . which tell of England's natural beauty, of the sylvan Thames, and of the Oxfordshire meadows."[29] The book's central tenets, he claims, are that "pleasure in work is the secret of art and of content" and that "delight in physical life upon earth is the natural state of man."[30] Quoting from Walt Whitman's poem "Give Me the Splendid Silent Sun" ("Give me solitude—give me Nature—give me again, / O Nature, your primal sanities!"), he agrees with Morris that "we must simplify ourselves" and turn away from modern puzzlement, sophistication, and complexity towards the more primitive sources of joy and strength found in nature.[31] Writing in *The Economic Journal*, William Graham found echoes of a Rousseauian state of innocence mixed in with Mikhail Bakunin's anarchism—a "new Arcadia" of open-air living predicated on a rejection of the sordid architecture of modern industry, "for Mr. Morris has an artistic quarrel with the Nineteenth Century which is quite as deep as his social quarrel."[32] And yet Graham also pointed out the impracticality of Morris's project, ignoring as it did problems of empire, inheritance, the state "reviving after civil confusion," imperfections of human nature, and the unlikelihood of an English working class "very sane on all practical questions" striking up a revolutionary civil war "on account of Labour and Capital disputes."[33] Such issues, however, did not prevent *News from Nowhere* from being selected as a book of the month in *The Review of Reviews*, confirming its appeal as a contemporaneous parable.[34]

Together, these reviews suggest that a certain way of thinking was shared between Morris and the folk revivalist milieu as it coalesced around the fin de siècle, notwithstanding differences in attitude toward nationalism and revolutionary change. They attest to a distinctive worldview that rejected conservative politics, liberal economics, metropolitan sophistication, and the ethically or aesthetically ugly aspects of Victorian industry, while embracing a historically dubious conception of Merry England characterized by virility, mirth, communal spirit, and pleasure in craft. Drawing on aspects of both English Romanticism and American Transcendentalism, as we've already seen, these values ultimately indicated a desire for simplification and solace in the natural world—calling to mind that other wistful waterborne journey undertaken by Thoreau that would become *A Week on the Concord and Merrimack Rivers*. Given the ways in which a folkloric imagination has since come to be associated with the consolation of tradition on the political right, it's sometimes hard to see just how close the association could be between pastoral nostalgia, folklore, and socialist thought during the late nineteenth century.[35] What we should remember is that Morris's Arcadian no-place in *News from Nowhere* is not merely elegiac, escapist, or backward looking, but also subversive, critical, and indeed utopian.

Such aims were recognized perhaps most acutely in an anonymous 1904 article for *The Speaker* criticizing Rudyard Kipling's short story "The Army of a Dream" that conjured up an English military utopia. In contrast to such a brutal and absurd wish, the author notes, Morris "makes clear to us what we desire. . . . He fills us with the divine discontent that alone can work great changes upon the life of man."[36] *News from Nowhere* was "a dream too beautiful ever to come true, but so vivid in its beauty that it might almost persuade the world to attempt its realisation."[37] In other words, the purpose of the novella was not to be an allegory or premonition, but a catalyst for the very changes it portrayed—a prototype of socialist realism aimed at instigating the eventual realization of a communist society through art:

> Morris imagined a society freed of all our present encumbrances and perversions, the waste of war and competition, the blind despotism of machinery, the baffling division of classes—a society in which everyone did what was worth doing for its own sake and delighted therefore in doing it. . . . We are a country-loving people, though crowded by our own folly and a perverse density into towns. The people in *News from Nowhere* live in cottages or country towns, with orchards and meadows close about the market place. They have regained our forefathers' love and genius for noble building and

> fine craftsmanship. They delight in the earth, in their gardens, in the harvest, in unpolluted rivers, and in forests freed from the gamekeeper.[38]

Here, we can begin to see Morris's utopianism for what it is: an unequivocal critique of *now-here*, not merely a fantasy escape into *no-where*.[39] Morris the socialist is also Morris the environmentalist and the champion of skills in danger of being lost to the boundless headway of industrial modernity. In the book, Morris "turned the best and simplest part of English life into the whole of it," giving his readers a glimpse of utopian experience, rather than a stilted portrait of mere governance.[40]

As a critique of the here and now of the nineteenth century, Morris's book shares a theme with Bellamy's *Looking Backward*. In a reversal of the classic utopian device, Bellamy's time-traveling protagonist Julian West dreams toward the end of the novel that he is back in 1887, before finally waking up at last to the realities of a utopian Boston in the late twentieth century. During this nightmare, West scans a daily newspaper summarizing "impending war," "great suffering among the unemployed in London," "great strikes in Belgium," "evictions in Ireland," an "epidemic of fraud," "shocking corruption," "bribery," "burglaries and larcenies," murder, suicide, illiteracy, and insanity—topped off by "Professor Brown's oration on the moral grandeur of nineteenth century civilization."[41] He is disgusted by such "fatuous self-complacency," the "prevalence of advertising," and the "repulsiveness" of "this horrible babel of shameless self-assertion and mutual depreciation."[42] What stands out in particular is West's abhorrence of the selfish, superfluous, and inefficient nature of free-market commerce epitomized by the countless stores with their elaborate window displays each competing to sell the same pseudo-individualized goods to a burgeoning mass market. Mirroring the infamous department store in Émile Zola's *Au bonheur des dames*, West primarily associates this rampant commercialism with women—"throngs of ladies looking in, and the proprietors eagerly watching the effect of the bait."[43] But although gendered in this way (as consumerism tended to be), the culprit was in fact blind individualism, a cult of the self pursued at the expense of social cohesion. In it, we can find the kernel of neoliberal ideology: British Prime Minister Margaret Thatcher's insistence that "there is no such thing as society" but rather the need to "take responsibility for ourselves."[44]

Bellamy is surely in agreement with Morris when he describes the din and disarray of industrial manufacturing as a kind of infernal combat, its "roar and rattle of wheels and hammers" sounding like "the clangor of swords wielded by foemen" intent on destroying their adversaries.[45] In "Useful Work *versus* Useless Toil" Morris elaborates on the social relations underpinning this denunciation of capitalist activity and the dismal, cacophonous soundscapes of urban industry. Labour under capitalism, he argues, is "slave's work—mere toiling to live, that we may live to toil."[46] The working class, who not only produce goods but also supply the profits that others live on, are locked into a position of structural inferiority "involving a degradation both of mind and body."[47] In Marxist language, they are suffering from false consciousness. Labourers are forced into consuming "shams and mockeries of the luxury of the rich" that serve to keep them in bondage—"slave-wares whose use is the perpetuation of their slavery."[48] This is precisely the same argument that, as we saw in the previous chapter, Hubert Parry uses in his inaugural address to London's Folk-Song Society to condemn the "sham," "vulgarity," and "tawdriness" of crowded conurbations.[49] Such hostility toward mass culture was often indivisible from this opposition to an exploitation of the urban proletariat. After a century of progress and triumph, most of the country still seemed to many to be as poor and exhausted as ever—tortured, in addition, with wants and desires it found impossible to satisfy. Bellamy paints an extraordinary picture of this dark underbelly of modernity when his protagonist wanders through slums filled with "pale babies gasping out their lives amid sultry stenches," "hopeless-faced women deformed by hardship," and "swarms of half-clad brutalized children."[50] "Crowded towns and bewildering factories," Morris likewise asserts, "are simply the outcome of the profit system" and have no place in utopia.[51]

Instead of slaving away in the service of profit, Morris writes, useful labour involves working for the good of the whole community—a community of equals who rejoice and take pleasure in their work, typified by the man who exercises "the energy of his mind and soul as well as of his body" guided by "memory and imagination" and "the thoughts of the men of past ages."[52] Such ideas foreshadowed and indeed set the terms for how folk song enthusiasts of the late nineteenth century and beyond would come to understand the nation's musical heritage. Discussing what he refers to as "Popular Art," Morris claims that the intense pressures of modern industry suppress those things made "by the ordinary workman while he is about his ordinary work":

> This art, I repeat, no longer exists now, having been killed by commercialism. But from the beginning of man's contest with Nature till the rise of the present capitalistic system, it was alive, and generally flourished. While it lasted,

> everything that was made by man was adorned by man, just as everything made by Nature is adorned by her. The craftsman, as he fashioned the thing he had under his hand, ornamented it so naturally and so entirely without conscious effort, that it is often difficult to distinguish where the mere utilitarian part of his work ended and the ornamental began.[53]

We find in this passage crucial elements of the folkloric imagination entwined with an ardent elevation of spontaneous, non-instrumental creativity: something made without conscious effort as a mirror to the inner workings of Nature; something that lives and flourishes but is later destroyed by capital and laid to rest by commerce; something in need of rescue and resuscitation. Morris's elegy for popular craft—seen not as something made *for* the people, but *by* the people out of their own necessities and imagination—is one and the same as the elegy for authentic popular song that sent generations of collectors out into the woods and fields in search of the folk.

At least one critic picked up on this point of intersection in the wake of the Edwardian folk revival. In his waggish book *Music Ho! A Study of Music in Decline*, Constant Lambert complains that there is something about folk song and the art music compositions it inspired "both unbearably precious and unbearably hearty": "Its preciosity recalls the admirably meant endeavours of William Morris and his followers to combat the products of those dark satanic mills with green and unpleasant handwoven materials, while its heartiness conjures up the hideous faux bonhomie of the hiker, noisily wading his way through the petrol pumps of Metroland, singing obsolete sea chanties with the aid of the Week End Book, imbibing chemically flavoured synthetic beer under the impression that he is tossing off a tankard of 'jolly good ale and old' in the best Chester-Belloc manner."[54] His mention of the *Week-End Book* is largely lost on us today, but this eccentric 1924 anthology edited by Francis and Vera Meynell was a bestseller at the time. The mention of "Chester-Belloc" is an allusion to George Bernard Shaw's chimeric coupling of G. K. Chesterton and Hilaire Belloc in a 1908 article for *The New Age*. This reference is a little more cryptic, but turns on two aspects of Shaw's reproach: first, that they denote an "addiction to the pleasures of the table" that jars with the vegetarian or teetotal aspects of socialist radicalism; and second, that they like to speak for and "pretend to be the English people . . . or 'the folk.'"[55] Lambert's distaste for the "hearty" aspects of folk music thus revolves around hypocrisy: its admirers hike rather than drive cars, fantasize that ersatz beer is craft ale, and sing obsolete leftist anthems while pretending to represent the

FIGURE 11. Bird design in woven wool by William Morris, 1878. Morris had designed this pattern for the drawing room of his family home, Kelmscott House, in Hammersmith, London.

common man. If theirs was a rejection of the modern world, it appeared to be a superficial and affected one.

The "precious" element that Lambert articulates, via a humorous pairing of William Blake's "dark Satanic Mills" not with the anticipated "green and pleasant Land" but green and irksome hand-woven textiles, is a reference to Morris's revival of traditional crafts such as embroidery, tapestry, and weaving. In this context, it's hard not to recall Parry's well-known setting of "And did those feet in ancient time"—a text imbued with a folkloric yearning for England's archaic landscapes untouched by the aesthetic pollution of industrialization. Lambert is, of course, using the word precious according to what the *OED* defines as something "aiming at or affecting refinement in manners . . . over-delicate, over-fastidious; affectedly refined."[56] His criticism, nestled demurely between the lines, is that it is naive at best and sheer stupidity at worst to believe that handwoven textiles can combat or surmount the products and practices of capitalist modernity, whatever the good intentions.

By the 1930s, it seems, the utopian aspects of Morris's aesthetic project had been almost entirely downplayed or overlooked. Lumped together, Morris and folk revivalism are reduced to laughably ineffectual attempts to resist the behemoth of socioeconomic advancement—the folly of an age of innocence. Folk music had, in Lambert's words, become one element within a broader "cult of the exotic" in which Orientalism "and the cult of the peasant are curiously intermingled" often with nationalistic intent, resulting in a "nostalgic world of escape."[57]

But for Morris's generation of radicals, folk song meant much more than this. We know from his daughter that he had "a genuine love for music" reflecting his distinctive tastes in literature.[58] "The music that never failed to reach his heart," she recollects, "was the music of the people—from the times when they were fortunate enough to have music in them; the English folk-songs, the Irish, the French, the Scandinavian airs."[59] He disliked "the mechanical quality of the piano," preferring instead stringed and woodwind instruments, singing, and the bagpipes.[60] Just like the folk revivalists who were to follow him, these were not simply aesthetic choices, but tastes that echoed, sustained, and sought to realize a unique political vision. For Morris, as Elizabeth Helsinger notes, folk traditions evoked a time when song was a craft "like that of the stonecarver or the weaver, allied to rhythmic gestures of voice and body"—a form exemplifying the pleasures of participation in a community that offered a means "to imagine a new kind of fellowship in a socialist future."[61]

In *News from Nowhere*, Morris sets out a vision of society that is at once both radically utopian and a return to precapitalist modes of production and consumption. Engels had described such a society in *Socialism: Utopian and Scientific*. During the medieval era, he writes, "the question as to the owner of the product of labour could not arise" because, as craftsmen, "the individual producer, as a rule, had, from raw material belonging to himself, and generally his own handiwork, produced it with his own tools, by the labour of his own hands."[62] Wants and needs were thus satisfied within communities on a small scale, and products "did not assume the character of commodities" because "the family of the peasant produced almost everything they wanted: clothes and furniture, as well as means of subsistence."[63] But these statements form part of Engels's "scientific" account of historical dialectics in which society evolves from a primitive medieval condition through capitalist revolution to a final proletarian revolution where the means of production are transformed into public property, classes dissolve, state authority withers away, and all contradictions are resolved. They point toward an "act of universal emancipation" in which "man, at last the master of his own form of social organisation, becomes at the same time the lord over Nature, his own master—free."[64] In contrast, he argues, the utopianism of Saint-Simon, Fourier, and Robert Owen had "governed the Socialist ideas of the 19th century" with a crude "mish-mash" of theories.[65] Engels is adamant that such projects were simply "propaganda" imposed on society from without: "These new social systems were foredoomed as Utopian; the more completely they were worked out in detail, the more they could not avoid drifting off into pure phantasies."[66]

Morris's nowhere, however, is unusual for including both this "scientific" model and the "utopian" dream of authentic communal existence. In a substantial chapter titled "How the Change Came," Morris's protagonist William Guest asks his newfound utopian comrade Hammond how communism first emerged, inquiring if this revolution was peaceful. Hammond's reply is that the "period of transition from commercial slavery to freedom" was in fact "war from beginning to end."[67] Yet this riotous epoch of change was inspired by a romantic, visionary longing:

> When the hope of realizing a communal condition of life for all men arose, quite late in the nineteenth century, the power of the middle classes, the then tyrants of society, was so enormous and crushing, that to almost all men, even those who had, you may say despite themselves, despite their reason and judgement, conceived such hopes, it seemed a dream. So much was this the case that some of those more enlightened men who were then called Socialists, although they well knew, and even stated in public, that the only reasonable condition of Society was that of pure Communism (such as you now see around you), yet shrunk from what seemed to them the barren task of preaching the realization of a happy dream. Looking back now, we can see that the great motive-power of the change was a longing for freedom and equality, akin if you please to the unreasonable passion of the lover; a sickness of heart that rejected with loathing the aimless solitary life of the well-to-do educated man of that time.[68]

Morris clearly finds it difficult to throw off the trappings of an educated man entirely, with this subtle nod to the opening scene of *Hamlet*—a sickness of heart that also calls to mind Blake's sick rose, indicating his sense of a deep moral and political decay lurking under the handsome exterior of modern wealth and prosperity.

Although a form of cultural elitism, this visionary ability served the interests of society as a whole. As Hammond goes on to note, the

FIGURE 12. *King David the Poet*, stained glass panel 83 × 50 cm by Edward Burne-Jones (figure) and William Morris (background), 1863. An early commission for Morris, Marshall, Faulkner & Co. (the firm that would become Morris & Co. in 1875), this piece was made for the breakfast room at Silsden, a Yorkshire house built for the textile manufacturer Charles Hastings.

working classes were "too much burdened with the misery of their lives . . . to be able to form a conception of any escape from it except by the ordinary way prescribed by the system of slavery under which they lived"—that being "nothing more than a remote chance of climbing out of the oppressed into the oppressing class."[69] Industrialization is blamed for this creation of opposing and unharmonious social factions—classes that would be impossible to reconcile save through revolutionary upheaval. To borrow Hannah Arendt's words, Morris was interested in offering solutions to rising forces of "social atomization and extreme individualization" within this class-ridden society "whose cracks had been cemented with nationalistic sentiment."[70] The role of socialist radicals and dreamers, according to Morris, was to lead the way out of this cycle of class antagonism, division, and subjugation with the aid of the imagination. Without such stimulus, the masses appeared to lack the inclination or ability to throw off their shackles of bondage and reach toward a better future. Art, in other words, could take on a role as a political tool to manufacture class-consciousness among the laboring population—a consciousness that would provoke uprisings against an exploitative system and answer the ideological calling of the proletariat.

In Morris's world, this revolution happens in stages, progressing from an incipient form of state socialism and labor federation in which the working classes nevertheless remain "ill-organized, and growing poorer in reality" through minor riots across the country to the "great crash" of 1952 triggered by mass suffering, government inefficiency, and industrial unrest.[71] After a skirmish in Trafalgar Square in which "the civic *bourgeois* guard (called the police)" are overcome with only a few fatalities on either side, men and women take to the streets on such a scale that they cannot be suppressed—a counterfactual reshaping of events that Morris had witnessed at first hand in London only a few years before as groups of radical socialists and Irish nationalists clashed with a Metropolitan police force augmented by armed troops on Bloody Sunday of 1887.[72] Although at first afraid to use force to subdue this "state of siege" in the capital, in Morris's account, the executive finally appoints a general—"a mere military machine"—whose soldiers proceed to set up "mechanical guns" in front of an unarmed multitude.[73] An eyewitness describes this event for the reader: "It was as if the earth had opened, and hell had come up bodily amidst us. . . . Deep lanes were mowed amidst the thick crowd; the dead and dying covered the ground, and the shrieks and wails and cries of horror filled all the air."[74] It is by far the most disquieting scene in an otherwise serene narrative, foreshadowing the violence of the First World War and acts of democide that have come to define the past century.[75] In what might strike us now as either a moment of faith in human compassion or egregious naivety, Morris paints this massacre as the turning point in which soldiers find themselves unable to continue inflicting carnage despite orders to the contrary. It marks the beginnings of a civil war and a realignment of political sympathies.

Grassroots networks of workmen's associations answerable to common interests instead of a hierarchical structure emerge in the wake of this conflict, depending "not on a carefully arranged centre with all kinds of checks and counter-checks about it, but on a huge mass of people in thorough sympathy with the movement, bound together by a great number of links of small centres."[76] This is the heart of Morris's vision of a genuinely communal society—a new social fabric woven out of myriad links and small regions, self-sufficient districts with no need for a powerful state apparatus or any source of coercive authority. It is the kind of society that Noam Chomsky describes arising from the "natural struggle for liberation"—one that "runs counter to the prevailing tendency towards centralization in economic and political life" in the modern world.[77] Morris, in short, was advocating for a form of libertarian socialism or anarchism. Indeed, to quote Chomsky (paraphrasing Marx), Morris was in complete agreement that "control of production by a state bureaucracy, no matter how benevolent its intentions" will not create "conditions under which labor, manual and intellectual, can become the highest want in life."[78]

As Morris attests in true anarchist spirit, "state ownership and management" will inevitably lead to "bureaucratic despotism."[79] In his review of the book, William Graham was thus correct to find in its pages traces of Bakuninian thinking. Indeed, Bakunin had insisted that there was a flaw in Marxist approaches to the state:

> There is a flagrant contradiction in this theory. If their state would be really of the people, why eliminate it? And if the State is needed to emancipate the workers, then the workers are not yet free, so why call it a People's State? By our polemic against them we have brought them to the realization that freedom or anarchism, which means a free organization of the working masses from the bottom up, is the final objective of social development, and that every state, not excepting their People's State, is a yoke, on the one hand giving rise to despotism and on the other to slavery.[80]

In Morris's fragile pre-utopian moment marked by civil strife between rebels and reactionaries, the state is slowly brought to its knees by a general strike and the dissemination of didactic literature among the population via socialist newspapers that (in a metaphor freighted with folkloric meaning) "came upon the public with a kind of May-day freshness."[81] It is in this context that "the sloth, the hopelessness, and . . . the cowardice" of the nineteenth century slowly gives way "to the eager, restless heroism of a declared revolutionary period"—and finally to peace.[82]

What I want to focus upon is Morris's attitude toward labor and alienation. For Morris, the problem of alienation was closely allied to his libertarian philosophy. Hammond tells Guest that the "spirit of the new days" is characterized above all by "delight in the life of the world; intense and overweening love of the very skin and surface of the earth."[83] Having swept away the unsightly façade of modernity, this existence instead evoked "the spirit of the Middle Ages."[84] How did the people regain this spirit in the wake of capitalism? According to the old sage, the remedy was "the production of what used to be called art, but which has no name amongst us now, because it has become a necessary part of the labour of every man who produces."[85] Such work recuperated a lost tradition: "What of art existed under the old forms," Hammond tells us, "*revived* in a wonderful way during the latter part of the struggle, especially as regards music and poetry."[86] Much like the splendid and stalwart utopians themselves, art in this utopia is healthy and imbued with new life—restored to its rightful place in the hearts of the common people just as folk song collectors desired, testament to a rediscovered awareness of the aesthetic.

Nowhere, in short, is a haven for craft and artistic work to such an extent that they cease to be referred to as such, emerging organically as a result of unalienated labor. In Morris's vision, work and pleasure are hence one and the same:

> The art or work-pleasure, as one ought to call it . . . sprung up almost spontaneously, it seems, from a kind of instinct among people, no longer driven desperately to painful and terrible overwork, to do the best they could with the work in hand—to make it excellent of its kind; and when that had gone on for a little, a craving for beauty seemed to awaken in men's minds, and they began rudely and awkwardly to ornament the wares which they made; and when they had once set to work at that, it soon began to grow. All this was much helped by the abolition of the squalor which our immediate ancestors put up with so coolly; and by the leisurely, but not stupid, country-life which now grew (as I told you before) to be common amongst us. Thus at last and by slow degrees we got pleasure into our work; then we became conscious of that pleasure, and cultivated it, and took care that we had our fill of it; and then all was gained, and we were happy.[87]

Here is the utopian dream in a nutshell. Art, happiness, and a desire for embellishment arise spontaneously like meadow wildflowers in spring, the instinctual outpourings of an economic system no longer seeking to exploit laborers as a social underclass—its allure and craving for beauty offering up a mirror to the abolition of urban squalor and a life lived communally, unhurriedly, and in tune with nature.

What Morris sketches via Hammond is thus a silhouette of the folkloric trope: an expressive practice springing up unconsciously among humans in a healthy, childlike state of body and mind (discernable from their unsophisticated ornamentation); something growing instinctively that is later cultivated (attesting to the etymology of the word *culture* itself); something given life and meaning as a result of its proximity to nature and the simple, unsullied pleasures of the countryside; something manifesting a set of social relations more ancient, honest, and communal than the present.[88] Through his utopians, Morris is offering us a picture of what creative practice would look like if society were to be arranged in a radically different way. He holds a fundamental faith not only in society's ability to right itself, but also in ordinary people's capacity to produce and admire beautiful things when treated justly and with respect. His utopia is an allegorical glass house in which we see human culture at its best—no longer deprived of the ingredients needed to flourish. In this world, poetry and music revive, coming back to life having been pushed to the brink of extinction and inanity by an unjust system obstinately valuing profit over people, quantity over quality, and efficiency over ethics. Nowhere is a hermetic Eden where commercial degeneration cannot exist—an earthly paradise that folk revivalists would desperately try to recapture as they sought to rescue and revitalize songs of the ancient past. What *News from Nowhere* affords is hence a way to map out and trace a particular understanding of culture located at the core of folkloric reasoning.

Central to this set of values and beliefs is the idea that art not only has the potential to function as prerevolutionary propaganda (disseminating the ideas of an enlightened minority) but also, and more importantly, that it thrives in the population at large only under utopian conditions. These conditions, as we have seen, are characterized by unalienated or re-enchanted labor. Morris knew full well that artisanal work of the kind he produced through Morris & Co. was the preserve of an elite able to afford such luxuries—quite the opposite of the situation envisaged in utopia. What prevented the working classes from adopting traditional techniques, of course, were the brutal demands of industrialized capitalism. Marx describes it thus in *Capital*:

> All means for the development of production transform themselves into means of domination over, and exploitation of, the producers; they mutilate the labourer into a fragment of a man, degrade him to the level of an appendage of a machine, destroy every remnant of charm in his work and turn it into a hated toil; they estrange from him the intellectual potentialities of the labour-process in the same proportion as science is incorporated in it as an independent power; they distort the conditions under which he works, subject him during the labour-process to a despotism the more hateful for its meanness; they transform his life-time into working-time, and drag his wife and child beneath the wheels of the Juggernaut of capital.[89]

It is not a pretty picture. Alienation mutilates, fragments, degrades, distorts, and finally destroys life. Under capitalist labor relations, the worker is not simply a machine, but the mere accessory to a machine, a slave to it and the owner of this means of production—more accurately portrayed as a "means of domination." Yet exploitation is not the only torment: equally pitiless, Marx claims, is the process by which industrial wage laborers have the *pleasure* of manual work and its intellectual aspects stripped from them. Their entire being, in essence, is instrumentalized.

The worker, Marx writes in his 1844 *Economic and Philosophic Manuscripts*, "sinks to the level of a commodity" within this "system of estrangement."[90] Their labor is reified as a product that serves in turn to enchain them and generate wealth for somebody else—the owner of private property. Both this product and this somebody else are always other, constituting the worker's alienation. Their estrangement, he argues, "manifests itself not only in the result, but also in the *act of production*, within the *activity of production* itself."[91] This is because labor under capitalism is forced upon the worker in return for wages as a way to satisfy external needs, engendering a system in which the thing produced does not belong to the worker who, in effect, no longer entirely belongs to him- or herself. Such work, in consequence, has an "alien character"—it is a form of "self-sacrifice" for the worker that "does not develop free mental and physical energy, but mortifies his flesh and ruins his mind."[92] Put simply, "estranged labour reduces spontaneous and free activity to a means."[93] For Marx, there is one final and paramount abuse that these forms of social organization and coercion bring about: the alienation of workers not only from labor per se, but also from nature and what he describes as "species-life" or "species-being"—the essence of what it means to be human characterized by "free conscious activity."[94] We can read his condemnation of capitalist labor relations, therefore, as an attack on their capacity to undermine and break apart the fabric of society, those bonds of cooperation and solidarity that make up a community of free individuals freely pursuing their own ends. The only solution, as Morris likewise believed, was "the *emancipation of the workers*" because "in their emancipation is contained universal human emancipation."[95]

We can thus begin to see just how high the stakes were surrounding something as ostensibly insignificant as a manufacturing process. Morris and Marx are concerned with emancipation not simply as the answer to structural inequality and class exploitation, but also as a way to put an end to forms of production that rob people of their spirit and humanity as well as their relationship to nature, society, and quotidian existence. Resisting endemic alienation in the capitalist economy was nothing less than opposing the existential servitude of mankind. Although Morris would not have been able to read the *Economic and Philosophic Manuscripts* (they were published in 1932, with an English translation only appearing in 1959), his utopian vision is a striking realization of Marxist "species-being" in which labor is no longer simply a means, but a pleasurable end in and of itself. Morris's Nowhere delivers a fictional inversion of alienation and estrangement—a domain of refuge, liberation, and recuperation from what John Ruskin portrayed as "the storm-cloud of the nineteenth century."[96] In fact, it is Ruskin to whom Morris owes his greatest debt with regard to these observations on the barbaric failings of industrialized labor. Having encountered his writings while at Oxford, Morris later admitted that "before my days of practical Socialism, [Ruskin] was my master towards the ideal aforesaid. . . . It was through him that I learned to give form to my discontent."[97]

In the second volume of Ruskin's *The Stones of Venice* we find a remarkable echo of Marx's ideas from the 1844 manuscripts. Ruskin's argument is concerned principally with defending the "rude and wild" Gothic architecture of northern Europe against a dull and degrading uniformity of style.[98] Given the freedom to create and make mistakes, he argues, stonemasons are saved from being a mere "animated tool," whereas if precision and perfection are demanded, making "their fingers measure degrees like cog-wheels, and their arms strike curves like compasses, you must unhumanize them."[99] Much like folklorists and song collectors, Ruskin was fascinated by raw and instinctual forms of creative expression that afford imagination and—in spite or rather *owing to* their "roughness," "dulness," or even "failure"—bring out "the

FIGURE 13. John Ruskin, "Temperance and Intemperance in Ornament," Plate 1 from *The Stones of Venice: Volume the Third, The Fall* (London: Smith, Elder, and Co., 1853).

whole majesty" of an individual worker as well as an ensuing "transfiguration" of sensibility.[100] Like Marx, he sees the industrialized division of labor as a form of slavery that smothers souls, erodes minds, and turns bodies into "leathern thongs to yoke machinery with."[101] Fineness of finish and exactness of execution are thus the outward signs of an inward ruination. "The degree in which the workman is degraded," he writes, "may be thus known at a glance."[102] Although unwilling to do away with conventional social hierarchies, Ruskin believed that life and liberty were to be found in the crude, free, and imperfect idiosyncrasies of invention.

What we should look for and support, he advises, are childlike products of "healthy and ennobling labour" that oppose the fragmented nature of factory work and class discord.[103] Undignified work, by way of contrast, results in strict regularity and "standardization," to use Adorno's favored term—the symptom, in Ruskin's mind, of a diseased attitude toward beauty.[104] A primary cause of this disorder, equally lamented by folk revivalists, was the separation of manual and intellectual activity:

> We are always in these days endeavouring to separate the two; we want one man to be always thinking, and another to be always working, and we call one a gentleman, and the other an operative. . . . As it is, we make both ungentle, the one envying, the other despising, his brother; and the mass of society is made up of morbid thinkers, and miserable workers. Now it is only by labour that thought can be made healthy, and only by thought that labour can be made happy, and the two cannot be separated with impunity. It would be well if all of us were good handicraftsmen in some kind, and the dishonour of manual labour done away with altogether.[105]

In this passage we find the fundamentals of Morris's civilization in which there are "neither brain-sick brain workers nor heart-sick hand workers," but rather brotherhood and "work-pleasure" for all.[106] It is a vision predicated on a medieval nostalgia with distinctively Ruskinian contours in which something is cherished for its age and inscription of time—"that deep sense of voicefulness, of stern watching, of mysterious sympathy" found in certain objects "that have long been washed by the passing waves of humanity."[107] Ruskin's attitude to such material is quintessentially folkloric:

> It is in their lasting witness against men, in their quiet contrast with the transitional character of all things, in the strength which, through the lapse of seasons and times, and the decline and birth of dynasties, and the changing of the face of the earth, and of the limits of the sea, maintains its sculptured shapeliness for a time insuperable, connects forgotten and following ages with each other, and half constitutes the identity, as it concentrates the sympathy, of nations: it is in that golden stain of time, that we are to look for the real light, and colour, and preciousness of architecture; and it is not until a building has assumed this character, till it has been entrusted with the fame, and hallowed by the deeds of men, till its walls have been witnesses of suffering, and its pillars rise out of the shadows of death, that its existence, more lasting as it is than that of the natural objects of the world around it, can be gifted with even so much as these possess, of language and of life.[108]

FIGURE 14. John Ruskin, *Study of the Marble Inlaying on the Front of the Casa Loredan, Venice*. Pencil and watercolour, 32 × 27 cm, 1845.

It is, quite literally, a golden age vision in which a building (and here we can equally read folk song) gains its glory by acting as a kind of palimpsest scrawled over and over again with a nation's deeds, heroes, sufferings, and public life. Connecting forgotten ages with the present and future, this talismanic object comes to constitute a people's collective memory as it stands firm and eternal through the sea changes of history.

In Ruskin and Marx—albeit in very different ways—we find the keystones of a folkloric value system later adopted by Morris and his devotees. Ruskin gives us this way of thinking at its most distilled in his autobiography *Praeterita*, recounting a trip to the Alpine foothills. For Ruskin, euphoric at his first sight of a picturesque cottage, the legend of William Tell becomes "mythically luminous with more than mortal truth": "here, under the black woods, glowed the visible, beautiful, tangible testimony to it in the purple larch timber, carved to exquisiteness by the joy of peasant life, continuous, motionless there in the pine shadow on its ancestral turf."[109] This cottage encapsulates his aesthetic theory and the broader political imaginaries of the folk song project: chivalric myth, nature, continuity, peasant life, and ancestral soil. Absent are the mills and factories of industrial England, the alienated labor of capitalist production, and the degenerate squalor of a swarming metropolis. It is a thumbnail sketch of artisanal, premodern existence—the faint, fairy-tale memory of a garden lost in the wake of a fall brought on and exacerbated by the unstoppable encumbrance of modernity. Ruskin's response was to establish what became known as the Guild of St. George—a failed utopian endeavor to protest against modern industry driven by his peculiar form of "Tory-mediaevalism."[110] Morris, however, continued to insist that what was needed to recapture that first fine careless rapture was a more radical change in political ontology. In either case, the folk appeared as signal fires on a pathway back to what Wordsworth saw as "the Paradise / Where I was reared; in Nature's primitive gifts," where people work freely "with choice / Of time, and place, and object."[111]

Throughout this chapter we've been tracing something delicate and difficult to pin down but nevertheless persistent. No one historical source gives us this folkloric trope in pure form, but grouped together they gesture toward a body of theories, aspirations, and aesthetic values that were shared widely across nineteenth-century political thought and continue to appear in various forms up to the present day. In this sense, the Victorian folk revival was never a parochial phenomenon, but rather the symptom of a node of deeply held assumptions about the past and the role of labor projected onto the imagined demos of the folk. The reforms anticipated by folk song collectors and aficionados share a profound similarity with *News from Nowhere*—a desire to rekindle the imagination in the service of achieving a better world based on recovering aspects of a lost, precapitalist past. Present in the folk revivalism of the 1890s, if we follow this reasoning, is thus a ghost of the socialist revival of the 1880s.[112] Morris's utopian vision and the radical counterpublic he helped to shape both haunt and prefigure what I've been calling the folkloric imagination, a nostalgic habit of thought that seeks to reinstate those archaic practices it eulogizes.

The penultimate chapter of *News from Nowhere* is titled "An Old House amongst New Folk"—this old house being Morris's beloved Kelmscott Manor (as he indicates in the frontispiece), and this new folk (infused with the double meaning of both friends and a *people*) a newly liberated community living a common existence in the English countryside. For Morris, Kelmscott Manor exists as a testament or harbinger, as if it "had waited for these happy days, and held in it the gathered crumbs of happiness of the confused and turbulent past."[113] Here we can see the Janus-like face of Morris's socialism most clearly, looking simultaneously backward at medieval craftsmanship and onward toward a brighter future for the fallen masses of the nineteenth century—both at Ruskin's ancient stones and Marx's call for revolutionary action. Such hope appears in the book always as a tantalizing, beguiling dream:

> There I stood in a dreamy mood, and rubbed my eyes as if I were not wholly awake, and half expected to see the gay-clad company of beautiful men and women change to two or three spindle-legged back-bowed men and haggard, hollow-eyed, ill-favoured women, who once wore down the soil of this land with their heavy hopeless feet, from day to day, and season to season, and year to year. But no change came as yet, and my heart swelled with joy as I thought of all the beautiful grey villages, from the river to the plain and the plain to the uplands, which I could picture to myself so well, all peopled now with this happy and lovely folk, who had cast away riches and attained to wealth.[114]

On the surface it appears to be a eugenicist fantasy foreshadowing elements of H. G. Wells's unsettling racial utopia.[115] But in fact these new folk are beautiful not on account of breeding, but as the organic upshot of a humane political system—just as the land and old buildings around them are beautiful. No longer geared toward the attainment of riches for the few, Morris's healthy body politic results in healthy utopian bodies and a wealth of artistic activity. In the folkloric imagination, likewise, politics and aesthetics are inseparable, one necessarily a reflection of the other.

Nature, creativity, and folk mythology are the lifeblood of Morris's rural utopia. His utopians revel in reading Grimm's fairy stories and in "the child-like part of us that produces works of imagination"; as good Ruskinians, moreover, they drink from handmade native glassware

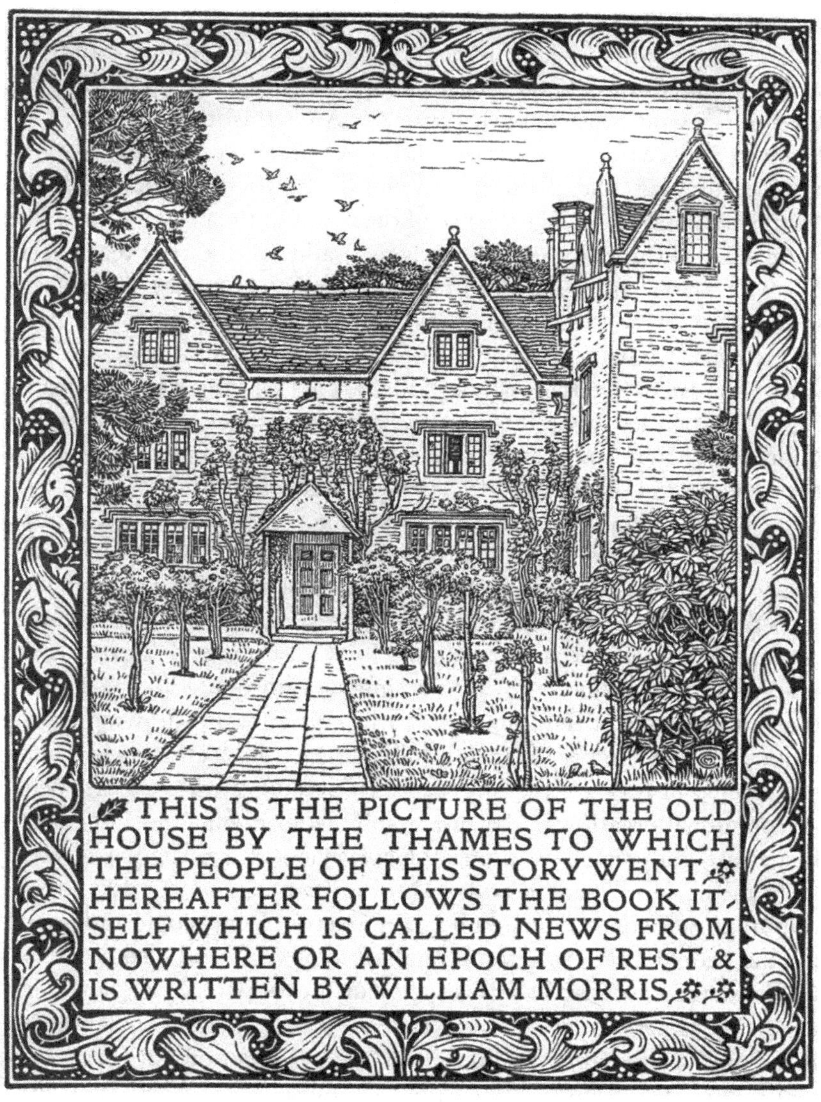


FIGURE 15. Kelmscott Manor as depicted by William Morris in the frontispiece to his 1892 Kelmscott Press edition of *News from Nowhere; or, an Epoch of Rest, Being Some Chapters from a Utopian Romance.*

"somewhat bubbled and hornier in texture than the commercial articles of the nineteenth century"; and they have all left the towns and city slums en masse for country villages, flinging themselves "upon the freed land like a wild beast upon his prey."[116] After this great exodus, they begin to replace the machines they had once been so reliant upon—"the old men amongst the labourers" teaching "the younger ones gradually a little artisanship, such as the use of the saw and the plane."[117] Just like these wise old men, bearers of a dying tradition, the true teachers in Morris's world and the realm of folk revivalism "must be Nature and History."[118] These tutors would instruct us that the best art is a peasant art that "clung fast to the life of the people."[119] In utopia, such art is for all, just as freedom is for all. Bad art is that which is enslaved by capital and either sequestered by the rich or produced cheaply for the poor; good art, in contrast, is produced freely for the many by the many themselves—constituting a "decorative, noble, *popular* art."[120]

It would be hard to find a more succinct definition of folk music than this—a "noble, *popular* art." Employing the ideal of communal creation as a way to criticize the present, it carries with it a seductive vision: a space and time in which humans are untroubled by division, commerce, and modern distractions. In this communal horde all are one—one people, one body, a folk singing with one voice. Writing in the United States at the same time as Morris and also drawing on the work of Jacob Grimm, Francis Child's former student Francis Barton Gummere put forward the most famous account of this folkloric belief in communal creation.[121] Tracing a shift from public and impersonal to private and subjective modes of creativity—mirroring a transition from medieval to modern and oral to written—Gummere drew attention to a "perpetual confusion between poetry of the people and poetry for the people, between a traditional piece of verse and a song written to please the casual crowd of an alley or a concert-hall."[122] For Gummere as for later figures such as Cecil Sharp and John Lomax, authentic ballads were free from commerce, modern conceptions of ownership, and the hand of individual artistry. "We must seek poetry," he insists, "which springs from the people, which belongs to no one poet."[123] This material was assumed to have emerged spontaneously from communities "as yet undivided by lettered or unlettered taste."[124] This idea was echoed by Child's successor at Harvard George Lyman Kittredge in his introduction to the widely read single volume edition of *The English and Scottish Popular Ballads*. Although careful to note the possibility of individual authorship and collective rewriting, Kittredge likewise points to a primeval environment where groups "in a low state of civilization" would fashion songs together: tracing the history of the ballad, he claims, leads the scholar "to very simple conditions of society, to the singing and dancing throng, to a period of communal composition."[125] It is both a nostalgic vision of an inscrutable past and a utopian vision of a potential future, the model for a community of equals.

In Britain, we find this communal theory adopted by the working-class intellectual and folklorist A. L. Lloyd in his 1944 wartime pamphlet *The Singing Englishman*, published by the Workers' Music Association (a cultural subsidiary of the Communist Party of Great Britain).[126] This organization's aims and objectives as stated at the time were imbued with a typically Morrisonian or folkloric attitude, at once nostalgic and utopian—both "to present to the people their rich musical inheritance," and "to foster and further the art of music on the principle that true art can move the people to work for the betterment of society."[127] Once again, folk music appears simultaneously as a form of future-oriented socialist propaganda and as the fossilized or slowly fading remains of a lost political unity. Lloyd is interested in documenting music produced by "men as a community, as a class even, not as solitary individuals isolated like weathercocks on a steeple of genius."[128] "Where you don't have private enterprise," he reasons, "communal art is no more unlikely than communal ploughing."[129] "Brave hardy tough songs," he imagines, once sprang up naturally from the folk in the "old idyllic concord of the village community"—a community devastated by urbanization and capitalist alienation, which gave rise to new songs "decadent and sad and sickly enough to suit an overworked and undernourished slum proletariat."[130] What Lloyd is describing is folkloric utopianism at its most elemental: a village community whose songs presage the dream of communism. We can trace this political vision from Morris through to the protest songs of radicals such as Ewan MacColl, Woody Guthrie, and Pete Seeger, along with other movements for social liberation dug deep into Marxist thought.[131]

There is a strange pull concealed within their folkloric vision—something elusive and paradoxical that I've described as janiform, something with two different faces looking in two opposing directions at once, torn between nostalgia and utopia, innocence and revolution, the finite past and the boundless future yet to come. Rather than seeing this tension as an irreconcilable fault line running through this labyrinth of ideas, however, we might try to recognize the ways in which nostalgia and utopia are in fact cognate. As Svetlana Boym has argued, "Nostalgia is not always about the past; it can be retrospective but also prospective"—a way to anticipate another world.[132] Unlike melancholia, she points out, nostalgia concerns the relationship between individual and collective memory and is thus inherently social. It "speaks in riddles and puzzles" and "tantalizes us with its fundamental ambivalence," the "repetition of the unrepeatable, materialization of the immaterial."[133] We can see such nostalgia as the symptom of an epoch, "a historical emotion . . . coeval with modernity itself"—a "mourning of displacement and temporal irreversibility" always lurking "at the very core of the modern condition."[134] Exile, loss, and estrangement, in other words, are fundamental constituents of modernity and progress. Although Morris did not experience anything like enforced dispersal or migration, his exile, just like that of folk revivalists, was above all imaginative, cast out of a vanished home to which he felt he (and society) properly belonged. This home was Ruskin's medieval world of pleasurable, imperfect labor; Marx's world of small, precapitalist communities; and the anarchist world of nonhierarchical communism.

Folkloric nostalgia incorporates a confluence of what Boym refers to as "restorative" and "reflective" elements. On one hand, folklore is yet another example of an "invented tradition."[135] Stressing *nostos*, this form of longing "attempts a transhistorical reconstruction of the lost home" but refuses to think of itself as nostalgic; instead, it claims possession of while also seeking to protect "truth and tradition," shading into the more sinister regions of nationalistic and religious belonging.[136] This is precisely the same mechanism animating folk music's political imaginary—a nostalgic drive concerned with origins, gaps in memory, rituals, and revival. At its darkest, it dwells in "antimodern mythmaking," conspiracy theories, and a "return to national symbols"—those telltale insignia of the far right that we shall encounter later on.[137] But on the other hand, folkloric discourse involves *algia* and an emphasis on the "longing itself," the ache or pain of loss.[138] Folkloric imagination oscillates between these two poles—between "total reconstructions of monuments of the past" and a fixation on "ruins, the patina of time and history, in the dreams of another place."[139] Morris's Nowhere is the dream of a place that never was, although one that is grounded in a return to a specific epoch and an escape into a longed-for future. Folk ideology has a similar structure, its material always exiled from a utopian nowhere of time and place—the mythic space of belonging and concord where unalloyed populations resound with one communal voice.

Ultimately, folk revivalism epitomizes what Boym calls the off-modern—a form of "critical reflection on the modern condition that incorporates nostalgia."[140] This "off," she notes, is a way to signal an exploration of the "sideshadows and back alleys rather than the straight road of progress."[141] Folklorists and song collectors were always more interested in these adumbrations and missed opportunities, crossroads and unrealized possibilities, than the onward march of modernity, defined as it was by the evangelical spread of capitalism and the development of technocratic power—what Raymond Williams characterizes as a "long dominative mode" culminating in "man's mastering and controlling his natural environment."[142] Emerging amid the backwaters and eddies of this society, folkloric discourse always aspired to draw attention to the palpable failures of modernity by refusing to join these highways of perpetual change and innovation, acting instead as a signpost for an alternative way of life rooted in history and the eroded landscapes of home.

Folk song gives us a kind of perpetual present, but in this present is an affective ache for the ruins of time as well as an as-yet-unrealized tomorrow. Its off-modern nostalgia involves both displacement from the past and distance from an idealized future where the conflicts of the present are resolved and a collective identity or community is finally reestablished. In the next chapter, we'll see how this form of hopeful remembering played out differently according to the position of the author at the troubled intersection of music and race in the United States.

CHAPTER 4

# Difference and Belonging

## *On the Songs of Black Folk*

Origin stories always have the flavor of myth. The narrative of something's awakening seems to acquire a crystalline form, incontestable and prophetic. Folk music is no different. The most memorable vignette in this regard is the stilted description Maud Karpeles gives of Cecil Sharp's first experience of collecting:

> The song was "The Seeds of Love" and the singer was John England, the vicarage gardener. And it was through this song and this singer that Cecil Sharp had his introduction to the living folk-song. It happened in this way. Cecil Sharp was sitting in the vicarage garden talking to Charles Marson and to Mattie Kay, who was likewise staying at Hambridge, when he heard John England quietly singing to himself as he mowed the vicarage lawn. Cecil Sharp whipped out his notebook and took down the tune; and then persuaded John to give him the words. He immediately harmonized the song; and that same evening it was sung at a choir supper by Mattie Kay, Cecil Sharp accompanying. The audience was delighted; as one said, it was the first time that the song had been put into evening-dress.[1]

The story is impossibly prescient, too well arranged to be true: the man who would go on to disseminate his adulation of English folk culture across the world begins by encountering a song called "The Seeds of Love"; not only this, but the singer from whom he heard it happened to be called (with a kind of Nabokovian fortuity) John England.[2] There is an air of the miraculous about it, something sacred and sacramental. It was because of England that scales fell from Sharp's ears and he came to know the living spirit of the folk. And, of course, it all happened in a vicarage garden on a summer's day in Somerset, encircled by birdsong and bucolic charm. It was as a result of this chance meeting, Karpeles reminds the reader, that Sharp "was to discover our glorious heritage" having "perceived immediately the value of what he had found."[3] Presumably John was happy just to keep on mowing, blissfully unaware in his rural innocence of the profundity and worth of this unobtrusive song.

But Karpeles's vignette has two halves: carrying a handy notebook, Sharp transcribes and instinctively arranges this melody like a German *Lied*—as if it were a lost song in Robert Schumann's *Dichterliebe* or Schubert's *Die schöne Müllerin*. A piano is introduced, and spectators listen in rapt attention as the song is uprooted from the vicarage garden and stuffed hastily into formal clothing. It isn't hard to see why Marxist critics such as Dave Harker saw this process as expropriative, a deceitful plundering of working-class culture for the entertainment and subsequent profit of the leisured bourgeoisie.[4] What I want to focus on in this chapter, however, is not class exploitation, but framings, affordances, and the ways in which folkloric thinking could be used to articulate powerful forms of difference and belonging.[5] We can say that John England's singing *afforded* Sharp the possibility of imagining a vanishing way of life grounded in the English soil, "The Seeds of Love" being *framed* both as folk and art song. In one framing we find a solitary gardener in a rural village, in another a professionally trained singer and the proscenium of the stage. Without admitting as much, Sharp was also framing the folk as white—their music a creation of the race and nation. But similar figures were busy during this era framing other forms of native musical expression in a variety of different ways. In 1903, the very same year Sharp collected "The Seeds of Love," W. E. B. Du Bois published *The Souls of Black Folk*, his seminal meditation on African American experience. Folk song afforded Sharp's Arcadian dreaming, yet it also afforded what Houston A. Baker Jr. describes as the invoking of "ancestral spirits and ancient formulas that move toward an act of cultural triumph."[6] In this sense, as we'll see, the folk could be simultaneously modern and premodern, romantic and modernist at once.

The vast majority of writing that came to constitute the field and idea of folk music exhibits what Joe Feagin has termed a "white racial frame."[7] Striving to move beyond familiar understandings of race in the social sciences, Feagin employs this concept as a way of marking out a systemic and socially dominant "frame of reference" or "frame of mind" that has come to characterize large parts of the Western world since the seventeenth century—an overarching worldview encompassing "*a broad and persisting set of racial stereotypes, prejudices, ideologies, images, interpretations and narratives, emotions, and reactions to language accents, as well as racialized inclinations to discriminate.*"[8] The United States, he reminds us, was founded on a racial basis with the conquest of indigenous land and the enforced labor of African captives integral to its history and governance. The white racial frame has been a way of rationalizing and legitimating this history of subjugation and genocide. It is impossible to avoid such a frame in folklore research during the late nineteenth and early twentieth centuries. Indeed, folkloric writing worked to secure this frame and its attendant politics of white supremacy—the belief in the innate superiority of light-skinned people, principally when compared to their darker-skinned neighbors, subjects of the colonial enterprise. Not only did folk song research entrench and reflect this white frame, but in so doing it also framed those others under its gaze *as* other.

In the first chapter, we touched very briefly on John Lomax's relationship with the singer Huddie Ledbetter—his attempts at collecting replicating in many ways the power dynamics of chattel slavery. The white racial frame that Lomax adopted, as he reveals in a 1910 request for ballads printed in the *New York Times*, was the sub-frame of a folkloric imagination conditioned by familiar Harvard school ideas:

> Whenever people, from whatever cause, live for a time in primitive isolation they make songs that reflect the feelings of the whole community. Such particular songs also spring up from groups of unlettered men following a particular occupation, especially one that calls for supreme physical effort. In most cases the authorship can be traced to no one person. The songs are perhaps rarely written out, and less seldom find their way to print. They are often crude in form and matter, sometimes vulgar, but always interesting as a reflection of the intimate life of the people. These are the folk-songs, either handed down by "word of mouth" from generation to generation, or entirely submerged in the rush of progress or lost through the dominion of the newspaper.[9]

It was his purpose, Lomax concluded, "to help save the native American 'ballad' from extinction"—not the Native American ballad, of course, but the songs of those other folk who occupied the former's lands to become the American people.[10] Much like Sharp, he was on the lookout for rare examples of songs and tunes produced by communities in embryonic isolation from education and mass media. Prime examples of such music were the "negro melodies of the southern States."[11]

Five years later, Lomax was still on the trail of these elusive melodies, having documented plantation ballads on the theme of the boll weevil (a deadly menace to the cotton crop), in which he felt "the negroes . . . sympathize with the puny boll-weevil against the attacks of the white man"—recalling old trickster tales such as "the weaker and shrewder Brer Rabbit against his stronger opponents."[12] By alluding to this tale, Lomax was situating himself in a long tradition of white-framed southern folklore epitomized by Joel Chandler Harris's bestselling 1881 collection *Uncle Remus, His Songs and His Sayings: The Folk-Lore of the Old Plantation*. This book contained the Brer Rabbit fables Lomax is referring to—a reminder that African American trickster tales such as these were received at large through the mediations of white folklorists and northern publishers. A significant aspect of such mediation was the use of phonetic dialect, as Harris puts it, to "preserve the legends themselves in their original simplicity."[13] Although he contrasts his work with "the intolerable misrepresentations of the minstrel stage" (aiming instead to capture the "really poetic imagination of the negro"), Harris's racial frame permitted him to acclaim what he portrays as Harriet Beecher Stowe's "wonderful defense of slavery as it existed in the south."[14] Indeed, he imagines his Uncle Remus character as an old man "who has nothing but pleasant memories of the discipline of slavery"—a comment that reveals Remus to be a vehicle for Harris's own form of racist antebellum nostalgia.[15] Much like Lomax's boll weevil transcriptions, his use of dialect inevitably recalls the enduring lineaments of blackface caricature, helping to set in motion the snares and performative practices that Matthew D. Morrison refers to as "blacksound."[16] Significantly, these songs were not deep-rooted fables at risk of disappearing (indeed Lomax dates them by the recent spread of the blight from Mexico), but rather seemed to manifest and give voice to some ancient or "primitive" emotional instinct.[17] It was this instinct above all that captivated white folklorists such as Lomax.

As he wrote in his field diary in the early 1930s on another ballad-hunting adventure through the south, "the simple directness and power of this primitive music, coupled with its descriptions of life where force and other elemental influences are dominating, impress me more deeply every time I hear it."[18] It was on this trip over the summer of 1933 that Lomax began to record African American music with a portable electric machine, subsidized by the Library of Congress and under the auspices of the Archive of American Folk Song.[19] Traveling through Texas, Louisiana, Mississippi, and Tennessee, Lomax claims to have "interrogated nearly ten thousand Negro convicts," as well as "groups of Negroes living in remote communities" and on several large plantations and lumber camps.[20] The purpose? "To record on permanent aluminium or celluloid plates . . . the folk-songs of the Negro—songs that in musical phrasing and poetic content are most unlike those of the white race, the least contaminated by white influence or by the modern Negro jazz."[21] These recordings, he insists, are "in a very true sense, sound-photographs of Negro songs, rendered in their own native element, unrestrained, uninfluenced and undirected."[22] In addition to a large number of recordings now archived at the Library of Congress, the result was *American Ballads and Folk Songs*, coedited with his son Alan Lomax—a collection that the *New York Times* portrayed as being deliberately aimed at a mass-market readership.[23] Lomax senior also published a more scholarly essay based on his fieldwork in *The Musical Quarterly* alliteratively titled "'Sinful Songs' of the Southern Negro."[24] In it, we find the clearest illustration of the paternalistic white racial frame through which this music was heard and the ways in which African American singers were in turn framed as atavistic, wild, and racially distinct.

What the Lomaxes were after was the sound of racial purity—a seemingly untainted expression requiring conditions of effective segregation and isolation that allowed a mythic folk essence to emerge. This vision was nevertheless predicated on the very racialized ontology it strove to document. In other words, there is a curious circularity at work here in which a stubborn belief in racial difference sharpens the folklorist's desire to find racialized forms of expression, which in turn justifies and then cements the concept of racial difference itself. Each time this circle is repeated, the complex relations that make up a culture are elided and a white racial frame is further entrenched—a process that Roland Barthes once described as "mythology." Scrutinizing a cover photograph from the magazine *Paris-Match* in which "a young Negro in a French uniform is saluting, with his eyes uplifted, probably fixed on a fold of the tricolour," Barthes finds a tautologous reciprocity in the relationship between empire and the boy soldier: "French imperiality condemns the saluting Negro to be nothing more than an instrumental signifier . . . but at the same moment the Negro's salute thickens, becomes vitrified, freezes into an eternal reference meant to *establish* French imperiality."[25] In such schemes, he argues, "things lose the memory that they once were made" via a kind of "conjuring trick" that has turned reality inside out, emptied it of history, and filled it with nature.[26] Myth's primary feat is this capacity to transform history into nature—depoliticizing memory by denying that any historical or performative constitution has taken place. In the case of folk song collecting during this era, it is the history of slavery and racist stereotyping that becomes mythically transformed into the "natural" qualities of African American expression.

Through his folkloric fieldwork, Lomax hoped to document what he describes as singers who "revert more and more to the idiom of the Negro common people" when removed from white society and modern innovation, and who thereby produce "pure Negro creations."[27] He was less interested in spirituals—too clean and close to white traditions of biblical worship and eschatology—than "sinful songs" that were assumed to divulge the inner experience and hidden lives of Southern Blacks:

> Of these two types of musical expression, distinctly separated into two definite classes by the Negro mind, one, the secular songs, is taboo, emphatically taboo, to all Negro ministers, all Negro teachers, and to practically all Negroes of any educational attainments whatever. They are "sinful songs," songs that definitely connect them with their former barbaric life. . . . Black-Sampson, a Negro murderer in the Nashville penitentiary, would not sing an innocently worded levee camp-song into our microphone until ordered to do so by the Warden. Even then, without telling me beforehand, he prefaced the song with an humble apology to the Lord . . . [for] his sin of setting down a delightful tune and story.[28]

This is a particularly telling passage for a number of reasons. First, as with other folk collectors before him, the songs were far more important to Lomax than the people from whom he collected. No matter that the prison warden had to force Black-Sampson to sing and that he felt himself morally condemned, his "delightful tune and story" were folklore and thus the property of the nation and community, not the individual. Second, and more importantly for our present purposes, Lomax frames these songs as evolutionary links back to some "former barbaric life"—not simply to an African ancestry, but to Africa portrayed in colonialist terms as a locus of exotic (i.e., non-Christian) belief systems and primitive brutality.[29] Through song, folklorists believed they could catch a glimpse of this past becoming ever more indistinct.

In the folkloric imagination and the white racial frame within which it moved, African Americans held a particular fascination given the close relationship they appeared to have with pure, rough, instinctual, or primitive forms of creativity. Recalling the well-worn trope we

FIGURE 16. African American convicts at Reed Camp, South Carolina, December 1934. Photograph by Alan Lomax.

encountered in chapter 1, Lomax believed "the Negro . . . is endowed by nature with a strong sense of rhythm": songs "burst from him, when in his own environment, as naturally and as freely as those of a bird amid its native trees. . . . His is the real art of simplicity and naturalness."[30] This indigenous environment, however, was a world defined by manual labor "without books or newspapers" or education in general—characterized, in short, by "the absence of 'free-world' conventions in prison life."[31] Those vocal quartets and smart clubs "representing Negro colleges," he felt, had simply become too civilized, imitating "some trait borrowed directly from conventional music of white origin."[32] By prizing folk expression and the peculiar conditions in which he believed ballads organically emerged, Lomax comes exceedingly close to suggesting that African American culture thrives only under conditions of illiteracy, incarceration, and white racist oppression. This contemptible idea would haunt the blues revival of the 1960s, echoed in a purist veneration of "country blues" and the world of sharecropping and disenfranchisement from which it arose.[33] Much like later blues revivalists, Lomax's vision of folk culture was unequivocally patriarchal without, of course, ever being defined as such. If we read between the lines his value system becomes clear: male over female, purity over hybridity, stasis over change, oral over written, secular over sacred, isolation over liberation, nature over artifice, savage over civilized. Although African American culture was being celebrated by Lomax in this way, such praise took the form of a racializing opposition in which Black becomes the low other to white even as it provides the antidote to the alienating prospects of modernity.

Viewed in this light, the white frame Lomax brought to folk song was effectively the frame of racial segregation—a cultural manifestation of Jim Crow.[34] We can see Lomax projecting the segregation he saw around him back onto the history of song as a way to discount the complex hybridities and interfusions of southern culture. Recording came to the aid of the Lomaxes in this regard. John notes that whereas it was "nearly impossible to transport Negro folk-singers from the south and keep them untainted by white musical conventions," an electrical recording machine "affords the best means of preserving this music" as it captured songs in an enduring and unalloyed form.[35] Black music, it seemed, was best when kept apart from white, offering an antidote to social and technological change—trapped not only in a primitive, untutored state, but also in literal confinement or abusive labor relations in a way diametrically opposed to Lomax's other paradigm of rugged folk authenticity, the white cowboy riding free over western plains.[36]

Although Lomax found it hard to believe, many African Americans were of the opinion that his folkloric vision was a substantial obstacle to dignity, liberation, and progress, as he notes defensively in his autobiography: "I'd like to protest again to the educated and the semi-educated Negroes of the south. Almost universally they opposed my project of collecting the folk lore and folk songs on the ground that 'we have got beyond that.'. . . Tuskegee and other Negro colleges politely refused to allow me to talk to their students."[37] We can find unmistakable traces of this opinion in Ralph Ellison's 1952 novel *Invisible Man*. Early in the book, the titular figure reflects mordantly on his time at a prestigious Black college in the south closely modeled on Booker T. Washington's Tuskegee Institute, where Ellison himself had studied music. When "special white guests" visited the school, a country ensemble led by a local sharecropper with the emblematic name Trueblood were at times called upon to perform "primitive spirituals" in the chapel: "We were embarrassed by the earthy harmonies they sang, but since the visitors were awed we dared not laugh at the crude, high, plaintively animal sounds Jim Trueblood made as he led the quartet. . . . I didn't understand in those pre-invisible days that [the faculty's] hate, and mine too, was charged with fear. How all of us at the college hated the black-belt people, the 'peasants,' during those days! We were trying to lift them up and they, like Trueblood, did everything it seemed to pull us down."[38] In such a context, Lomax's emphasis on low and iniquitous forms of Black vernacular expression met with contempt owing to their incompatibility with ideals of racial uplift. In contrast to the contemporaneous work of Lawrence Gellert—who deliberately solicited material featuring expressions of protest against racial subjugation—the Lomaxes' work shows them to have been more interested in a conception of Blackness that willingly accepted a subordinate status.[39] Their folk song collecting, in other words, did nothing to advance the cause of African American self-definition.

Such ideas were by no means exceptional at the time. Prefaced with an epigraph by Cecil Sharp, a pocket-sized book by the singer Bentley Ball entitled *The Song-A-Logue of America* claimed that folk songs were "an index to race, thought, and character, and tend to reveal the aptitudes of a people"—albeit at the same time (and somewhat paradoxically) attesting to "the universal brotherhood of man."[40] "No one," Ball writes, "could fail to recognize a typical negro melody, for no other nation has produced music of this sort."[41] Unlike Lomax, however, Ball thought spirituals were the archetype of African American folk music—a genre "born of the black race . . . from the wilds of Africa" attesting to the fact that this people had "in so short a time" developed a "deep religious sense" under conditions of slavery.[42] Ball was drawing on established research to make such claims, including *Afro-American Folksongs: A Study in Racial and National Music* by the American music critic Henry Krehbiel. Echoing the paradigm shift away from antiquarianism toward empiricism that we encountered earlier, Krehbiel states that his primary aim in this book was to bring "a species of folksong into the field of scientific observation."[43] For Krehbiel, authentic Black folk songs needed to be understood as properly distinct from those related but undesirable forms propelled by syncopation, the "debased offspring" of authentic plantation music—ragtime and "coon" songs.[44] Defined by "rhythmical intoxication . . . almost to the exclusion of melody and harmony," ragtime was a "degenerate" craze, the sign of a "careless music" pervading Britain and the United States.[45] African American folk song, in contrast, was the pure and precious root of Black music to be used as a bulwark against the incursion of racialized rhythm into the popular sphere—the sounds of slavery ranged against the modern world.

In Krehbiel's scientific framing, African American folk songs are once again something primeval, one constituent of "a body of evidence" relating to "the science of ethnology, such as racial relations, primitive modes of thought, ancient customs and ancient religions."[46] Such music was an intriguing survival of "primitive superstitions which the slaves brought with them from Africa" manifest in "wild and lascivious" dances—a faint but still discernible reverberation of "their savage ancestors."[47] Shadowing the teleological fantasies of Herbert Spencer, such music appeared to be uncultivated, undeveloped, and apparently unable to reach the "more refined aesthetic sensibilities" of Western man.[48] Indeed, this music was portrayed as a failure or aberration on the terms of Western tonality. "To avoid the abnormal interval of a second consisting of three semitones," Krehbiel writes, "European theorists also raise the sixth, thus obtaining the conventional ascending minor scale—the melodic minor . . . [but] a primitive melodic sense seems to have led the negroes to rebel at this procedure."[49] In a white racial frame, Black music was thus not simply unusual but openly rebellious and deviant, always heard through an evolutionary lattice that situated it at a temporal and developmental remove from the norms of common practice. This idea that music betrayed something deep about a culture, nation, or race whether flattering or not was predicated on the conveniently abstract qualities of sound. As Krehbiel puts it, music preserves things "more truthfully" than other media, as it "cannot lie, for the reason that the things which are at its base, the things without which it could not be, are unconscious, unvolitional human products."[50] The rules of European harmony and rhythmic restraint, in short, became ways to ensnare African-derived traditions in a permanent condition of backwardness, creating and justifying a racialized hierarchy through recourse to the ostensible candor of sound.

These writers were not simply dismissing African American music as barbaric nonsense, however, but rather attempting in their own way to document and celebrate traditions that they felt were uniquely evocative of US history. As Natalie Curtis Burlin writes in the foreword to a 1918 book of songs collected with a phonograph, her fieldwork had been "a reverent and dedicated love-labor" in the service of protecting "that spontaneous musical utterance which is the Negro's priceless contribution to the art of America."[51] These songs, she states in contrast to Krehbiel, were the result of an instinct "transplanted to America and influenced by European music"—a confluence that "flowered into the truly extraordinary harmonic talent found in the singing of even the most ignorant Negroes of our Southern States."[52] Such material was nevertheless caught up in a romantic racial framework:

> Into the "Spirituals," the prayer-songs of the days of slavery, was poured the aspiration of a race in bondage whose religion, primitive and intense, was their whole hope, sustenance and comfort, and the realm wherein the soul, at least, soared free. At stolen meetings in woods or in valleys, at secret gatherings on the plantations, the Negroes found outlet for their sorrows, their longings and their religious ecstasies. No one can hear these songs unmoved. The childlike simplicity of the verse in "Couldn't hear nobody pray" and "Ev'ry time I feel de Spirit," but throws into sharper relief the touching, poignant poetry—a poetry born of hearts that sang beneath heavy burdens, and of a faith as radiant and certain as the sunrise.[53]

Burlin's writing demonstrates something akin to what Eric Lott refers to, in his classic study of blackface minstrelsy, as "love and theft"—a glorification of racial difference and concomitant desire to tame, own, and represent it (here, via notation in dialect for vocal quartet).[54] Although fundamentally American, slaves were still "childlike" in simplicity, bound to nature, and "primitive" in conviction.

We find this copresence of love and condescension, primitivist thinking and wide-eyed allure in Percy Grainger's review of Burlin's song books in the *New York Times*. Following in Sharp's footsteps, Grainger juxtaposes what he calls "conscious" and "unconscious" music along the lines of notation and orality, dividing European art and popular spheres from "folk-music and primitive music the world over"—a category uniting the traditions "of such otherwise divergent types and origin as Russian, British, Scandinavian, Kashmiri folksongs, native Australian, Greenlandic, Rarotongan (Polynesian), and American negro musics."[55] But he is at pains to point out that this juxtaposition does not necessarily imply an aesthetic hierarchy, "for what is gained on the one hand is lost on the other": "What is gained in harmonic expressibility, for instance, is lost in melodic inventiveness, and what is gained in rhythmic definiteness is lost in rhythmic subtlety and variety."[56] What was at stake was unconscious music's propensity to deteriorate when exposed to the modern world—in a word, its fragility. This quality was its most seductive feature:

> Of all the various kinds of beautiful and thrilling music, classical or popular, primitive or cultured, that it has been my good fortune to hear in the United States, this negro folk-music easily occupies the first place in my mind, as regards its sheer acoustical beauty, its emotional depth, and by reason of its musico-historical import. This is the most truly vocal of music, ideally adapted for singing by choirs and solo organizations. It is the most American music imaginable, breathing the spiritual fervor and abandonment and the fragrance of sentiment so strangely typical of this wondrous, this generous-souled continent; yet worldwide in its applicability—as is all truly great emotional music.[57]

What characterized this tradition above all was its apparent naturalness. It was ostensibly "uncultured," not cultivated through musical notation and formalized theory. Here we might return to Raymond Williams's definition of culture as "the tending of natural growth"—a concept intimately associated with ideas of agronomy, husbandry, and cultivation, a confluence of organic flux and calculated activity.[58] What Grainger's colonial dichotomy misses is that this so-called primitive music was also a product of aesthetic cultivation. Such music was not uncultured; its cultivation was merely hidden and dispersed through generations of oral circulation, its refinements inaudible to those listening through a white racial acoustemology.[59]

Black and white responses to these folk traditions differed markedly—the latter always eavesdropping, as it were, on a social world that seemed intriguingly alien and yet also somehow distinctively American. Whereas white folklorists tended to admire Black folk song at a distance as something of wild and uncultivated beauty, African American writers themselves, turning to document and interpret the nation's musical past, fashioned a strikingly different frame. Central to this perspective were the Fisk Jubilee Singers as they ushered the spirituals into the global limelight. When a scholar such as John Wesley Work, professor of Latin and History at Fisk University, writes about such music in 1915, it takes on an entirely new meaning, gifting us with a momentary glimpse from a horizon beyond a white racial frame:

> We know for a fact that it was never intended that the world should understand the slave music. It was a kind of secret pass-word into their lives. In some instances their secrets are protected by dual meanings to their songs.

> "Steal Away to Jesus" meant to the slave a secret meeting which the master had prohibited; and to the overseer and the rest of the world, a longing for the quiet communion with God. "Rise! Shine! For the Light is a-Coming!" meant to the slave, freedom approaching! To the world it was the Messianic prophecy. . . . "Great Camp Meeting in the Promised Land" and "Good News, the Chariot's a-Coming, Don't Yer Leave Me Behind" were to the slaves prophecies of the joys of freedom; to the uninitiated, anticipations of joy in Heaven.[60]

There is something especially ironic about these pervasive double-voiced utterances when we remember how white authors had framed Black Christian expressivity as a paradigm of guilelessness—this "deep religious sense" of the slaves, as Ball had put it, revealed to contain a surreptitious logic of deceit. Through a white racial frame, we might see sorrowful obedience with eyes trained on the Promised Land, but from another angle, a people unjustly bound in servitude with eyes trained less on divine redemption than on worldly liberation. Slipping the yoke, this joke was on the ignorant overseer or white slave owner, entirely unconscious of the supposedly unconscious musical outpourings of their Black bondsmen and women.[61]

The stereotypes, prejudices, and images formed through a white racial frame, Work argues, are a "tangled waste" needing to be torn up by the roots, "for some of the traits which men call characteristic of Negro soul, are the plain excrescences of civilization; which, although they influence him, are not essential but accidental."[62] There is a foreshadowing here of Frantz Fanon's claim that "what is often called the black soul is a white man's artifact"—an "existential deviation" or mythic livery that had enslaved minds the world over.[63] And yet Work himself was not free of such racialized thinking, opting to cleave African Americans from their African kin on colonial terms. "The American Negro," he writes, "has, because of an intelligence superior to that of his African brother, evolved some more beautiful tunes by more effective arrangements of the notes of his scale," polishing and refining "some of the barbaric tendencies" of the latter.[64] The Negro's freedom, it appears, came at the cost of the African's confinement within an imperialist vision. Clothed in a European language of difference, the Dark Continent remained a sign of alterity beyond comprehension—employed, in Work's case, as a strategic foil to set off the modernity of his New World brethren struggling for recognition in an inequitable land. This new Negro music developing on US soil was no longer "savage" and "heathen," but a modern "portrayal of his soul," a "sublime improvement upon the song

FIGURE 17. Jubilee Singers of Fisk University, Nashville, Tennessee, early 1870s. Albumen print, 6 × 10 cm. Photograph by James Wallace Black for the American Missionary Association. From left to right: Minnie Tate, Greene Evans, Isaac Dickerson, Jennie Jackson, Maggie Porter, Ella Sheppard, Thomas Rutling, Benjamin Holmes, and Eliza Walker.

of his ancestors."[65] Work was not interested in a pan-Africanist vision of unity, but Black pride based on a "race character" that revealed African Americans' embodiment, during the horrors of slavery, of Christian ideals of love.[66] To those living in the present and willing to face up to this traumatic past, folk songs offered "a source of encouragement" to be valued not for antiquarian or picturesque reasons, but as cultural memory and inheritance—"ever calling us from discouragement and fears," he writes, "they lead us to face with confidence the hostile forces of life."[67]

As a conductor of the Fisk Jubilee Singers in a later incarnation, Work was familiar with these songs not simply as texts, but as living lore and conduits of memory brought to life and reframed for the concert hall stage. It was during the early 1870s—not fully a decade after President Abraham Lincoln's Emancipation Proclamation—that the initial group of singers had formed to campaign for much needed funds at Fisk University, their legacy the majestic Jubilee Hall erected on the foundations of a former slave pen. This original group, as Work notes, was "the first to sing these songs to the world," garnering attention not only in New England but also across the Atlantic where "they sang their way into the good graces of the whole of Great Britain from the queen down to the peasant."[68] The Jubilee Singers, as Work points out, were seen not as comedic entertainers, but as an ensemble that "made a deep impression upon the hearts of all who heard them."[69] This view is borne out by a review in the *Musical Standard* of their London debut in May 1873:

> There is something altogether novel in the music sung by these real black minstrels, and their performances have nothing in common with "nigger-mongery," with its accompaniments of faces blacked with cork, bones, tamborines, and other characteristics. Rude the music unquestionably is, but it is at least genuine, and though it may not perhaps satisfy the artistic standard of educated musicians, it is impossible not to feel a certain amount of charm with the novel and natural effects produced. The music somewhat resembles Gregorian tones in its character. . . . The voices of the singers are of sweet, bell-like quality, and the expression they sing with, though unstudied, is singularly pathetic and striking.[70]

Here was African American folk song received as "an expression of real emotion"—the genuine article when compared with the populist folly of blackface entertainment.[71] Similar opinions on this series of concerts were expressed in the *Musical World*, which remarked on the "hushed attention" and "frequently moistened eye[s]" of an audience demanding repetitions of "nearly every piece set down in the programme." "It may be safely asserted," this reviewer noted, "that nothing like the plantation songs of these 'Jubilee Singers' has been before heard in this country."[72]

Having enthralled British audiences across the nation sympathetic to abolition and the plight of emancipated slaves, the Jubilee Singers returned in 1875 with a new lineup. Their unfailingly positive reception framed the group on this occasion as both epitomes of folkloric authenticity and as consummate professionals. An article in the *Tonic Sol-Fa Reporter*, for instance, found similarities "between their songs and the old melodies of Wales" while noting that "the training of the singers is almost perfect; there is an exactness in time, and a chordal sweetness that gratifies every ear" particularly evident in "the sudden transitions from *forte* to the most delicate *piano*."[73] Terms such as primitive and savage are entirely absent—the Fisk singers positioned instead as archetypes of grace, dignity, and talent. Even on their first appearance, reviewers had remarked on their "perfect unity of Attack" and "beautiful Quality of voice."[74] An extended piece in *Chambers's Journal* from 1878 likewise praised the ensemble and their charitable enterprise, commenting that "amidst the frauds and commercial rascalities of pompous pretenders that are becoming a scandal to the age, the unselfish

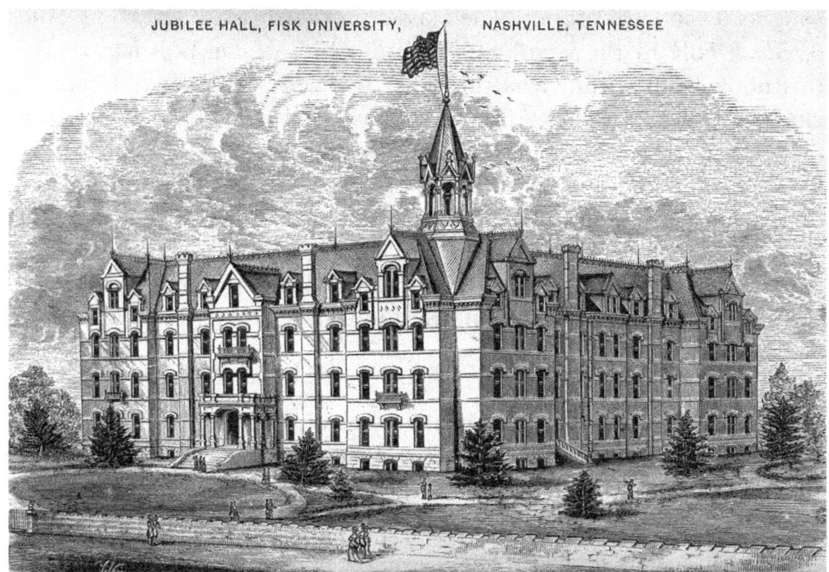


FIGURE 18. Engraving of Jubilee Hall at Fisk University from J. B. T. Marsh, *The Story of the Jubilee Singers; with their Songs* (Boston: Houghton, Mifflin and Company, 1880).

and noble endeavours of these humble melodists stand out in marked contrast, as something to applaud and to redeem human nature."[75] It is hard to imagine much higher praise: African American singers positioned as saviors of human decency, reformist antidotes to the decadent excesses of Victorian society and its scandalous preoccupation with minstrelsy. Seen as purveyors of music akin to "the simpler class of national ballads and songs," the Jubilee Singers were received by British audiences on the terms of a folkloric imagination—guardians of a sad but splendid tradition that appealed to "high and low" alike.[76] By the 1890s these celebrated vocalists had toured the world, receiving acclaim at the Framjee Cawasjee Institute in Bombay, for instance, where one reviewer observed that "they sang with such full and complete harmony, their voices being so evenly blended and well balanced that it gave one an idea that the sounds were produced by an organ under the manipulation of a master hand."[77]

This idea of mastery—of Black music as the spectral workings of a hand that had effortlessly mastered the forms and expressive tools of the white world—is at the heart of an African American reading of folk song as a mode of affinity. The classic text in this regard is *The Souls of Black Folk* by the sociologist W. E. B. Du Bois. Du Bois had written this book from within what he calls "the Veil" of racial difference, a cloak pulled down over African American existence that he aimed to raise "that you may view faintly its deeper recesses."[78] The spirituals—what he refers to unforgettably as the Sorrow Songs—pervade his book with echoes "of haunting melody from the only American music which welled up from black souls in the dark past."[79] These "weird old songs," Du Bois writes, were the medium through which "the soul of the black slave spoke to men," a mystical necropolis of lost voices:

> After years when I came to Nashville I saw the great temple builded of these songs towering over the pale city. To me Jubilee Hall seemed ever made of the songs themselves, and its bricks were red with the blood and dust of toil. Out of them rose for me morning, noon, and night, bursts of wonderful melody, full of the voices of my brothers and sisters, full of the voices of the past. Little of beauty has America given the world save the rude grandeur God himself stamped on her bosom; the human spirit in this new world has expressed itself in vigor and ingenuity rather than in beauty. And so by fateful chance the Negro folk-song—the rhythmic cry of the slave—stands to-day not simply as the sole American music, but as the most beautiful expression of human experience born this side the seas. It has been neglected, it has been, and is, half despised, and above all it has been persistently mistaken and misunderstood; but notwithstanding, it still remains as the singular spiritual heritage of the nation and the greatest gift of the Negro people.[80]

These songs were a means for southern slaves to meet northerners and the world at large "for the first time . . . face to face and heart to heart."[81] They enabled something like a splintering of the white racial frame or a rending of the veil, and in their place the foretaste of an African American *culture*—a Black tradition of witness to the trauma of race that held up a mirror to systemic terror and prejudice.

In Du Bois, we find folkloric ideals remixed and reclaimed as a strategic elucidation of Black essence. Slaves are still rendered as "primitive," their spirituals manifesting "the restlessness of the savage," but their expression (unlike lucrative white appropriations) was "the true Negro folk-song," and therefore provided a beacon of reassurance: "through all the sorrow of the Sorrow Songs," he proclaims, "there breathes a hope—a faith in the ultimate justice of things . . . [of] triumph and calm confidence."[82] This hope, in concrete terms, was that "sometime, somewhere, men will judge men by their souls and not by their skins"—a phrase echoed exactly sixty years later in Martin Luther King Jr.'s visionary anticipation at the 1963 March on Washington that his four

FIGURE 19. Dr. W. E. B. Du Bois, early twentieth century.

children "will one day live in a nation where they will not be judged by the color of their skin, but by the content of their character."[83] "With this faith," King proclaimed amid shouts of assent, "we will be able to transform the jangling discords of our nation into a beautiful symphony of brotherhood."[84] Here, at the very apex of the civil rights movement, we find an invocation of Du Bois's vision of folk song as the culmination of King's address, his voice at its most lyrical and uplifting merging imperceptibly with "the words of the old Negro spiritual: 'Free at last! Free at last! Thank God Almighty, we are free at last!'"[85] By strange, prophetic coincidence Du Bois had passed away in Ghana at the age of ninety-five on the eve of this historic march.[86] The momentous social and legal changes of the 1960s, he would surely have affirmed, would not have occurred had the Fisk Jubilee Singers not sung "the slave songs so deeply into the world's heart that it can never wholly forget them again."[87] Their songs of sorrow and hopeful anticipation of the future were "the articulate message of the slave to the world," their joy, though eclipsed by grief, not undimmed—"the music of an unhappy people, of the children of disappointment" telling "of death and suffering and unvoiced longing toward a truer world."[88]

The difference between Du Bois and white folklorists such as Sharp and Lomax was not necessarily in the language employed (Du Bois, for instance, claims in typically folkloric manner that the spirituals were "the siftings of centuries," their music "far more ancient than the words," the slaves who made them "primitive folk" who "stood near to Nature's heart"), but in the *framing* of such material.[89] Du Bois was far less concerned with theories of origin, preservation, future revival, or the subtle bonds of blood and soil than with African American folk song as a cipher of present belonging—the sign of a community forged through diasporic experience and imagined through music.[90] Unlike the masses conjured up by anxious white folklorists, Du Bois's Black folk were a thriving populace looking toward a bright future distinct from and yet imbued with the ancestral spirits of the dark, colonial past. Du Bois was well aware of the utter impossibility of cultural purity—Black experience in the United States always inexorably hybrid, dialogic, a changing same. First there is African music, then "Afro-American," then "a blending of Negro music with the music heard in the foster land" (something "still distinctively Negro . . . [and] original" although "the elements are both Negro and Caucasian"), then the final truth that "the songs of white America have been distinctively influenced by the slave songs or have incorporated whole phrases of Negro melody."[91] This, in potted form, is the history of American music—a history that folklorists have repeatedly sought to separate out into racial strands, following them in isolation to what seemed to be their innate features and descents. In a white racial frame, the folkloric imagination afforded a way to do battle against unwanted interfusion; for Du Bois, in contrast, it was inseparable from an embrace of hybridity and two-way cultural interaction.

This reciprocal transaction, of course, was never equal. As Du Bois points out at the rhetorical climax of his book, the United States was built on the lacerated backs of African captives and their descendants, its culture always already entwined:

> Before the Pilgrims landed we were here. Here we have brought our three gifts and mingled them with yours: a gift of story and song—soft, stirring melody in an ill-harmonized and unmelodious land; the gift of sweat and brawn to

> beat back the wilderness, conquer the soil, and lay the foundations of this vast economic empire two hundred years earlier than your weak hands could have done it; the third, a gift of the Spirit. . . . Actively we have woven ourselves with the very warp and woof of this nation,—we fought their battles, shared their sorrow, mingled our blood with theirs, and generation after generation have pleaded with a headstrong, careless people to despise not Justice, Mercy, and Truth, lest the nation be smitten with a curse. Our song, our toil, our cheer, and warning have been given to this nation in blood-brotherhood. Are not these gifts worth the giving? Is not this work and striving? Would America have been America without her Negro people?[92]

They are answers too evident to need stating. The sorrow songs are the folk art of this long and excruciating history—a gift, a warning, and a witness of the nation's past. To Du Bois, these were songs not just of belonging to an African American *folk*, but of belonging to the American *people*; not of primitivism, but of modernity.

Du Bois would return to this theme again twenty years later in *The Gift of Black Folk*. His aim was to challenge the white supremacist view of the US as "a continuation of English nationality" in which a series of others are "looked upon as a sort of dilution of more or less doubtful value'—communities needing to "be assimilated as far as possible and made over to the original and basic type."[93] It is a resilient myth and Du Bois is right to sense the ease with which "casual thinkers" assume its veracity.[94] I write this paragraph in the wake of two mass shootings, one of which (in the border town of El Paso, Texas) appears as a horrific realization of the white nationalist rhetoric associated with the presidency of Donald Trump—nativist, anti-immigrant terrorism that aims to rid America of those others who threaten the fragile fiction of a racially and culturally pure nation. To be American in this vision (as we shall see in the book's coda) is to have a white heritage; nonwhite others are thus intruders or imposters. Yet as Du Bois insists, "America is conglomerate."[95] It is "high time," he writes, "that this course of our thinking should be changed" and the reality of a profoundly crossbred spirit be acknowledged as the result of diverse "threads of thought and feeling coming not only from America but from Europe and Asia and indeed from Africa."[96] The so-called "Negro problem," the problem of the color line, he argues, is ultimately "the failure to recognize this fact and to continue to act as though the Negro was what we once imagined and wanted to imagine him—a representative of a subhuman species fitted only for subordination."[97] It was this institutionalized subordination that not only removed the liberty of enslaved Africans, but also annulled the very possibility of freedom. As Hannah Arendt writes, slavery's true act of criminality began "when it was forgotten that it was man who had deprived his fellow-men of freedom, and when the sanction for the crime was attributed to nature"—another example of historical experience being erased by myth.[98]

As memory entails forgetting just as much as it involves recollection, Du Bois is concerned to foreground those at risk of being overlooked or nullified when the monuments of cultural memory are erected. He is mindful that an entire people's history is at risk of being washed away as the nation's mythic self-identity hardens into sculptural form—those very people who laid the foundations upon which such monuments are built. Now that the "deep but bare" underpinnings of the country have been constructed, he writes, "there are those as always who would forget the humble builders, toiling wan mornings and blazing noons, and picture America as the last reasoned blossom of mighty ancestors."[99] This is the primary reason for Du Bois's veneration of the folk and their lore—what he described in 1898 as "those finer manifestations of social life which history can but mention and which statistics can not count, such as the expression of Negro life as found in their hundred newspapers, their considerable literature, their music and folklore and their germ of esthetic life."[100] Folk songs such as the spirituals were to be remembered and integrated into the national imaginary just as African Americans themselves must be reintegrated into the fabric of society. It is not folk material that Du Bois worries might be lost, therefore, but a people's role in the making of a nation's history—a racialized erasure of the "splendid sordid truth that out of the most lowly and persecuted of men, Man made America."[101] By dwelling on the folk, Du Bois elevates the commonplace and the lives of those anonymous men and women whose unwaged labor composed a nation.

It is in this regard that the African American folk turn from romantic exemplifications of primitivism to become key players within Afro-modernism and the Harlem Renaissance—emblems of what Houston Baker terms "renaissancism," the expressive makings and maskings of Black modernity that begin around the turn of the century and come to fruition during the 1920s.[102] Vernacular culture is central to this expressive paradigm and the "resonantly and continuously productive set of tactics, strategies, and syllables" upon which it rests.[103] Du Bois, in Baker's words, deploys a cunning "deformation of mastery" that creates "the contours of a field of Afro-American phonics" marking "the birth of Afro-American modernism."[104] Du Bois deconstructs or "de-forms" the illusions of racial mastery and inequality through his prose, steadfastly refusing to participate in the charade of minstrel stereotypes and soundings. Within this field, Fisk University and the Jubilee Singers epitomize a modernist vision of uplift, freedom, and progress inspired by inherited spirits of slavery and suffering. This is precisely how the ensemble was received across the world: not as regressive blackface entertainers, as we've seen, but as skilled and even masterful performers outdoing Western musicianship on its own terms. The Jubilee Singers had learned the game and in so doing wrested selfhood from prior conditions of bondage. As Baker puts it, "the birth of such a self is never simply a coming into being, but always, also, a release from a BEING POSSESSED."[105] Slaves were literally possessed beings—the deformation practiced by Du Bois and the Fisk singers working to repossess a stolen past, enacting liberation through song.

Du Bois's work, Baker notes, "refuses a master's *nonsense*" by returning to "the sound and space of an African ancestral past."[106] It is a kind of "cultural performance" much like that of the Jubilee Singers themselves, a "diorama of the folk" laid out by an author who emblematically "*knows the score*."[107] The Black folk that materialize within his writing are the indication of "a distinct social mind"—a body of people on the move propelled into new territories by the spiritual power of the sorrow songs.[108] And yet, as Baker points out, *The Souls of Black Folk* simultaneously "implies that any conceivable global modernism in an age where "the color line" is preeminent must be articulated through Caliban's expressive traditions"—a language enforced, as in Shakespeare's late play *The Tempest*, upon colonial subjects who employ this very language both to curse their condition of enslavement and to out-perform their masters in displays of linguistic eloquence.[109] During the course of his book, Du Bois actively *fashions* a folk out of the remnants of shattered heritage and racialized terror, showing that African Americans are not defined by the typecasts of blackface minstrelsy but by enactments of cultural belonging. This vision of the folk is diametrically opposed to that offered by Lomax, keen as he was to accentuate the stereotypes of a white racial frame—barbarism, violence, illiteracy, primitivism, and vice. In contrast, Du Bois's project is one of *mastery* and *critique*—of turning such imagery inside out and upside down. It is a conception of the folk, as Baker suggests, "possessed of a guiding or tutelary spirit."[110] The African American folk that emerges, phoenix-like, from these embers of historical oppression can lay claim to a culture entirely of their own making containing within itself the hard-won seeds of uplift, identity, and freedom.

Throughout this chapter we've seen African American folk song framed in a variety of different, even paradoxical, ways. For white folklorists, it appeared to be something elemental, pure, and racially distinct, connecting African Americans to a savage past; a survival of primitive, premodern rituals and superstitions; an archetype of indigenous American music made by groups living close to nature; or something uncultivated and unconscious. Many of these strands of reception arose as a direct result of horizons of expectation shaped within a white racial frame. African Americans were innately rhythmical but lacking in tonal sophistication, their culture defined by orality rather than writing, their nature most clearly manifest when circumscribed among others of their race, their religious impulse always crude but intense, their expression innately genuine and unmediated.[111] But rather than African American folk song possessing these so-called "primitive" or "savage" qualities, such qualities were in truth projections by white folklorists—ways of framing Black folk song *as* primitive and savage. Although African American music afforded the view that its melodies and rhythms were rebellious by Western standards, it was a white racial frame that made these differences of intonation, accent, and tonality into an aural signworld of racial alterity. Difference, in other words, was a given, but it was the frame of a folkloric imagination that gave this difference meaning. Folk song was thereby imbued—for many white writers on the subject—with the charm and intrigue of African mysticism dressed up as living proof of racialized ontology.

For Black writers, by way of contrast, such music was often the portrait of a community's very soul and being—less a biological fact than a result of history and shared experience. But we also find a fissure within African American culture between the spirituals as a potential source of fear or embarrassment along the hard road to racial uplift and the spirituals as a sad but proud emblem of descent, a lantern of fellowship to carry into the future. For Work, these songs manifested aspects of secret, in-group communication that would later be styled as "signifyin."[112] For Du Bois, they were a precious crucible of memory that held the capacity to create a modern and estimable *people*, a full-fledged citizenry out of the scattered ruins and atrocities of the American past. This spirit of folkloric renaissancism flourished across the arts during the early twentieth century, from books such as the 1925 anthology *The New Negro* edited by Alain Locke and the paintings of Aaron Douglas

FIGURE 20. W. C. Handy, July 1941. Photograph by Carl Van Vechten.

to the poetry of Langston Hughes and the tent show blues of Gertrude "Ma" Rainey and Bessie Smith.[113] As Du Bois puts it with typical virtuosity, the "musical soul of a race unleashed itself violently" from the inhibitions of "conventional morality," and "in the saloons and brothels of the Mississippi bottoms and gulf coast flared to that crimson license of expression known as 'ragtime,' 'jazz' and the more singular 'blues' retaining with all their impossible words the glamour of rhythm and wild joy."[114] It is a bold vision squarely at odds with white efforts to segregate authentic Black folk music from the perversions of the mass marketplace. Symptomatic of this unbridled soul was the composer and bandleader W. C. Handy, who frequented the very world that Du Bois is describing here. Hearing for the first time what he calls "low folk forms," Handy was overawed not least for the lucrative potential he sensed in "the beauty of primitive music" and the haunting strains of "folk blues" he encountered in the south.[115] Amid "a rain of silver dollars" for a disheveled upstart trio that had asked to perform in place of his band, Handy notes that "a composer was born, an *American* composer"—one more in touch with both a Black popular audience and "the essence" of African American musical expression.[116]

For Handy, the folk opened up the possibility of a distinctively Black form of popular culture, as well as the unseen underworlds of Mississippi in which it thrived:

> Across the tracks of the Y[azoo]. & M[issippi]. V[alley]. railroad in Clarksdale there was a section called the "New World." It was the local red-light district. . . . As musicians . . . hired to play music rather than to discuss morals, we kept our mouths shut. We knew that big shot officials winked at the New World, but that was neither here nor there to the men with the horns and the fiddles. What was important was that these rouge-tinted girls, wearing silk stockings and short skirts, bobbing their soft hair and smoking cigarets in that prim era, long before these styles had gained respectability, were among the best patrons the orchestra had. They employed us for big nights, occasions when social or political figures of importance were expected to dine and dance with their favorite creole belles.[117]

The "contacts made in these shady precincts," Handy points out with evident glee, "often led to jobs in chaste great houses of the rich and well-to-do."[118] Such music was referred to at the time as "Boogie-house music"—a style he describes as later being "fumigated and played in the best of society."[119] This was a world of unsettling double consciousness that demanded mastery, deformation, and tact in equal measure. One moment Handy could be supporting a white racist gubernatorial candidate, and in another acting as a clandestine distributor of seditious northern newspapers and magazines such as *The Chicago Defender* or *The Voice of the Negro*. His blues compositions penned during these early years of the twentieth century heralded the blossoming of race records during the 1920s, Parisian "Negrophilia," and a global vogue for Black culture—what Baker describes as a "folk energy" that "can only be called a black and classical sound of the self-in-marronage," unbounded.[120]

This spirit animated African American musicians, writers, and creative artists across the aesthetic spectrum. A figure who likewise sought to "mine a southern Afro-American tradition with dedicated genius" and render a Black folk voice "in its simple, performative eloquence" (to borrow Baker's portrayal of the poet Sterling Allen Brown) was the Harlem Renaissance writer Jean Toomer.[121] Structured as a series of thematically connected vignettes of narrative prose, poetry, and theatrical dialogue interspersed (much like Du Bois's "singing book") with fragments of song, his 1923 novel *Cane* is an Afro-modernist archetype.[122] Writing to the editors of the radical labor magazine the *Liberator* shortly before *Cane* was published, Toomer describes how turning to the folk had stirred and renewed his creativity:

> Within the last two to three years . . . my growing need for artistic expression has pulled me deeper and deeper into the Negro group. And as my powers of receptivity increased, I found myself loving it in a way that I could never love the other. It has stimulated and fertilized whatever creative talent I may contain within me. A visit to Georgia last fall was the starting point of almost everything of worth that I have done. I heard folk-songs come from the lips of Negro peasants. I saw the rich dusk beauty that I had heard many false accents about, and of which, till then, I was somewhat skeptical. And a deep part of my nature, a part that I had repressed, sprang suddenly to life and responded to them. Now, I can not conceive of myself as aloof and separated. My point of view has not changed; it has deepened, it has widened.[123]

For Toomer, as for Handy, meeting the Black folk spirit in the flesh was a moment of profound awakening—a recognition of cultural and ancestral kinship, however mixed the blood and history. But the folk led Toomer and Handy in opposite directions: one toward modern popular entertainment and profit, the other toward modernist literary technique and folkloric preservation. As Toomer notes, the folk music he so admired was demonized by "the Negroes of the town" with their "victrolas and player-pianos" and their embrace of "industry and commerce and machines"; the spirituals, he felt, would be certain to perish in this brave new world of technological innovation, their "folk-spirit . . . walking in to die on the modern desert."[124] *Cane*, he writes, "was a swan-song . . . a song of an end."[125]

The term *swan-song* appears again in a letter Toomer writes to the novelist Waldo Frank in early 1923. "The Negro of the folk-song," he worries, "has all but passed away"—a figure at risk of dissolving into the lifeless mainstream of white modernity.[126] The motivating force behind the Harlem Renaissance movement, he states, is "a vague sense of this fact," the loss of something that "America needs."[127] In familiar folkloric fashion, he laments the rise of industrialization and "mechanical civilization"—transformations that rob African Americans of something vital, forcing them to conform "to the general outlines of American civilization, or of American chaos."[128] In marked contrast to Du Bois, the dominant mood of his own writing aligned with this folk spirit is "a sadness derived from a sense of fading."[129]

Rather than "the buoyant expression of a new race," Toomer finds dissipation and creeping homogeneity.[130] He goes so far as to suggest that such loss is bound up with a collective turning away from an "emotional allegiance to the soil."[131] It is this closeness to the landscape of the south that he seeks to reconstruct in the literary mosaic of *Cane*—where hills and valleys are "heaving with folk-songs" that spark between distant cabins "like purple tallow flames" spreading "a ruddy haze over the heavens" until "the whole countryside is a soft chorus."[132] A full moon rises and we find that "Negro women" have "improvised songs against its spell."[133] Folk songs in Toomer's South seem always to be associated with nightfall and evening, signs of waning and the unknown. These songs emerge not only from the folk, but also as if from the land itself, its panorama set singing by "night's womb-song" and the breath of wind.[134] It is as if these songs are born like children, or made up in harmony with nature, communal call-and-response hymns commemorating the vernacular:

> Smoke is on the hills. Rise up.
> Smoke is on the hills, O rise
> And take my soul to Jesus.[135]

Sometimes we are aware of Toomer himself as a poetic vessel for this folk, as in two poems "Song of the Son" and "Georgia Dusk" that dwell on legacies of servitude and mourning, sugar cane a persistent reminder of plantation life:

> In time, for though the sun is setting on
> A song-lit race of slaves, it has not set;
> Though late, O soil, it is not too late yet
> To catch thy plaintive soul, leaving, soon gone,
> Leaving, to catch thy plaintive soul soon gone.[136]
>
> A feast of moon and men and barking hounds,
> An orgy for some genius of the South
> With blood-hot eyes and cane-lipped scented mouth,
> Surprised in making folk-songs from soul sounds.[137]

His simple rhymes here call to mind end-stopped stanzas set to music, his repetition of lines alluding to the blues form. They are elegies for this "song-lit race" whose souls seem to be attuned to the night, captured in their final days.

Whether *Cane* or *The Souls of Black Folk*, Black renaissancism of this era is often imbued with this same folkloric spirit as an act of remembering—of attempting, quite literally, to re-member a race, bringing together through shared recollection of the sorrow songs the scattered remains of a diverse social body torn apart by the traumatic histories of imperialism, slavery, and exile. It is a similar undertaking to Zora Neale Hurston's anthropological fieldwork weaving together webs of

African-derived folk medicine variously termed "hoodoo," "*juju*," "conjure," "obeah," or "roots."[138] Her work, like that of Du Bois, Toomer, and other artists of the Harlem Renaissance, is also a form of re-membering—of documenting the diffuse and distinctive customs once shared through family ties and tribal affiliations, since dispersed across the continent and found interspersed with elements of white religious practice. These strategies were all efforts to hold on to something precious: a collective identity in the face of displacement and the prospect of assimilation.

Folklore and modernism are routinely cast as antithetical, two opposing aesthetic paradigms—one nostalgic, egalitarian, and quaint; the other vanguard, elitist, and willfully disobedient; one rural and the other metropolitan; one ancient and the other always striving to blast new tunnels into the future. The term *modernism* thus hardly ever appears in discussions of folk music, despite its importance to poets such as Carl Sandburg, an associate of John Lomax.[139] One rare exception is provided by William Roy, who uses the term to identify the "frame of mind that has informed European thinking since the Enlightenment"—that is, as a synonym for modernity, a concept that encompasses but extends well beyond the artistic experimentations of the modernist nexus.[140] Roy is nevertheless correct to note that folk song, as an idea, is something like a symptom of modernity, as we've seen—one aspect of its own "self-critique" highlighting "the anxieties, disquiet, emptiness, and alienation of the modern condition."[141] And yet folkloric discourse in an African American context is far more complicated than this statement suggests. In one framing, the Black folk are cast by white writers as primitivist antidotes to modernity, situated as exemplifications of racial difference; but in a concurrent framing, they appear as the raw material for modernist literary poetics as well as crucial markers of African American modernity and belonging—guiding spirits of liberation and ancestral memory used to stage a critique of worn-out stereotypes and racialized disempowerment. As such, Black folk song is a not an element of modernity's own self-critique, but a critique from without seeking to emancipate the past as the groundwork for an egalitarian future.

In the final chapter, we shall look at the ways in which folkloric thinking could be used for precisely the opposite end, betraying its underlying affinities with fascist thought. Although folk music afforded minorities a way to speak out and resist forms of hegemony, homogenization, and oppression, when wielded rhetorically by a dominant culture that feels under threat from these very figures or rapid cultural change, the result can be a grim and obdurate inversion of Du Bois's aspiration.

CHAPTER 5

# Soul through the Soil

## *Cecil Sharp & the Specter of Fascism*

One of the most remarkable things about folk music is the way it has managed to shake off, almost entirely, the more sinister aspects of its history. Folk dances and songs seem to dwell in a timeless rural idyll. White-shirted figures perform quaint remnants of a forgotten ritual calendar; bohemian singers give voice to timeworn ballads of love and magic, tragedy and gallantry; fairy tales tell of wild, childlike adventure and mythological fantasy. The political ideal that emerges between the lines is a conspicuously leftist vision of Arts and Crafts nostalgia and popular resistance to power exemplified by William Morris's utopianism. Haunting the revival of the 1960s, for instance, are legends such as Woody Guthrie, his guitar emblazoned with the phrase "THIS MACHINE KILLS FASCISTS" (now available as a sticker for $4 a piece).[1] In Britain, Guthrie's counterpart would be Ewan MacColl—a vociferous anti-fascist and proud, card-carrying communist.[2] This union between folk culture and the left is so apparent and long-standing that we rarely ever think to question it. In the public imagination, the folk revivalist is a dyed-in-the-wool radical whose commitment to the betterment of the common man was forged in the furnace of anti-capitalist hostility. These figures rage against commerce and coercion with songs of social injustice, their feet firmly planted in the territory of home.

But this tradition carries on its shoulders a dark encumbrance that casts a disconcerting shadow over the idea of folk music as tool of resistance. With few exceptions, volkish celebrations of the past contain a call not simply to equality, peace, and harmony, but also to blood-and-soil nativism. We'll see in this chapter that when nineteenth-century dreams of communism were abandoned or revised by those with an interest in the nation state, folkloric elements could be put to very different uses. Another way of saying this would be to point out that far more links socialist ideals of folk community and fascist visions of tribal unity than we like to imagine. Above all, what remains a thorn in the side of the left is what the Italian political exile Giuseppe Borgese described in 1934 as "the spiritual chemism of nationalism."[3] Published in translation the year before, an essay by Mussolini noted that fascism had arisen from the embers of war "in opposition to all political parties" as "a living movement"—a force based on the denial of economic or materialist conceptions of history, the notion of "an unchangeable and unchanging class-war," and the "democratic ideology" of liberalism.[4] Its solution to the contradictions of capitalism and party rivalry was an elevation of the state into an organic, populist entity that would be "custodian and transmitter of the spirit of the people, as it has grown up through the centuries in language, in customs and in faith."[5] Such ideas, Borgese suggests, appealed primarily to those "lower intellectuals" hungry for spiritual fulfillment "degraded to emotional appetite."[6] In Britain, this collectivist vision in which the state educates the people who in turn become an ethnic nation rooted in tradition sparked the interest of Cecil Sharp, whose theories on song and dance—despite severe criticism from a range of contemporaries—eventually won out as the dominant way of understanding folk heritage across the Western world.

In June 1905 a note appeared in the *Musical Times* reporting that London's Folk-Song Society "seems to have entered upon a new lease of life" under its new Honorary Secretary Lucy Broadwood; it went on to state that a recently issued volume of the Society's *Journal* contained a significant "harvest" contributed by that "enthusiastic collector" Cecil Sharp.[7] Founded in 1898, the Society had indeed been suffering from a substantial decrease in revenue and a general inertia due to Kate Lee's deteriorating health.[8] The turning point came in 1904. An Annual Report noted that several new members had been elected and that Sharp, "who has lately collected some hundreds of songs in Somersetshire and North Devon, joined our Committee."[9] Sharp had neither participated in the Society's foundation nor shown any public interest in the subject during the 1890s. Educated at Cambridge—where he read mathematics—he had become principal of the Hampstead Conservatoire of Music and was busy carving out a career in the capital as an educator and choral conductor. In 1902 he had published a miscellany entitled *A Book of British Song for Home and School*, prompting one reviewer to comment on its "large sprinkling of folk-songs" and remark in astonishment that "although this collection of school songs is designated 'British,' no fewer than sixty-six of the seventy-eight ditties contained herein are English."[10] From the outset, as we've seen, Sharp appeared to be set on the promulgation not only of folk song in wider society, but of folk song as a means to cultivate a specifically English nationality—utilizing a handful of singers from "three small districts" as indicators of the southwest, the southwest itself as a microcosm of England, and England as a politicized synecdoche for Britain.[11] It would be Sharp, more than any other collector, who would come to dominate folkloric discourse and practice in the new century—initiating a paradigm shift away from antiquarianism toward resolute doctrine, pedagogy, and deliberate cultural intervention.

Although he aimed for a scientific approach when publishing material in the Society's *Journal*—printing (as Francis James Child had done) "with each ballad all the variants and different versions of it," along with singers" names, location, and the date of collection—Sharp began to construct an elaborate theory of folk song that not only contradicted this meticulous collation of data, but also served to erase the presence, experience, and voices of the individual singers he encountered.[12] As reported by the *Musical Times*, he outlined this Darwinian model of origin, variation, and selection in an address to the social reformist Tonic Sol-fa Association: "The lecturer boldly applies the doctrines of evolution to explain the adoption of final forms (if there are any). He thinks that many of the existing tunes began with mere inflection, and that gradually, in the course of generations, they have assumed their existing form. So we have geometrical increase, constant variation, struggles for existence, and survival of the fittest—the communally made tune, embodying the rhythmic and tonal likings of the race and district."[13] What set Sharp apart from previous collectors was not only this framework, but also the extent to which he wished to see such material restored to the nation as a whole. Whereas the Folk-Song Society "is doing its best to collect the ballad before it dies," he stressed, "it remains for others to restore it, and place the ballad in the mouths of the people."[14] Within this scheme, however, the folk themselves appeared merely as ghosts, usurped by revivalists and rendered silent. Although showing "upon the lantern screen a number of photographs of the old singers who contributed to his collection"—including figures we encountered in chapter 1—Sharp chose to illustrate his talk with performances featuring the singer Mattie Kay, with himself on piano.[15]

Vociferously rebutting anyone who claimed that England had no pleasing or authentic songs with proof from his own fieldwork, Sharp's voice became a familiar point of reference in public debates over folk song in the press.[16] Such ideas were elaborated in his 1907 monograph *English Folk-Song: Some Conclusions*—a book, he states, the "main thesis" of which is "the evolutionary origin of the folk-song."[17] This theory was to become the linchpin of his revivalist vision. Folk song and popular song, he emphasizes, are to the expert "two distinct species of music" differing "not in degree but in kind"—one the result of cultivated enterprise, the other the result of an unconscious communal process.[18] Establishing a global spectrum of subalterns in familiar ethnological manner, such instinct supposedly united "ancient" music with rural "peasant" singers and "the natives of New Guinea, China, Java, Sumatra, and other Eastern nations"—their modes, as Sharp points out, "may be called *natural* scales."[19] The folk he imagined were likewise not simply illiterate, but an entirely unschooled group akin to Lomax's African American convicts "whose mental development has been due . . . solely to environment" and who have thus "escaped the infection of modern ideas."[20] What Sharp was interested in, consequently, was a kind of prosopopoeia in which folk song was the expression not of heterogeneous modern civilization, but of Nature itself. Despite admitting that pages of his field notebooks were "filled with scraps of imperfectly remembered broadside versions" and sometimes even an entire ballad, Sharp refused to engage with evidence that might have rendered this thesis incorrect. "To search for the originals of folk-songs amongst the printed music of olden days," he declares, is a "mere waste of time."[21]

Sharp was far less concerned with documenting vernacular culture on its own terms than "unsealing the lips" of rural singers in order to induce them, as he puts it, "to unlock their treasures at our bidding"—culminating in what one critic astutely described as the "transference of the songs and dances from one class to the other."[22] Indeed, Sharp openly acknowledged that his principal goal was not ethnography, but to change the "pessimistic attitude towards the musical prospects of our country."[23] As "the natural musical idiom of a national will," folk song could provide a rebuttal both to foreign musical dominance and to unwelcome internationalism arising from Britain's history as the world's preeminent imperial power.[24] Here is Sharp at his most fervent in a particularly revealing passage that's worth quoting in full:

> There are many ways of stimulating the feeling of patriotism. Education is one of them. Our system of education is, at present, too cosmopolitan; it is calculated to produce citizens of the world rather than Englishmen. And it is Englishmen, English citizens, that we want. How can this be remedied? By taking care, I would suggest, that every child born of English parents is, in its earliest years, placed in possession of all those things which are the distinctive products of its race. The first and most important of these is the mother tongue. Its words, its grammatical constructions, its idioms, are all characteristic of the race which has evolved them, and whose ideas and thoughts they are thus peculiarly fitted to express. The English tongue differs from the French or German precisely as the Englishman differs from the Frenchman or the German. Irish patriots are fully alive to this, and, from their own point of view, are quite right in advocating the revival of the Irish language.
>
> Then there are the folk-tales, legends, and proverbs, which are peculiar to the English; the national sports, pastimes, and dances also. All these things belong of right to the children of our race, and it is as unwise, as it is unjust, to rob them of this their national inheritance.
>
> Finally, there are the folk-songs, those simple ditties which have sprung like wild flowers from the very hearts of our countrymen, and which are as redolent of the English race as its language. If every child be placed in possession of all these race-products, he will know and understand his country and his countrymen far better than he does at present; and knowing and understanding them he will love them the more, realize that he is united to them by the subtle bond of blood and kinship, and become, in the highest sense of the word, a better citizen, and a truer patriot.[25]

In contrast to the cheap patriotism of professionally authored patriotic songs, folk songs seemed to provide a deeper, more mystical and organic, and hence more authentic patriotism based on language, kinship, and the soil. As such, they were to be introduced into elementary schools "to effect an improvement in the musical taste of the people, and to refine and strengthen the national character"—mitigating the "very serious national shortcoming" of the country's presently weak patriotic spirit.[26]

Folk music accordingly placed "in the hands of the patriot, as well as of the educationalist, an *instrument* of great value."[27] Recalling ideals we encountered in chapter 2, Sharp regarded the material he collected as the means to a specific political end—that of making "the streets a pleasanter place for those who have sensitive ears" by "civilizing the masses."[28] Such ideas anticipated R. Murray Schafer's much later disgust with the Dionysian "vulgarity" of modern soundscapes and his belief that "the general acoustic environment of a society can be read as an indicator of social conditions"—something that obliged Apollonian listeners to rage against all manner of "insouciant and distracting sounds."[29] Sharp's project represented a similar attempt at an orderly, undemocratic rearrangement of the public sphere. With their apparent rejection of drinking songs, comic songs, sentimental songs, and crass jingoism, the rural folk were everything the metropolitan masses were not. Their songs were thus a device with which the English people could be "purged" of their unnatural attachment to commercial entertainment and Continental composition, their culture redirected along national lines, no longer "to lisp in the tongue of the foreigner" but to "repeat in the future what we have accomplished in the past."[30] Repurposed as what Sharp calls an "educational force," folk melodies offered up the possibility of a cultural "resuscitation," inspiring "that love of country and pride of race, the absence of which we now deplore."[31] The reintroduction of folk song into schools, he felt, would create "virgin soil" for a revival of tradition comparable to that following in the wake of Bishop Thomas Percy's *Reliques of Ancient English Poetry*, a text that had inspired (as he points out) writers from Scott to Wordsworth.[32] In simple terms, then, Sharp viewed folk revivalism as a mechanism for mass social reform.

Such designs, we should remember, bore scant relation to rural working-class experience during the early twentieth century, grounded as they were in conjecture and a puritanical conception of rustic life beholden to a period before music hall and the railways.[33] Where Sharp saw a so-called "peasant" song culture in terminal decline, other sources tell a different story.[34] One text that discusses vernacular singing in the countryside during this era is Fred Kitchen's *Brother to the Ox: The Autobiography of a Farm Labourer*. Born in Edwinstowe, Nottinghamshire in 1890, Kitchen had moved with his family to Yorkshire, where they lived as tenant farmers on an aristocratic estate. After the death of his first wife and a number of different jobs (including employment as a cowman, miner, and railway navvy), Kitchen had enrolled in evening classes at the Workers' Educational Association, where he began writing *Brother to the Ox*—a book that would go on to win a Foyles literary prize.[35] In marked contrast to Sharp's uneducated ideal, Kitchen recalls that owing to early encouragement from his schoolmistress and a chaplain he had "always been fond of poetry, and could recite off-hand much of Burns, Keats, Shelly's Skylark, and many of the great poets," and had also read "most of George Eliot's works, several Dickens, Thackery's *Vanity Fair*, and Emily Brontë's *Wuthering Heights*."[36]

Kitchen recounts many evenings spent with other farm laborers in the stables "until nine o'clock, when we had a basin of bread-and-milk, and so to bed":

> Usually one of them would bring a melodeon, and he was considered a poor gawk who couldn't knock a tune out of a mouth-organ or give a song to pass away the evening. We had rare times in the "fotherham," seated on the corn-bin or on a truss of hay. Tom fra' Bennett's would strike off with, "Oh, never go into a sentry-box, to be wrapt in a soldier's cloak," while someone played away on the melodeon. He was a merry sort of lad, was Tom, and his songs always had a spicy flavour. Harry Bates, Farmer Wood's man, always sang sentimental ballads. Harry was a Lincolnshire chap, and their singing, I always noticed, was of a more serious vein than the rollicking Yorkies. . . . He knew no end of good songs—as did most of the farm lads—but his were mostly about "soldiers sighing for their native land," and "heart-broken lovers," and that sort of stuff, so that as a rule we liked to get Tom singing first. They were all good singers, and good musicians too, and it must not be supposed, because they were farm men and lads, they were just caterwauling.[37]

These gatherings would typically involve songs such as "Heart of Oak" (composed in the eighteenth century by William Boyce and David Garrick), broadside ballads such as "The Sentry Box," and sentimental music hall material such as "The Volunteer Organist" (published by Wm. B. Glenroy and Henry Lamb).[38] Although Kitchen was fond of what he calls the "meat and poetry of our old songs," the concept of folk song never figures in his worldview and his evidence fails to support Sharp's evolutionary supposition.[39] In fact, Kitchen was at pains to point out that the pastoral visions of outsiders tended to support preconceptions. Although "artists have drawn some pleasing pictures of the shepherd leading his flock on the grassy uplands, or gazing pensively at a setting sun," he points out, there are somewhat fewer portraits of the rough, undignified, and frequently grueling aspects of country life.[40]

What is yet more striking, however, is that Sharp's ideas were not accepted among his fellow folk song enthusiasts. The Folk-Song Society's own advice at the time, for instance, was that collectors should ask a singer "whether he possesses, or knows of anyone who possesses, old song-books or ballad-sheets, as these (more especially the latter) are most valuable in connection with the subject of Folk-songs."[41] Broadwood had instructed collectors to go "back, through the broadsides of the eighteenth and seventeenth centuries, to the earliest black-letter ballad-sheets in our museums, and you will find, on *these*, words still sung *to-day*."[42] Conversant with such material and thoroughly unmoved by Sharp's theorizing, the antiquarian Frank Kidson published a review of *English Folk-Song* voicing restrained concern over the author's "zealous devotion" to his subject and conclusions that "bear upon the face of them an assured conviction as to their soundness."[43] Kidson probed Sharp's evolutionary hypothesis of origin, variation, and selection, arguing that "there remain many puzzling things about folk-song—or rather folk-melody—which are not solved by such obvious reasoning."[44] As Miss A. E. Keeton pointed out in 1906 during a lively debate with Sharp in the *Morning Post*, "these songs—with, on the one hand, their absence of any special racial characteristics, and on the other, certain distinctly modern snatches of rhythm and melody—had drifted in scraps from our towns, or many of them more probably equally in scraps from the Continent."[45] She was spot on, finding this popular material therefore "no more indigenous to an uncultivated English soil than is the popular air of 'Home, Sweet Home.'"[46]

The psychologist C. S. Myers, whom we encountered in chapter 1, likewise protested Sharp's definition, given that it seemed to imply that all music "of the untrained mind" was folk song, whereas Sharp himself had stated that this was not the case.[47] Myers felt it necessary to draw attention to several major flaws and at least one passage that was "demonstrably inaccurate" in the book.[48] J. A. Fuller Maitland's review of what he dubbed Sharp's "professedly scientific treatise" in the *Times Literary Supplement* was no less unflattering, dryly recommending that given his "comparatively late advent into the ranks of the collectors" the subtitle be amended to "Some Beginnings."[49] The model of individual creation followed by communal selection specified in its pages, he noticed, was in truth far less radical than the "strange theory" of collective authorship that Sharp liked to advance "in the heat of controversy."[50] Musing on why the versions of songs Sharp considered most authoritative always happened to be his own discoveries, Fuller Maitland concludes his review by noting that although Sharp deserved credit for his eagerness, "he might well leave to others the work of analyzing the treasures he finds."[51]

Beyond the world of folk collecting, the nationalistic proclivity that Sharp exemplified had also been subject to critique. Several years earlier, the music critic Edward Baughan had ceremoniously pulled the rug out from under this trend, uncovering a paradox at the heart of Sharp's political vision. Sharp believed that English folk music was the expression of an unalloyed national identity in a country that had, for centuries, extended its colonizing dominion across the globe—and was thus the postcolonial product of what Edward Said calls "intertwined histories."[52] As Hubert Parry was delivering his inaugural address to the Folk-Song Society, Baughan published the following under the title "A Plea for Cosmopolitanism":

> It will, perhaps, seem rather far fetched to trace the influence of our genius for colonization on our music, but in these days, when our foremost composers show a decided inclination to apologize for the cosmopolitan character of British music, and to dig into the mine of Folk-song, it is necessary to point out that Great Britain is not as other nations, that her sons have carried her flag to every part of the habitable globe, and that the country itself is nothing more than a large warehouse with a thriving brokerage business attached.[53]

It would be absurd, Baughan continues, to suppose that such a history had no effect on national character, and "equally absurd to speak of one character" given the self-evidently hybrid nature of human descent and the questionable place of England itself within a "National British School."[54] Although in broad agreement with Sharp and Parry regarding the evolutionary nature of musical development, Baughan used this same teleological argument to arrive at a diametrically opposite conclusion—that an infatuation with unsophisticated folk song was "a reversal of the proper order of things."[55] As the outpouring of "a people . . . lower in the scale of human culture" containing "little of that healthier, broader, and more sublime thought that is characteristic of man when educated and civilized," folk song was stubbornly out of touch with "modern complexity" and its devotees too inclined to think that "all the virtues of mankind lie in the simplicity of the untutored mind."[56]

The most acerbic critique of Sharp and the folk song movement as a whole, however, came from the pen of celebrated music critic Ernest Newman. A short article in the *Observer* in May 1912 commented that Newman had been "discoursing eloquently on the many fallacies connected with the aims and claims of folk-song partisans": appearing in the *English Review*, his arguments, it noted, "are strong and, if you are not sentimental on the subject, entirely conclusive."[57] The idea of "the" Englishman, Newman asserts, is simply "a fiction"; Sharp's ideas on folk song, in consequence, were crude, superficial, and built upon a wholly untenable foundation.[58] Unearthing the abundant contradictions in his work, Newman reasons that "the whole theory of 'racial characteristics' in music is flawed to the very centre" as nations could never be "summed up in this style under a single simple formula."[59] Challenging what he refers to as Sharp's "facile and foolish generalizations," he notes that "the supposed fixity of type within a given territory is a myth, there being all possible variations of it observable when we study it in detail. Still less can we predicate any such fixity of type among the nations of Western Europe, or such starkness of type-contrast between one nation as a whole and another. . . . The theory that even in a simple community—to say nothing of complex communities like ours—there is any one type of mind or body that can claim to be 'the' national type is absurd."[60] Drawing on Frank Kidson's work Newman points out, furthermore, that "patient research proves the foreign *provenance* of many a melody that has always been accepted as unquestionably 'national.'"[61] These songs, he suggests, were not the outcome of communal selection, as individual singers always performed the same material differently—something that Sharp himself confessed. Warning against this idealization of the past and fetishization of "sheer musical incompetence," Newman finally objects (much like Baughan had) to a form of colonialist déjà vu—folk song discourse being merely "a revival of the eighteenth-century theory of the divine rightness of the noble savage and the corruption of civilization."[62]

Sharp thought Newman's "serious and reasoned attack" provocative enough to warrant an extended reply in the same periodical two months later.[63] His rebuttal amounted to a defense of the very "national characteristic" that Newman had so conscientiously criticized: "Although we cannot define it," Sharp proclaims, we "recognise it when we come across it."[64] This essence was the wellspring of culture "found in its purest, crudest, and least diluted form" in traditional song: "Just as the mixture is strongest at the bottom of the bottle, so are the peculiar characteristics of a nation concentrated in its humblest class. This is natural enough; because the peasantry, as a class, is, of all the others, the most homogeneous and the least affected by alien and outside influences. Unlettered and untravelled, the peasant has had no opportunity of producing an imitative, sophisticated art. What art he does create must of necessity be spontaneous, natural, and un-selfconscious."[65] Comparing this "primitive" creation of "uncultivated minds" to the aesthetic splendor of "all elemental things, the trees, clouds, hills, and rivers," he urges Newman to "silence his analytical mind" and try instead "to *feel* the beauty of the folk-song."[66] Newman was not impressed. In a final rejoinder, he points out that Sharp "simply repeats the old fallacies . . . with the addition of one or two new ones, . . . imagines he has proved things when he has merely said them, and that the arguments against a theorem can be refuted by a bold reassertion of it."[67] Attempting to shift attention away from these confrontations over theory and ideology, Sharp had concluded his article by noting that the worth of folk song would ultimately not be decided by bothersome intellectuals such as Newman: "the verdict" instead "rests with the public."[68]

Herein lies the reason why Sharp would become one of the most authoritative folk song gatekeepers of the twentieth century. As an educator, he had a keen sense for what the public desired from the folk and a judicious ability to capitalize on this desire for his own personal and political gain. An official report by the Board of Education on state elementary schools presented to the Houses of Parliament in 1905, for instance, had enthusiastically encouraged the use of "national or folk-songs" as they satisfied criteria including the teaching of singing, mother tongue, emotional expression, and history to infants.[69] In collaboration with the priest and antiquarian Sabine Baring-Gould, Sharp responded by swiftly publishing a book of arrangements the following year—a collection the editors stated explicitly was "made to meet the requirements of the Board of Education."[70] Yet whereas the Board's report recommended that children sing material from different countries in order "to convey an impression . . . of the characteristic traditions of other races," Sharp and Baring-Gould intended their edition to help English children acquire "that which is their very own" in preference to what they describe as "foreign models."[71] A review in the *Musical Standard* observed that as this book was "tastefully got up and extremely cheap" there was "little doubt that it will achieve the popularity it deserves."[72] This text is just one example of the ways in which Sharp utilized his vast collecting experience across the south of England to establish his reputation as a public authority on folk culture—an identity that would enable him to develop a countrywide network of instructors, graded vacation schools, rules, and adjudicated competitions.[73]

~

Unlike prior folk song devotees, Sharp became increasingly dictatorial, taking it upon himself to represent qualified expertise over and above the modest utterances of the Folk-Song Society—a body lacking clear directorship and corporate sway more concerned with forging ties with elite establishments such as the Library of Congress and the Bodleian. The music critic Percy Scholes noted in his obituary that although Broadwood, Kidson, Fuller Maitland, Ralph Vaughan Williams, and others had produced admirable work, Sharp "left them all far behind in one activity"—the "re-popularisation of English folk-song and folk-dance."[74] Scholes continues: "He published enormously, and published in practical form, providing cheap editions of songs, with simple accompaniments, such as were within the financial means and artistic resources of the elementary school. He founded the English Folk Dance Society, and trained and sent out teachers hall-marked by himself. I remember during the war, at Havre, being made to dance vigorously immediately after dinner by a party of soldiers taught by an instructress sent out by the society. This brought home to me the extent of Sharp's success."[75] Unlike many other collectors, Sharp was adamant that folk song was not merely a testament to loss and the charming patina of time, but when suitably revived would be something akin to "an ancient building newly restored."[76] Sharp, in other words, positioned himself at the helm of a movement serving as a gatekeeper to the folk. In so doing, he was able to establish a new orthodoxy that shaped vernacular custom into attractive, reproducible forms.

Indeed, Sharp achieved momentous popular success despite his critics, as Kidson noted rather euphemistically in 1915: "The part that Mr Cecil Sharp has taken in the advancement of folk-song is well known. . . . His vigorous methods of bringing the subject before the public have caused "folk-song" to become a household word."[77] In Broadwood's opinion, Sharp had made the ungentlemanly move of becoming a professional spokesperson, overstepping former pioneers in the field. In a letter to her sister she complains that "he puffed and boomed and shoved and ousted and used the Press to advertise himself"; crowning himself "King of the whole movement," she protests, he "was by the general ignorant public taken at his own valuation."[78] These brash tactics evidently worked, much to the chagrin of his more learned or demure colleagues. A 1912 article in the *Musical Times* noted that "no one has been more distinguished than Mr. Cecil Sharp" in the revival of songs and dances, while another article portrayed him as "the greatest authority on both these branches of folk-lore."[79] By this point, his work had become known across the Atlantic and absorbed by American scholars, preceeding his involvement in Harley Granville-Barker's acclaimed production of *A Midsummer Night's Dream* and various collecting trips to the Appalachian Mountains.[80] It was in this region, his companion Maud Karpeles later wrote, that he encountered the "England of his dreams"—a utopian enclave where a population descended from the English folk appeared to exist in a state of "arrested degeneration" owing to their isolation from the hazards of modernity.[81]

From unpublished diaries, it becomes clear why Sharp decided to focus his efforts on this particular area, ignoring other types of American

FIGURE 21. Cecil Sharp and Maud Karpeles collecting songs from Lucindy Pratt in Knott County, Kentucky, 1916. Reproduced by kind permission of the English Folk Dance and Song Society.

folk music. He held openly racist opinions about African Americans (twice penning the word *nigger*) and was deeply insensitive to the history of slavery, disenfranchisement, and white supremacy. Writing on 8 December 1918 regarding a conversation with John M. Glenn of the philanthropic Russell Sage Foundation, he remarks with indignation that Glenn "resented my dubbing the negroes as of a lower race & maintained it was a mere lack of education etc.!"[82] Earlier that year, he comments in unbelievably poor taste that the town in North Carolina in which he was staying was "stuffed full with negroes," pondering "whether they are attracted to this tobacco industry by their similarity in colour."[83] The only folk worthy of the name and thus of conservation, in Sharp's view, were white: Black music was either "distracting" or of absolutely no value as heritage.[84] Betraying this act of erasure, Evelyn Wells reminisced about the "new world [Sharp's collecting] opened out for us" and the "cultural roots of America which he laid bare," recalling "the spread of enthusiasm through the country, as the contagion caught on in Buffalo, in Pittsburgh, in Cincinnati and St. Louis and Chicago and Toronto, to say nothing of New York and Boston."[85] He was praised in the *Journal of American Folk-Lore* for this "persevering effort" in collecting "folk-dances and melodies of very ancient origin," and described as having "the acumen of the scholar in publication, and the enthusiasm of the teacher in instruction."[86]

His theories would eventually find their way into the disciplinary heart of folklore study as anonymous axioms. At the seventh conference of the International Folk Music Council in 1954, a plenary session was convened to discuss a delineation of the Council's remit proposed by Karpeles. A rubric was then drafted and put to a vote, with the result that "the Congress agreed that this definition be accepted":

> Folk music is the product of a musical tradition that has been evolved through the process of oral transmission. The factors that shape the tradition are: (i) continuity which links the present with the past; (ii) variation which springs from the creative impulse of the individual or the group; and (iii) selection by the community, which determines the form or forms in which the music survives. The term can be applied to music that has been evolved from rudimentary beginnings by a community uninfluenced by popular and art music and it can likewise be applied to music which has originated with an individual composer and has subsequently been absorbed into the unwritten living tradition of a community. The term does not cover composed popular music that has been taken over ready-made by a community and remains unchanged, for it is the re-fashioning and re-creation of the music by the community that gives it its folk character.[87]

The legacy that Sharp bequeathed to folk music's discursive formation is etched unambiguously throughout: it is the unwritten survival of oral tradition; it results from an evolutionary process of variation and selection; and it exists within the confines of a communal milieu entirely removed from mass culture and high art.

Sharp's posthumous authority, moreover, was felt in a reformist statement on education passed unanimously during this same congress stating that "folk music (which includes dance as well as song) is the basis upon which should rest the musical education of the ordinary citizen."[88] This resolution openly admitted that "the knowledge of experts should be utilised in the selection of material in the training of teachers and in the control of the diffusion of folk music by popular methods such as radio, television, records, films and public performances."[89] Predicated on a chain of decisions requiring folk material to be vetted by professional folklorists as if it were a kind of propaganda, the process necessary for the translation of vernacular culture into folk music could not be more concisely laid out. The overriding issue, however, was not simply that folklore is always mediated in this way, but that it carried with it a series of dynamic political affordances. Retracing these patterns of thought reveals a disturbing vision lurking within Sharp's hostility toward the present.

On the one hand, Sharp was providing scientific corroboration for the late Victorian and Edwardian vogue for evocations of an Arcadian past—crystallizing a prevailing mood of pastoral nostalgia manifest in the Arts and Crafts movement, conservationism, the garden city movement, the Merrie England Society, and the Peasant Arts Society, of which he was an active member. Social life, as one reviewer put it, had "undergone a reconstruction" still not complete: "just as the invention of gunpowder blew an old order of things to the winds, so the introduction of machinery and rapid locomotion have brought in a new epoch."[90] The poet John Masefield likewise felt that Sharp's songs were fading flowers of "the old beautiful peasant life from which they came"—rare objects that stirred his melancholy imagination:

> I have often wished that I could be a minstrel, or strolling ballad singer, in a country less orderly than England, with a peasantry sufficiently critical to make me careful of my craft. . . . When it rained, I should get into a barn, or into an alehouse if I had any money, and I would sit among the hay and the clucking hens, or by a good fire, and I would make up ballads of my own to tunes of my own. Then I would sing these to the country people at fairs, or weddings, or funeral feasts, or after executions. . . . Alas, that sort of fame will never be mine, . . . I shall never have the thrill that must have come to many a hedge-poet, as he walked the roads, past the taverns, and heard his songs coming rousingly from the folk by the fire.[91]

For an era negotiating the dawn of a new century and with it new technologies, the entrenchment of mass culture, the expansion of capital, and a globe poised on the brink of conflict, such music sounded an agreeably reassuring note of stability while simultaneously revealing a world divided by race, nation, and empire. Myers notes, for instance, that "it was exceedingly interesting for one who has worked at the music of savage peoples to find many points of resemblance between them and the peasant folk-singers of our own country."[92] As we've seen throughout this book, folk song theory sutured "peasant" to "primitive" as twin incarnations of organic and thus potentially restorative musical expression. Symptoms of an attempt to reverse the baleful intrusions of modernity, the material Sharp collected became the spur to a revitalization of lost tradition—a bulwark against the "evil days" of music hall entertainment with its "debased art" of "cake-walks and skirt-dances."[93]

On the other hand, revived songs and the broader epistemology of folk music attest to a history that has passed almost entirely without notice. On the surface, Sharp's political commitments may appear contradictory. We know, for instance, that he was a member of the conservative and imperialistic Navy League, that he was also a committed socialist who joined the Fabian Society in 1900, and yet (as Karpeles points out) "was at no time a keen Party man."[94] Founded in London in 1884, the Fabian Society was an influential gathering of middle-class intellectuals aiming, as described in an 1891 report, "at the reorganisation of Society by the emancipation of Land and industrial Capital from individuals and class ownership, and the vesting of them in the community for the general benefit."[95] Disseminated through a vast number of statistical and didactic tracts, the Society's reformist principles revolved around three related desires: to see the establishment of an efficient and centralized state, to replace individualism with collectivism, and to work toward the "cessation of class distinctions."[96] The Fabians' overriding objection was that wealth and the means of production had been kept unjustly "in the hands of a class instead of in the hands of the nation as a whole."[97] In contrast to figures such as Morris, however, greater economic equality was not to be achieved through revolutionary uprising, but via gradualist democratic means utilizing established systems of government.

Diversity of opinion of course existed, and Sharp did not support all aspects of Fabianism. In contrast to their manifesto's commitment to gender equality, for example, he was staunchly opposed to women's suffrage.[98] Indeed, Sharp seems to have been less keen on achieving political equality than on a spiritual call to national unity. Significantly, Karpeles notes that Sharp "did not regard democracy as a fetish to be unreservedly worshipped" and feared (writing in a letter to his son Charles from the United States in 1918) that "the evils of democracy" might bring about rule "by a tyrannous majority."[99] He was not alone in holding such views. As Mussolini later pointed out, new political movements emerging during the early twentieth century appeared to be similarly "anti-Liberal" and authoritarian in outlook, focused on the state and the organic collective but declining to accept "that the majority, by the simple fact that it is a majority, can direct human society."[100] Sharp likewise abhorred the masses but praised the notion

FIGURE 22. Cover design by Walter Crane of *Fabian Essays in Socialism*, edited by G. Bernard Shaw (London: Walter Scott, 1889). Here, indolent Privilege sits atop the ladder of Capital, propped up valiantly by Labour, who are kept in check by the threat of violent coercion.

of collectivism articulated by Fabian Christian Socialists—the way, as he wrote in 1893, in which they were "endeavouring to disseminate the grand and ideal truths of Socialism" by "leaving these principles to take concrete form themselves."[101] His views were echoed by the Reverend John Clifford in an 1897 Fabian Tract claiming that "a new ideal of life and labour . . . is most urgently needed."[102] Reacting to a century of "hard individualism" that bred "caste feelings," hollowness, indolence, contempt, and serfdom, Clifford extolled "the unity of English life . . . an ideal that is the *soul* at once of Collectivism and of the revelation of the brotherhood of man in Jesus Christ."[103] Aligned with his identity as a self-styled "Conservative Socialist," Sharp's membership of the patriotic Navy League begins to make sense from this perspective.[104] Encompassing a significant number of Liberals despite its distinctly right-wing tenor, this popular lobbying group saw itself as a nonpartisan platform dedicated to securing British military supremacy at sea in the decades leading up to the Great War—a movement, as Matthew Johnson argues, "based on a conception of naval power not simply as a legitimate arm of national defense but as the basis of national might and prestige."[105]

In fact, Sharp's simultaneous support for authoritarian, nonrevolutionary socialism and militant, organic nationalism in conjunction with his antipathy toward liberal democracy, fascination with social Darwinism, ideas on racial kinship, and dabbling in Christian Science, theosophy, and spiritualism are by no means inconsistent.[106] In a powerful series of books, Zeev Sternhell has argued that such a confluence must be seen not merely as the precursor to fascist movements, but rather as the ideological nexus within which fascism was constituted as an alternative political culture. Our unwillingness to see fascism as an integral element of European history belonging to the nineteenth and early twentieth centuries, he stresses, has arisen from the exigencies of Cold War historiography, strategic amnesia, and a desire to treat the 1930s and '40s as an aberration rather than the extension of long-standing habits of political thought. Fascism at its most simple is "a latent ideology" grounded in a revision of Marxism: "Before it became a political force," Sternhell emphasizes, it was "a cultural phenomenon."[107] Coalescing in Europe at the fin de siècle, this framework involved the synthesis of new forms of virile nationalism with a socialism no longer beholden to proletarian revolt. The result was a doctrine and a mode of action revolving around the nation-state; glorification of communality; warfare; religion; denigration of liberal democracy; and a rejection of individualism, philosophical materialism, and the social ills of capitalism (though not necessarily private property or profit). Behind these interlaced factors was the desire to unify and mobilize all classes of society through the idea of the nation viewed as a tribal population with sacred ties to the soil—a community modeled on the native folk.

Sharp's views are undeniably bound up with and indebted to these complex intellectual currents that would later give rise to fascist regimes. He was familiar with the political landscape in both Europe and the

United States at the time, and his diaries are full of references to "long arguments" with friends and acquaintances about democracy and the war. Two particularly telling passages from early 1918 reveal how a committed socialist could reject a key facet of Marxist thinking:

> This is going to be a very critical year for the whole world and almost anything may happen. My constant fear is that the war will not reach a definite conclusion with a signed treaty of peace as wars in the past have done, but that it will gradually assume a general revolution in this and any belligerent country and perhaps neutral countries as well. War, weariness [?], and general dislike to return to the unfair almost savage economic conditions which existed in pre-war days will very likely lead to something of this kind—a world revolution following up on a world-war. Well, we shall see!![108]

> Then to Miss [Gertrude] Schoepperle's Celtic tea where I have a long argument—political—with [Roger Sherman] Loomis, Miss S. cutting in inconsequently in Celtic fashion. Take the conservative view in politics, or rather the value of a conservative party to act as a drag, and point to Russia as a hideous example of a nation which lacks one.[109]

As a subscribing reader of the Fabian *New Statesman*, in other words, Sharp abhorred the brutal economic inequities produced by laissez-faire capitalism, and yet also espoused a conservative position against the dangers of a socialist revolution. What his view signposted instead was a different kind of revolutionary ambition.

Fascism, Sternhell reminds us, aimed for "a revolution of the spirit."[110] Its advocates sought "to lay the foundation of a new civilization, a communal, anti-individualist civilization that alone would be capable of perpetuating the existence of a human collectivity in which all layers and classes of society are perfectly integrated."[111] The nation was to take on this stabilizing role in the modern world, "a nation that boasted a moral unity that liberalism and Marxism—both productive of factionalism and discord—could never provide."[112] Offering new relationships "between man and nature," this prevailing ideology of rejection and renewal demanded "new forms of social organization and cultural expression."[113] It is in this light that Sharp's work and the project of folk revivalism he instigated must be seen. Via his theories, the songs and dances he collected became anonymous tokens of organic collectivity, the natural emanation of the nation's soul over and above the individualist products of an unchecked capitalist economy. This philosophy explains the curious discrepancy between his theory and collecting praxis. Rural songs and dances were envisioned as tools capable of forging new relations of kinship between people and nature, as well

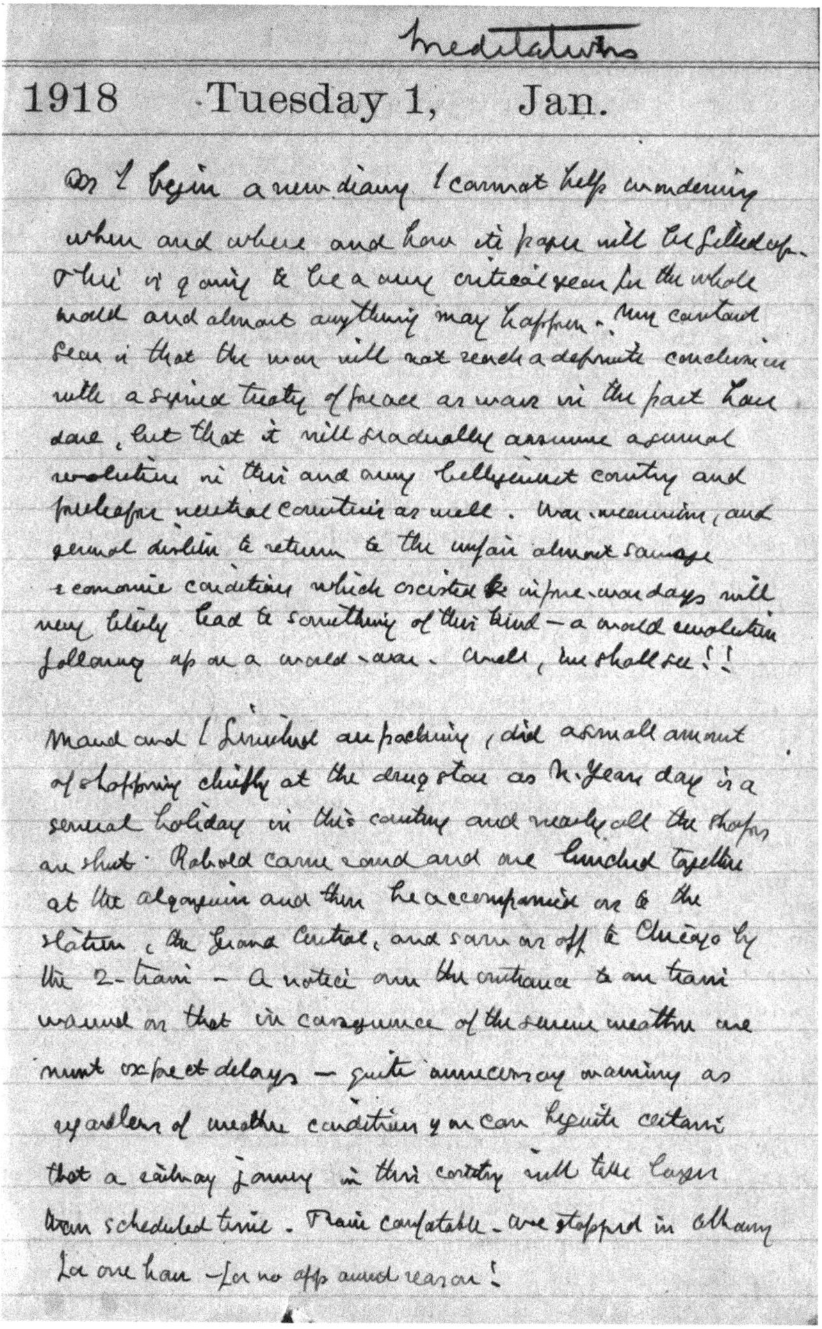

Meditations

1918 Tuesday 1, Jan.

As I begin a new diary I cannot help wondering when and where and how its pages will be filled up. This is going to be a very critical year for the whole world and almost anything may happen. My constant fear is that the war will not reach a definite conclusion with a signed treaty of peace as wars in the past have done, but that it will gradually assume a social revolution in this and every belligerent country and perhaps in neutral countries as well. War weariness, and general dislike to return to the unfair almost savage economic conditions which existed in pre-war days will very likely lead to something of this kind — a world revolution following up on a world war. Well, we shall see!!

Maud and I finished our packing, did a small amount of shopping chiefly at the drug store as N. Year's day is a general holiday in this country and nearly all the shops are shut. Rabold came round and we lunched together at the Algonquin and then he accompanied us to the station, the Grand Central, and saw us off to Chicago by the 2- train — a notice over the entrance to our train warned us that in consequence of the severe weather we must expect delays — quite unnecessary warning as regardless of weather conditions you can be quite certain that a railway journey in this country will take longer than scheduled time. Train comfortable — we stopped in Albany for one hour — for no apparent reason!

FIGURE 23. Cecil Sharp's handwritten diary entry from Tuesday 1 January 1918 (unpublished). Reproduced by kind permission of the English Folk Dance and Song Society.

as between citizens and classes—unifying the nation as a new tribe of patriots restored to the expressive contours of their birthright and the dead. It was no accident that Sharp's Folk Dance Society wished to instruct British soldiers during the First World War. As Sternhell notes, fascist ideology was galvanized by the masculine virtues "of heroism, energy, alertness, a sense of duty, a willingness to sacrifice, and an acceptance of the idea of the pre-eminence of the community over the individuals who compose it."[114] Such ideas were not lost on the rural revivalist Rolf Gardiner, who was openly sympathetic to fascism.[115] Our tendency to treat such figures as eccentrics or exceptions is symptomatic of the very revisionism Sternhell identifies; folk song is thereby able to retain its politically innocuous identity as a form of pastoral nostalgia and intangible heritage.

A final clue to Sharp's political vision can be found in his ideas on the global roots of folk poetry and modality. In *English Folk-Song*, he notes that the subjects of many ballads can be "traced to an Eastern origin," a "common storehouse" he defines as "the heritage . . . of the Arian race."[116] Fuller Maitland lands a joke at Sharp's expense on this point in his *TLS* review, concluding that "it is charitable to suppose that the printer was responsible for the allusion to the 'Arian' race" (Arianism being an unorthodox view of Christian divinity).[117] But Sharp knew exactly what he was referring to—Arian being an accepted, if uncommon, spelling of the term Aryan. Indeed, we find this spelling in a well-known *Cyclopaedia of India* edited by the Scottish orientalist Edward Balfour. This text has a ten-column entry on "Arian," describing a "peasant race" that has been "the mightiest engine of civilization" and "uninterruptedly masters of the world."[118] This myth concerned an ancient people from Central Asia encompassing Persian Zoroastrians and Indian Hindus spreading across northern Europe, drawn in contrast to the Semitic. For Balfour, this race anticipated Western civilization: "The tendency of the Arian race is to form national and political communities, marry one wife; and worship one supreme and spiritual deity."[119] "Aryan" was, at the time, interchangeable with "Indo European," a term Sharp also employs in *English Folk-Song*—further proof that he was conversant with such theories.[120] Sharp finds evidence for his claim that the human mind "at equal levels of cultivation is everywhere the same" in the fact that several "Indo-European nations have arrived at the same scales . . . independently of one another."[121] Folk modality was, in consequence, a witness to racial patrimony—the sign of an Aryan seed from which European folk melody and poetry had evolved. This perspective helps to explain why Sharp could find Indian songs "highly interesting" and dine so affably with the philosopher Ananda Coomaraswamy, while holding explicitly racist views of African Americans.[122] Sharp, in short, believed in Aryan supremacy.

One possible source for such views is the preface to Louis-Albert Bourgault-Ducoudray's collection *Trente Mélodies Populaires de Basse-Bretagne*, published in 1885—a book Sharp had read and cites on several occasions during *English Folk-Song*, predominantly in relation to modal theory. Sharp's belief in Aryan musical heritage is essentially a paraphrase of Bourgault-Ducoudray's ideas: "Numerous collections of folk melodies from these different countries enable us to note, from a *modal* and *rhythmic* point of view, an obvious family resemblance. It seems now proven that identical characteristics can be found in the primitive music of all the peoples who make up the Indo-European group, that is to say the Aryan race. . . . Today, the study of folk song brings a new argument to the consciousness of Aryan unity: the musical argument."[123] Much like Bourgault-Ducoudray, Sharp was invested in the idea of folk song as an Aryan artifact, giving voice to a vague but discernable "racial character" sprung from the ancient past.[124] Connections between this way of thinking and the specter of racism that animated European politics are unequivocal. As Hannah Arendt writes, this "purely imaginary distinction" became central to Nazi ideals of *Volksgemeinschaft*—a mythic folk commune founded on racialized exclusion that offered a counter to communist visions of a classless society.[125]

~

We can see this confluence most plainly when viewed from the early 1930s, just under a decade after Sharp passed away. A major *New York Times* article from 1931, for instance, signaled in its title the ominous unfolding of the ideas Sharp and other folk revivalists had been seduced by and in turn propagated: "The Tune Hitlerism Beats for Germany: It Sets the Street Vibrating to Wotan and Valhalla and Stirs the 'Unknown Folk' of Village and Countryside."[126] The author, Miriam Beard, points out that this new demagogic movement was defined above all by "arts of mass-suggestion" practiced on a hitherto unknown scale.[127] Central to such propaganda was the idea of racial and national singularity. Hitler knew "that while some may be roused by earnest talks on finance and agriculture, many are set vibrating best by mention of Wotan and Valhalla, a denunciation of African jazz, or a crusade against flat roofs as symbols of insidious Orientalism among Germany's peak-tops."[128] In this worldview "ghosts of long-laid racial passions" were "called forth to stalk again the dark lanes of medieval towns."[129] Sharp's colleague Rolf Gardiner had felt its allure while an undergraduate at Cambridge—folk dancing and singing providing a way to answer, as he puts it, "the need to renew the roots of our culture, to revive religion of the soul through the soil."[130] Gardiner had traveled to Germany, where he found inspiration in the Hitler Youth and made close alliances with its leaders, remarking that "the new Germans are young, brave, ardent, enthusiastic, alive," whereas "the modern British are mature, cautious, over-critical, over-prudent, tired."[131]

The Hitler Youth, as Beard writes, had been "captured by a philosophy that rolls the Superman, the Front Soldier, William Tell and Hiawatha all into one"—a virile archetype modeled on folk heroism.[132] Much like Sharp's revivalist project, Nazism aspired to be "sociological rather than political," shunning the urban intelligentsia and their calm rationality in favor of wild mysticism, nature, youthful vigor, and sheer fanaticism.[133] Nazism likewise found solace in racial ideology, glorified "the precapitalistic, hand-worker age," and was moved by "sermons on love and destiny" recalling "that folk-longing, through the war-torn Middle Ages, for a utopian unity and the figure of Barbarossa waiting in a mountain cavern, as legends say, for the millenium"—something that appeared as a wistful dream and a revelation of the future.[134] Such ideas meet in a nostalgic attachment to rural community: "Small towns thrilled to the trumpets of the Third Empire. On them, not the proletariat, rests the Nazi movement; of the eleven most enthusiastic urban districts last September only one was a big city and the rest markedly non-industrial. And the program offered all a small-towner could very well ask: away with industry, away with big cities and their immoral habits, away with proletariat. Bind everybody by law to his home spot. Return to small towns and the handicraft age."[135] This is the very same call that issued from folk revivalists of the late nineteenth and early twentieth centuries: picturesque villages over filthy industrialized capitalism, artisanal peasants over mechanized labor, the noble folk of the countryside over the urban proletariat with their degeneracy, vice, and dormant seditious potential. The revival spurred on by a folkloric imagination is this entreaty to return home and revive a simpler way of life—a way of life, not coincidentally, in which women are cast out of politics and returned to the role of maid, wife, or servant, just as Sharp seemed to desire.

Consisting of "religion, hero stories and gymnastics" orchestrated by "culture dictators," moreover, education under the Third Reich offers up an illuminating parallel with Sharp's aspirations for revivalist dance and his obsession with getting songbooks and authorized folk rituals into British schools.[136] His views in this area were later reflected not only in Germany, but also in Italy, where Mussolini saw state-sponsored education as a vital tool to weld citizens "into unity" by developing their consciousness "of its members who have died for its existence" and "the geniuses who have illuminated it with glory as an example to be followed by future generations."[137] Folk culture, suitably controlled, offered a unique way to instill this sense of "holiness and heroism" always rooted in a nation's mystical past.[138]

Sharp's ideas thus bear witness to what Sternhell describes as the "great ideological laboratory of the end of the nineteenth century and the beginning of the twentieth" that laid the groundwork for totalitarianism and genocide.[139] His work is an example of what Raymond Williams characterizes as "idealist retrospect"—a way of measuring change and resisting capitalist injustice nevertheless in danger of reinforcing undemocratic hierarchies "in the name of blood and soil."[140] Such thinking is particularly noticable in Sharp's sensuous ruralism, anti-intellectualism (evident in his exchange with Newman), elevation of the peasantry, and attempts to tie national identity to the "social life of the English village," in which folk material was "part and parcel of a great tradition that stretches back into the mists of the past in one long, unbroken chain" now under threat.[141] The nation's salvation, in this view, lay in what Robert Paxton describes as a "vast collective enterprise": "the warmth of belonging to a race now fully aware of its identity, historic destiny, and power."[142]

It would thus be counterproductive at best and dangerously revisionist at worst to suggest that folkloric notions of racial collectivity, purity of origin, and spiritual renewal combined with Sharp's vociferous rejection of cosmopolitan internationalism and his desire to reenergize a unified Aryan nation through the idea of a "fatherland" are distinct from the history of European fascism.[143] Edwardian folk revivalism and the heroic revivification of an imagined racial community are inextricable. Driven on by this political imaginary, Sharp's gatekeeping activities worked to erase the very traditions he was safeguarding—transforming the vernacular practices he found into circumscribed artifacts untethered from their original histories of meaning and use, repurposed for the sake of forging a new national socialist consciousness.

The roots of Sharp's vision for this spiritual revival are plain to see. Turn to the first page of his 1907 monograph and what do we find? Not a commentary on the intricate histories of popular music making and consumption in Britain, but a strange discourse that appears far more concerned with nation and racial ontology:

> All forms of mental activity are due to the development and specialization of qualities that are natural and inborn. Education can create nothing; it can only develop those natural and instinctive faculties which already exist in rudimentary form. When these aptitudes are pronounced they will, under favourable conditions, reveal themselves without the aid of conscious or formal education, and in some cases achieve results of a very remarkable kind. Indications, therefore, of those special gifts for which a nation is renowned will usually be conspicuous in the output of its lower and unlettered classes.[144]

It is an odd claim to make for someone so involved with and professedly interested in education, but it makes perfect sense when we read it in light of Sharp's commitment to racial determinism and how fascism would later view the nation state. The race exhibits certain instinctive characteristics that are found at their most elemental in the untaught folk—inherited traits that can be restored to the population at large only by means of nationalistic education inspired by folk material. This is the model upon which Sharp's entire revivalist project rests. Folk song simply *had* to have evolved communally among "the native and aboriginal inhabitants of . . . remote country districts" for his theory of racial kinship to work.[145] This scheme was hence pure ideology in which folk song is necessarily "peasant-made," an unconscious oral product that proceeds organically from "the heart and soul of a nation."[146] Sharp, it is tempting to conclude, worked backwards from this premise to his source material rather than letting these songs tell him a different story—not of purity and political identity, but of myriad complexity, material culture, and aesthetic sensitivity.

Many contemporaries saw straight through such ideas. The most famous of these was none other than T. S. Eliot, who reviewed Sharp's 1924 book *The Dance* in the *Criterion* the following year. Eliot begins by stating that as Sharp was neither a philosopher nor an anthropologist, his notes "are not only inadequate, but are even conducive to error."[147] Initially restrained, Eliot soon begins digging in critical barbs, joining the chorus of others who found that "Cecil Sharp's limited knowledge—and of course limited interests—lead him to a very partial view, and to very doubtful conclusions."[148] It was "obvious," Eliot writes, "that Sharp had never really understood the modern ballet," a point that called into question "both his judgment and his sensibility."[149] Prejudiced against the experiments and virtuosities of modernism and convinced of the supremacy of his own material, Sharp came across as "smug."[150] But most significantly, Eliot proclaims, "Cecil Sharp is a confirmed—and I must say dangerous—radical."[151] Why? "For he seems to have wished to substitute for the traditional ballet a *native* ballet . . . 'founded on folk-dance technique.'"[152] For Eliot, this was an absurdity given that ballet was "so completely international."[153] The idea of building on "a dead ritual," he notes, was flawed, as "you cannot *revive* a ritual without reviving a faith"—what you get instead is a facsimile of tradition, something that merely serves "as a Saturday afternoon alternative to tennis and badminton for active young men in garden suburbs."[154] You can almost hear Eliot's sneer.

But this dismissal of folk dance as a petty bourgeois leisure activity fails to account for the fanatical nature of Sharp's underlying motivations.[155] His folk revivalism, like fascism more broadly, sought to create "a new calibre of man"—a "moral transformation" of society issuing from the deliberate interconnection of ethics and aesthetics.[156] As Sternhell notes, this was the basis of the spiritual revolution for which "antibourgeois, anticapitalist, and anti-individualist nationalism had always fought," propelled by its "revulsion toward a society that has lost sight of any goal except capitalist profit and sullied itself with a sordid materialism."[157] For revivalists it was folk culture and a return to the bedrock of a communal, collective identity that paved the road to salvation. Folk song and dance were to be the great stimulus to national renewal and moral transformation, linking the present population with its deep racial past and a culture that existed entirely outside the bounds of industrialized drudgery and the new world of mass entertainment arriving in its wake. This "disgust for capitalism"—characteristic of folk revivalist movements across the political spectrum—is, as Sternhell points out, really "the expression of a contempt for a materialism that degrades the human soul."[158] As Sharp puts it, folk music was a way to nurture the imagination and a sense of tribal allegiance in opposition to the "materializing tendencies" of those things that "appeal to the intellect only"—collected songs and dances exercising "a purifying and regenerative influence" on the masses and the "material age" they exemplified.[159] Here, at last, is the clearest indication of the undeniable interweaving of folk revivalism and fascist thought, their rejection of materialism a refusal of the spirit-deadening conflagrations of modernity.

Looking back on the heyday of the movement five years after Sharp's death, Robert Hull observed that the "label 'folk-song' is regarded as a talisman capable of sustaining any attack": such music, he suggests, had "been exalted to a position which it was never intended to occupy."[160] Hull is right on both counts. The folk have now become a figure impossible to ignore, the music encased in their magical insignia elevated from mere common popular songs of the olden time to revered symbols of national identity and ethnic heritage, with each country or community entitled to their own folk traditions traversing the inconstant topographies of kinship. What is surprising is the extent to which such ideas—deeply conditioned by the lingering histories of racism, colonialism, and fascist ideology—have managed to circulate without having their political meanings fully scrutinized. In this sense, Sharp has been supremely effective as a gatekeeper to cultural memory. His ideas reverberate silently and therefore all the more powerfully within objects and cultural practices that, for many, exist simply as innocent tokens of the past. In the current climate, it is worth pausing to reflect on how many of our own ideas, assumptions, and institutions remain indebted to these very same habits of thought. The coda takes up this question in relation to the contemporary political philosophy of the alt-right.

# Coda

## *Blood Sings: A Soundtrack for the Alt-Right*

The vernacular harbors a persistent allure. Occasionally, when we hear a folk-like melody or a field recording issuing from the depths of imagined time, it is as if we are privy to a revelation, an aural epiphany. Dylan compares his first encounter with the music of Lead Belly to "an explosion . . . like I'd been walking in darkness and all of a sudden the darkness was illuminated . . . like somebody laid hands on me."[1] These songs appear numinous, "more vibrant and truthful to life" than something on the charts, where performers are mere gamblers hoping for a shot at the top.[2] The vernacular was thus, for a young Dylan, something to internalize and embody in his writing—its rhetoric and devices, its secrets and mysteries, "I could make it all connect and move with the current of the day."[3] But these currents have now changed, their eddies swirling in new and ominous directions. Whereas the 1960s revival rode on the crest of a wave propelled by the countercultural left, folk music today has been adopted by a resurgent right-wing nationalism bound to the intellectual tideways we have been exploring throughout this book.

To get a sense of how this reactionary embrace of the folk on the part of the self-styled "alt-right" is not a betrayal of the past, but rather an entirely consonant echo of prior folkloric thinking, I want to begin with Proust. Not readily associated with the folk revivalism of the fin de siècle, Proust nevertheless turns to folk song momentarily during the opening pages of volume five of *À la recherche du temps perdu* in a passage distinctive for its evocation of nationalist retrotopia:

> Mme de Guermantes seemed to me at this time more attractive than in the days when I was still in love with her. Expecting less of her (I no longer went to visit her for her own sake), it was almost with the relaxed negligence one exhibits when alone, with my feet on the fender, that I listened to her as though I were reading a book written in the language of long ago. I was sufficiently detached to enjoy in what she said that pure charm of the French language which we no longer find either in the speech or in the writing of the present day. I listened to her conversation as to a folk song deliciously and purely French. . . . It is not in the bloodless pastiches of the writers of today who say *au fait* (for "in reality"), *singulièrement* (for "in particular"), *étonné* (for "struck with amazement"), and the like, that we recapture the old speech and the true pronunciation of words, but in conversing with a Mme de Guermantes.[4]

For Proust's narrator, it is the Duchesse, Oriane, who is a storehouse of French folk culture—her conversation akin to a book written in a long-forgotten language, her pronunciation true to the history of a people, this sound "a folk song deliciously and purely French." Such purity and charm are predictably contrasted with the "bloodless pastiches" and debasements of the present—of an untethered modernity.

It is as if the aristocracy preserves the customs of a land or a particular region in their latent affectations better than those rural folk to whom they attest. In Proust's words, there was an "earthy and quasi-peasant quality that survived" in the accent of the Duchesse de Guermantes, a hint of long-lost ties to the blood and soil of an imagined political community.[5] As Katharine Ellis points out, by the final decade of the nineteenth century, "simplicity combined with a certain earthiness" had come to rank "among the greatest of French virtues"—a value system in which "the unpretentious simplicity of folk song" was "a mirror of the French musical spirit."[6] Oriane displays this quality as an aesthetic preference, a knowing and momentary rending of society veneer. As these aristocratic figures speak, they conjure up "a whole map of France, historical and geographical," their pronunciation and vocabulary "a regular museum of French history displayed in conversation."[7] However, "it is in this aspect," Proust continues, "that the nobility shows itself truly conservative . . . being at once slightly puerile, slightly dangerous, stubborn in its resistance to change, but at the same time diverting to an artist."[8] Here, in essence, is everything the folk stood for during the modern era: purity, vigor, history, stubborn simplicity, landscape, earthiness, and the nation. It is a nexus that offers hope and peril in equal measure, as well as a continuing source of creative inspiration.

Indeed, only a few pages later Marcel is recounting a quarrel between Oriane and her husband, the Duc de Guermantes, on the Dreyfus affair. Oriane suggests that the Jewish community were rightly incensed, as they "knew quite well that if he hadn't been a Jew people wouldn't have been so ready to think him a traitor *a priori*"; Basin's response, in marked contrast, is to point out that France "ought to have driven out all the Jews" in the first place.[9] Coming so soon after a passage on the longed-for charm of folk song, it is impossible to separate the echoes of Oriane's "pure" native tongue from the chauvinistic anti-Semitism of her husband. It is only with a similarly folkloric conception of place, culture, and language that the Duc is able to envisage an unsullied France purged of its disagreeably "cosmopolitan" strangers.[10]

We don't have to look very far for the legacy of such ideas. We are currently living through an era of resurgent right-wing populism in which repeated references are made to tribal belonging saturated with blood-and-soil rhetoric. One of the clearest indications of this link between twenty-first-century patterns of political prejudice and the legacy bequeathed to us by folk song can be found in an American balladeer by the name of Paddy Tarleton. Type his name into Reddit and you'll find links to songs with titles such as "Battle of Sacramento," "Charlottesville Ballad (War is Coming)," and "Shut Your Lyin' Jew Mouths." These links have been posted to subreddits including r/Nationalism, r/punk, r/IndieFolk, r/ARMusic, the openly anti-Semitic r/fashysongs, and r/PussyPass, a popular forum dedicated to proving that being a woman gives you undue social benefits. Some posts are met with hostility—"What is this white supremacist shit?" and "Nazi punks fuck off (that means you)"—but mostly they act as a centrifuge for a variety of extreme positions united by shared hatred of a perceived liberal, elitist hegemony.

The fact that many of Paddy Tarleton's songs have been made unavailable or removed for violating official policies on hate speech only seems to add to their appeal for the online alt-right and the perception that such views are being unjustly marginalized by the mainstream media. Tarleton's ballads are at once anti-establishment rants against ubiquitous state authority and hard-line defenses of an ultraconservative status quo—both punk-like and reactionary, a new kind of skinhead folk. The Southern Poverty Law Center has branded his work a "soundtrack of hate," reluctantly applying the label "folk" with the heaviest of scare quotes.[11] Indeed, Tarleton is made out to be an imposter on the folk scene—a singer who barely deserves this appellation owing to its radical heritage. Yet Tarleton works skillfully not only within the voice and guitar idiom, but with a keen sense of tradition. He explains this aesthetic in an interview with Trey Knickerbocker for the website altright.com, where he is introduced as a "Volkish Folk Singer" and "one of today's most influential and popular White-Identitarian" artists.[12] Knickerbocker frames this discussion by noting that Tarleton's music "speaks directly to the heart of the Alt-Right's current issues and plight" by combining "traditional Americana music with a contemporary subject matter" to "create and shape an artistic culture that our movement so desperately wants and needs."[13] Significantly, he claims, Tarleton's style "represents the true musical embodiment of the word folk in the venerable sense of the word, which means people or kindred tribe."[14] Cecil Sharp's ears would surely have pricked up: his theories of racial patrimony are thriving in the digital age.

A simple dismissal of Tarleton as a purveyor of white supremacist hatred fails to heed the ways in which he grounds his songwriting in a folkloric imaginary as a means to enlighten and resist. As we saw in the last chapter, Sharp would have been well acquainted with the distinctive confluence sustaining his born-again beliefs: "Politically, I tend to lean more towards social nationalism but I have friends and allies in every camp of the Alt Right/New Right. The more time passes, the more I see we are fighting a war that is spiritual as much as it is cultural and political. I'm [Eastern] Orthodox, having recently been baptized by Father Matthew Raphael Johnson, my priest, and I am now a member of the Catacomb church whose metropolitan is based in Moscow."[15] Tarleton fuses his commitments to social nationalism—a form of kinship distinct from both official state nationalism and more narrow ethnic nationalism—with an adherence to Christian faith of a distinctively esoteric and subversive bent.[16]

Matthew Raphael Johnson is a renegade scholar whose work is hosted on websites including *The Orthodox Nationalist* and *The Russian Orthodox Medievalist*.[17] Johnson describes himself as a proponent of "ethnic nationalism, Eurasianism and the Orthodox tradition as forms of rebellion against globalism," believing that Vladimir Putin is "a necessary balance to the American empire and the liberal authoritarianism it enforces."[18] The term *globalism* should be read in this instance as thoroughly anti-Semitic, an allusion (via figures such as the billionaire philanthropist George Soros, lightning rod of far-right conspiracy theories) to age-old myths in which Jews are seen as a secret force working to undermine social structures.[19] Indeed, we find in Johnson's work the tell-tale insignia of fascist thought: on one hand, a recourse to communal belonging, a love of the medieval, embrace of authoritarianism, and nominalism set against ultimate religious truth; and on the other, a frenzied rejection of globalized capitalism, commodity culture, and the hollow ideology of bourgeois individualism—"a demonic, serpentine Leviathan spreading the postmodern acid of American-sponsored mass-zombification to the world," as Johnson puts it, unintentionally mimicking the Frankfurt School.[20] Tarleton draws all these ideas together by noting that the underlying problem is above all spiritual—the very signature of the anti-materialist revolution fascism strove to instigate.[21]

Tarleton goes on to elucidate how, after college, his political opinions began to take shape in relation to music, echoing ideas we've encountered repeatedly:

> I finally began to wake up in my mid-twenties. This was around '08, going into '09. My social and political beliefs were forged simultaneously as they were intertwined. I knew I hated modernity, cosmopolitanism, and liberalism, and this could be seen even before I decided to exert my political convictions through the music I made. It was around those years that I started getting back into a lot of the Anglo-Celtic and old-time Americana/Country music I'd heard as a kid. Roots music. I do hate that term, though. "Roots" music. So much traditional forms of music have been hijacked by deluded leftists that even once appropriate terms like that tend to irk me.[22]

The value that trumps all others is tradition and its embeddedness in history—in short, its perceived age. Tarleton "hated anything new," instead following "that natural urge to hear authentic, sincere, quality music" rather than "newer styles" and "progressive" ideas," which are "trash," "garbage," "mindless," "modern," and "ugly."[23] It is only ostensibly odd that immediately after this answer he confesses to being influenced by the late Ewan MacColl, foremost Marxist songsmith of the Cold War era, proud anti-fascist, and longstanding member of the Communist Party of Great Britain.[24] What links these otherwise radically dissimilar artists is not only their mutual claims on traditional Anglo-Celtic and old-time roots music, but also a fervent rejection of the modern, the Americanized, the global, and the menace of mass culture. Much like Tarleton, MacColl's dedication to what he describes as an "incredibly rich repertoire of traditional songs" was spurred by a feeling that "genuine" forms of creative expression "were being eliminated by the mass media and particularly by Tin Pan Alley and Denmark Street."[25] Indeed, MacColl too rages against the "vacuous, dreary and utterly mediocre" sounds of what he calls "imbecilic teeny-boppers' pop-music," declaring that true folk music "would help English, Irish, Scots and Welsh workers to assert their national and class identity."[26] Both these figures employ folk song to indict feminized pop culture and rootless capitalism in favor of ritual, place, nation, political revolt, and the virile traditions of manual labor undercut by modernization.[27] Both recall the arguments put forward a generation earlier by folk enthusiasts such as Sharp and Hubert Parry, who raged against the commercial music hall and those who were seduced by its spurious allure.

Perhaps figures such as MacColl (the "deluded leftist") and Tarleton (voice of the "woke" alt-right) have more in common than either would care to admit fully. They meet and diverge at the same point: a search for what Tarleton describes as "our true, organic identities" over and above the "insta-identity" available to anybody in a world of hybridity and dislocation.[28] But whereas MacColl, the brazen Marxist, saw this as tied to collective class-consciousness (albeit intersected by nationality), Tarleton sees it as a shoring up of whiteness against unwanted incursions by a racialized other. When Tarleton proclaims that "the North American is very much an Anglicized person" he is purposely erasing the history and legitimacy of the African American—not to mention the Native American or any other variety of US citizen not self-identifying as white. In fact, *citizen* is a word he vehemently rejects:

> Blood sings. . . . It is the natural state of things. A nation isn't just a confined space with borders wherein a people remain citizens. God, I hate that word. "Citizens." It's so meaningless. A nation is not so much a state as it is a transcendental entity. It lives and it breathes. Blood and soil. If you do not have this, you have nothing. You have no culture, no protection, no commonality, no communal soul. This is exactly why we're under the boot of oligarchy today. This mechanistic view of life and linear view of history. A homeland is something special, it is yours and no one else's, and white peoples, wherever they live, deserve their own homelands as much as anybody else.[29]

What Tarleton is advocating here is no mere patriotism, it is what Hannah Arendt referred to as "tribal nationalism"—an emotional drive wishing to transcend the geopolitical limits of the nation and envision an Aryan or pan-white homeland devoted to nurturing a mysterious and ill-defined racial soul, a utopian community "which it proposes to realize fully in the future."[30] This attitude, she notes, is distinctive for its insistence that its people are "surrounded by 'a world of enemies,' 'one against all,' that a fundamental difference exists between this people and all others."[31] Operating hand in hand with a violent anti-Semitism supposing Jews to be the agents of organized foreign oppression, it forms the kernel of fascist ideology. Tarleton fuses this form of anti-Semitic nationalism with other fascist tropes tied up with an antipathy toward Marxism—the rejection not only of a mechanical conception of society and historical unfolding driven by class, but also what Mussolini dismissed as a "materialist conception of happiness."[32] The alt-right's reinstatement of fascism aspires to rearrange the global political landscape anew along these lines of spirit, origin, and divine chosen-ness—emulating the Jewish diaspora it despises.

In this sense, Tarleton is deceiving us when he says that his views lean toward social nationalism: his comments are in fact paradigms of ethnic nationalism. Such belonging is defined, as James Kellas points out, "in exclusive terms, mainly on the basis of common descent" and involves "tests and other restrictions for suitability."[33] Just like Sharp, then, Tarleton sees folk music as both the organic expression of a nation's communal soul and a means of disseminating and cultivating that identity for subsequent generations. They both also share the view that traditional American music provides a crucial link back to a common white ancestry—something "rooted in the British Isles."[34] Tarleton consciously uses such melodies in his writing "to rail against modernity through the music itself," "because that is the folk tradition."[35] The concept of revival is thus central to his outlook—a revival harnessing the "rawest appeal to the emotions" to kick-start a deep social transformation:

> Look, we live in terrible times. . . . Most of us come from small towns or cities with rootless, degenerated populations of whites who have been conditioned their entire lives to work against their own interests and to hate their own, or to at least not recognize any significance or importance in their own blood. . . . The normalization of every degenerate ill under the sun, from porn to media promotion of racially mixed relationships (almost always pushed and advertised using non-European males with European females) and castigating those who reject these things, as we saw with the Left's "punch a Nazi" sensation last winter, even if they do so peaceably, should tell anyone with an IQ above room temperature all they need to know about who is in the wrong and why.[36]

Just as tradition is the answer to junk food, pornography, mass media, advertising, an avaricious pharmaceutical industry, feminism, and interracial relationships, so traditional song helps "degenerated populations of whites" sense their racial kinship, solidarity, and right to the land—echoing a paranoia surrounding degeneration that suffused European thought during the late nineteenth century, as we saw in chapter 2.[37] According to Tarleton, although their anger is rational, the left just doesn't get it: they should instead turn to recognize their shared racial ties, stop picking fights with neo-Nazis, grow up, give up empty virtue signaling, and engage together in liberating a "brainwashed" population from the system.[38]

The problem is that it's Tarleton himself and the alt-right who are in truth mistaken and tirelessly fighting the wrong battles. As scholars such as Benedict Anderson and Eric Hobsbawm established so cogently during the 1980s, the nation is anything but a "natural state of things"—rather, it is predicated on eliding its palpable modernity and incoherence via imaginative or quasi-religious recourse to a deep historical past. The nation, in short, is a product of the very modernity Tarleton claims to reject. We are left with a series of unresolved paradoxes, as Anderson points out: the nation's modernity for historians versus its "subjective antiquity in the eyes of nationalists"; its universality as a concept versus its unique and incompatible manifestations; its political efficacy and dominance versus its "philosophical poverty" as a concept.[39] Nations are in essence forgeries or performative fictions brought to life through ritual. As innovation drives societies ever forward into apparent chaos, these creations tend to emerge from the depths in their wake. The current rise of tribal nationalism around the world, from Donald Trump and Nigel Farage to Viktor Orbán, Marine Le Pen, Narendra Modi, and Jair Bolsonaro, for instance, can be read as the fallout of neoliberal economics, interventionist foreign policy, income stagnation, polarization of wealth, rapid population growth, forced displacement, mass migration, globalization, and an increasingly interconnected mediascape. What we're witnessing is the shattering of former stabilities and indexes of belonging. Nationalism, as Hobsbawm argues, works under such conditions as a "substitute for social cohesion" or a "new secular religion" among groups lacking unity—something that thrives "in proportion to its success in broadcasting on a wavelength to which the public [are] ready to tune in."[40] As Derrida might put it, "the more the period is in crisis, the more it is 'out of joint,' then the more one has to convoke the old, 'borrow' from it."[41]

And yet, as we've seen, the alt-right's vision has less to do with narrow state nationalism than the tainted legacy of scientific racism—the belief that distinct races exist in some kind of hierarchical order. Tarleton (a pseudonym alluding to a medley of ciphers from a thirteenth-century Lancashire village to an English revivalist band named Tarleton's Jig, a popular Elizabethan clown, a ruthless British army officer during the American Revolutionary War, and a claim on Irish ancestry) insists that his self-professed "Anglo-Celtic" descent "absolutely" influences his music.[42] His reference to an unenlightened white man "who loves his football teams full of Africans who would otherwise hate him" is carefully, cruelly worded: "Africans" denotes a racial alterity and homeland set explicitly against the white American and "Anglo-Celtic."[43] It is the very same gesture that Trump made when he suggested on Twitter in July 2019 that a number of Democrat Congresswomen should "go back and help fix the totally broken and crime infested places from which they came."[44] The four women he was referring to were Alexandria Ocasio-Cortez, Ilhan Omar, Ayanna Pressley, and Rashida Tlaib. Tlaib was born in Detroit to a Palestinian family; Omar was born in Mogadishu, Somalia, but has been a US citizen since 2000; Ocasio-Cortez was born in the Bronx to a Puerto Rican family; and Pressley is African American and was born in Cincinnati, Ohio. What was most significant for some on the extreme right was the insinuation that African Americans do not belong in the United States. Run by Andrew Anglin, the website *Daily Stormer*—which features a "Demographic Countdown" banner indicating a declining white population—published an ecstatic post stating "This is the kind of WHITE NATIONALISM we elected him for. . . . Trump is literally telling American blacks to go back to Africa."[45]

Anglin's website gives us an insight into the dark and dispiriting world of the alt-right. From a leaked style guide made available in 2017, it becomes clear that this faction views itself as a movement with a propaganda (or "outreach") arm targeting neophyte sympathizers online—people with an "8th grade vocabulary" that they hold in contempt as members of an "ADHD demographic."[46] Drawing explicitly on Hitler's ideas in *Mein Kampf* concerning weaponized information calculated to sway the emotions of an unintelligent mob, Anglin writes that the aim of such propaganda is (paradoxically) to "awaken" readers to reality. The means to this end is to "always blame the Jews for everything"—feminism, poverty, war, social dynamics, "the behavior of other nonwhites," "the destruction of the rainforest," and so on. Such tactics attest to what Slavoj Žižek describes as "a unique cause of Evil who 'pulls the strings' behind the scene," a terrifying but fascinating *point de capiton* (or "quilting point') that "*explains everything*."[47] Their anti-Semitism is thus pure ideology—an idea or ism, as Arendt defines it, "which to the satisfaction of [its] adherents can explain everything and every occurrence by deducing it from a single premise."[48] Racism is the axiomatic premise from which the alt-right derives its understanding of the world and in turn spreads its message of enmity; repeated as slogans or mantras, these abhorrent beliefs are envisaged as tools to unlock the world's secrets. The key to such indoctrination is what is often referred to as "lulz," a cultivated lightness and humorous ambiguity serving to lessen the shock of racist ideology—a ploy to divert attention from the horrors of terrorist violence and their stated wish to "dehumanize the enemy, to the point where people are ready to laugh at their deaths." As Anglin puts it, ironic mockery and the fusion of Nazi iconography with pop culture has "the psychological purpose of removing it from the void of weirdness that it would naturally exist in . . . something like adding cherry flavor to children's medicine." The alt-right views racism as the bitter pill needed to heal and reshape a society in thrall to nihilism, resisting what they see as the Jewish-inflected legacy of the 1960s.[49]

Such thinking is brought to the fore in Tarleton's song "Charlottesville Ballad (War Is Coming)," written in response to the 2017 "Unite the Right" rally held at Charlottesville, Virginia, where James Alex Fields Jr. drove his car into a crowd of people, killing a young woman named Heather Heyer and wounding nineteen other counterprotestors. It is a difficult song to listen to. Tarleton's demure objection to the "punch a Nazi" phenomenon becomes increasingly difficult to square with his snarled refrain "Come out you antifash / Come out and get your faces smashed." The song is a grim litany of abuse: Heyer is labeled a "scumbag," counterprotestors are "faggots," the mayor of Charlottesville, Michael Signer, is branded "that Jew Mayor," and African American vice mayor Dr. Wes Bellamy is referred to as a "monkey." It is a song calculated to provoke, a musical troll with a video of tiki torch parades, Nazi symbols, Confederate battle flags, street brawling, and fascist salutes.[50] As with many of Tarleton's other songs, the melody is borrowed from a traditional source—on this occasion, the Irish rebel song "Come Out, Ye Black and Tans" by Dominic Behan.[51] In his lyrics, Tarleton replaces "black and tans" (a pejorative reference to Royal Irish Constabulary soldiers in the Irish War of Independence and, by extension, pro-British factions in working-class Dublin during the 1920s) with antifa, the alt-right's anti-fascist nemesis. Borrowing not only the song's rousing tune but also Behan's message of defiance, "Charlottesville Ballad (War Is Coming)" aligns the alt-right with the IRA, indirectly condoning acts of violent resistance in the service of nationalist sovereignty—viewed not as terrorism, but as rightful liberation from tyranny. Antifa, then, are portrayed as the disloyal enemies within, traitors to the true cause, red "cowards" who "take refuge in the system" side-by-side with "cops and Feds."

At the heart of the song lies the concept of "white genocide," a term Tarleton deploys repeatedly in the chorus—the racist anxiety that white populations around the globe are at risk of being obliterated by a culture of liberal self-hatred, mass immigration from faster-reproducing nonwhite others, and declining birth rates.[52] Despite sharing her view that "the pollution of American space, with gadgetry and cars and TV and box architecture, brutalizes the senses," Tarleton is referring to an attitude epitomized by Susan Sontag's attack on American imperialism made in the context of extolling the counterculture's "turn toward the East" during the 1960s:

> If America is the culmination of Western white civilization, as everyone from the Left to the Right declares, then there must be something terribly wrong with Western white civilization. . . . The white race *is* the cancer of human history; it is the white race and it alone—its ideologies and inventions—which eradicates autonomous civilizations wherever it spreads, which has upset the ecological balance of the planet, which now threatens the very existence of life itself. What the Mongol hordes threaten is far less frightening than the damage that Western "Faustian" man, with his idealism, his magnificent art, his sense of intellectual adventure, his world-devouring energies for conquest, has already done, and further threatens to do.[53]

In the theory of white genocide, it is this kind of abject intellectualism among a liberal elite combined with their enthusiastic embrace of multiculturalism that must be resisted. What is to be avoided at all costs is a so-called "great replacement" of white populations.[54] Although it appeals most to those whom Dirk Moses describes as harboring "catastrophized subjectivities" (such as the terrorists Anders Breivik and Brenton Tarrant), it is a discernible undercurrent in right-wing thought.[55] Tarleton's spiritual guru, Matthew Raphael Johnson, has his own eccentric take on the question. Repudiating what he sees as an overriding "anti-white contempt" amid "the Leftist American ruling class," Johnson explains that "hatred for another race is justified" before going on to quote statistics concerning "migrant criminality," "non-white gangs," interracial rape, black murderers, and "the Jewish media"—something that adds up to "the planned destruction of European [read: white] culture."[56]

To call out such ideas as racist in the eyes of the alt-right is (to borrow Johnson's own words) mere "pseudo-intellectual virtue signaling," attesting to "university diversity-office pabulum" that refuses to recognize the nation as "a real, tangible and biological reality that must be respected."[57] But of course it *is* racist. Indeed, it would be hard to find a clearer example of white supremacist paranoia—conspiracy theory dressed up as critique.[58] It is disheartening to have to underscore that portraying Jewish people as a "disease"; using Christianity as a retort to Judaism; implying that African Americans are inherently criminal or comparing them with monkeys; fearing miscegenation via rape of white women; promoting racial hatred; advocating apartheid; and propagating Nazi ideology are archetypes of racism.[59] Employing the intellectual and emotive power of folkloric thinking, what the alt-right advocates is precisely racial discord and prejudice, its tendentious tactics resulting in the opposite of respectful dialogue, harmony, and understanding. Their vision is a modern-day incarnation of the National Socialist fantasy of *Volksgemeinschaft*—a "conceptual projection and an operational term," as Michael Wildt notes, that emerged during the early twentieth century representing an "enthusiastic and emotionally laden inclusion linked with a vehement and violent exclusion."[60] *Volksgemeinschaft* under Hitler came to mean not simply a unifying "people's community" but a fanatical and transcendent national belonging predicated on the ostracism and eventual extermination of the Jewish population. In their fear of white genocide, the contemporary alt-right erases the Nazi genocide while in the same gesture co-opting genocidal thinking characteristic of *Volksgemeinschaft*.

The racial characteristics this community invests in so deeply either via hating or safeguarding are, of course, the debris of pseudoscience and historical error.[61] The idea of race, as Stephen Jay Gould notes, was always "imposed from without, but falsely identified as lying within"—the result of enduring asymmetries of power and observation.[62] Its genealogy is inextricable from the history of empire building, early anthropology, the nation-state, and the Atlantic slave trade. Given credence by social Darwinism, race thinking is an anachronistic and yet extraordinarily obstinate phenomenon—what Paul Gilroy characterizes as an "afterimage," a "lingering effect of looking too casually into the damaging glare emanating from colonial conflicts at home and abroad."[63] In simple terms, the idea that distinct races exist emerged from and in turn helped to legitimate the project of European colonialism. Race acquired this meaning largely on account of the sheer incomprehensibility of difference as imperialists ravaged the Dark Continent of Africa—an "emergency explanation," Arendt writes, "of human beings whom no European or civilized man could understand and whose humanity so frightened and humiliated the immigrants that they no longer cared to belong to the same human species."[64] Appearing to be an extension of the natural world, they were somehow less than human, and thus all the more easy to massacre and exploit. But, as with nationalism, demonstrating its philosophical poverty does not rid the world of race as a lived reality. As Arif Dirlik argues, "If colonialism racialized both the colonizer and the colonized, the persistence of these racialized identities is a sign of the persistence of colonial modernity under the rubric of globalization."[65] The alt-right is a symptom of this persistence, even as it uses racialized ontologies to combat globalization in the name of isolationism.

As figures such as Tarleton search tirelessly for the pure and authentic sounds of white nationalism, they unwittingly stumble upon the postcolonial geographies of the musical past—those "overlapping territories" and "intertwined histories" that Edward Said identifies.[66] To imagine these hybridities away is a sign of willful self-deception. Consider the banjo, for instance. Tarleton describes it as his favorite folk instrument, associating it with the Irish traditional singer Margaret Barry.[67] The banjo, however, has an intriguing history. The modern instrument used in white bluegrass music is, as Gerhard Kubik points out, really "an American derivative of western and central Sudanic plucked lutes."[68] How did an African instrument end up in the Ozark Mountains or paired with fiddles and bones in blackface minstrelsy? The answer is obvious: chattel slavery. Slave ships on the Middle Passage carried not only African captives, but also musical instruments including drums and banjo-like lutes to the New World—traces of material culture inscribed with precious cultural memory nevertheless used within a violent stagecraft of enforced performance.[69]

The banjo is just one example of the kinds of global circulation that a white nationalist vision must downplay in order to sustain the colonialist fantasy of cultural and racial autonomy. There is a pleasing irony in an American "white identitarian" artist accompanying his proudly Anglo-Celtic songs with an African instrument—a sign of the undeniably composite and creole interracial heritage of southern musical culture.[70] As I've suggested over the course of this book, it is a folkloric imagination that covers over these palpable inconsistencies and contradictions, affording access to the mysticism of cultural purity, untainted origins, and the prospect of utopia. For Tarleton's fans such incongruities hardly matter; instead, what makes his music valuable is its ability to carry and hammer home a political message. Indeed, his recordings function largely as propaganda, not only in the sense of fostering ideological connections between past, present, and future but also in the more familiar guise of protest song. One reader of the interview from

FIGURE 24. *The Old Plantation (Slaves Dancing on a South Carolina Plantation)*, attributed to John Rose, c. 1785–95. Watercolor on paper, 30 × 45 cm. Note the stringed instrument on the right.

which I've been quoting remarks that "some of the choruses stick with you through the day and are useful slogans."[71] Tarleton's listeners see him as "a tremendous asset to the alt-right movement" and an "American treasure" on account of lyrical hooks that "would set people off" at rallies.[72] His music is the sound of left-wing protest movements of the twentieth century being turned against themselves, twisted inside out and flung back through a bullhorn with the same lexicon and syntax employed for diametrically opposite ends.

Turn to YouTube and we find his alt-right rendition of the 1930s labor song "Which Side Are You On?," written by Florence Reece to a traditional tune and recorded by the Almanac Singers on the album *Talking Union*.[73] Instead of beginning with the line "Come all of you good workers / Good news to you I'll tell," Tarleton's song begins with an inelegantly scanned rewording: "Come all of you nationalists / And let your ranks swell." Toward the end of this recording a spoken broadcast emerges from behind Tarleton's voice and is left alone above his guitar as the song comes to an end: ". . .to combat these Jewish media bosses and their collaborators in the government, in the schools, in the churches, and wherever else we find them." It is the voice of the prominent neo-Nazi leader William Luther Pierce, founder of the white supremacist National Alliance—an organization that once developed a first-person shooter game called *Ethnic Cleansing*.[74] The top-rated comment on this track reads, "I am on the side of my brothers and my ancestors of course," while other comments point toward "heritage preservation," "the white side . . . born of EUROPE," and the infamous "14 words" slogan, "we must secure the existence of our people, and a future for white children."[75] One potentially ambivalent comment cuts to the heart of the song's intended message: "White men didn't choose a side they were born into one." In other words, the song is making two interlinked assertions: first, you (a white person) are either with us or against us; and second, you (a nonwhite person) will have no choice in the matter. It is a characteristic illustration of the kind of black-and-white thinking that motivates extremist violence—something that Tarleton unearths within the original agitprop anthem and translates into fascist dogma. "Battle Hymn of the Republic" in his hands likewise becomes "Sovereignty and Blood Forever," its title usurping Ralph Chaplin's original Wobbly anthem "Solidarity Forever."[76]

These videos have been uploaded alongside a clip of Oswald Mosley under the Education category—a sign that they are not merely intended to embolden and unite the right but to gain converts and spread a creed, following in the footsteps of the folk protest tradition. Once the quintessence of a totalitarian system, the far right now frames itself as bold dissidents and defenders of free speech *against* the system, trading historical places with the "reds" they loathe. Tarleton has been dubbed "the alt-right Bob Dylan," and this is nowhere more evident than in a song titled "The Battle of Sacramento" commemorating a violent neo-Nazi rally outside the California State Capitol in June 2016.[77] Advocating a stance in direct opposition to Dylan's "finger-pointing songs" of the early 1960s, Tarleton mimics his persona and delivery mixed with a dash of John Lydon.[78] We might hear warped echoes of "Bob Dylan's Blues," "When the Ship Comes In," and "Talkin' John Birch Paranoid Blues" in which a young Dylan skewers communist paranoia epitomized by the far-right John Birch Society, impersonating a man who joins this Society only to end up investigating himself. The irony is that Tarleton is a present-day equivalent of this very figure—a paranoiac who sees a leftist conspiracy behind every toilet bowl. The alt-right revives these residues of the Cold War, endorsing a civil war (as one commentator on "The Battle of Sacramento" puts it) between US patriots and "the country's enemies of Antifa, Afrofascists, Libtards, and the Loony Left generally."[79]

But rather than an alt-right Dylan, Tarleton is perhaps closer to the lesser-known Phil Ochs—his song "Hallelujah I'm a Boomer" an inverted image of Ochs's satirical "Love Me, I'm a Liberal." Once again uploaded to the "Education" category on YouTube (this time by an account called "Plato Rising" with a Pepe the frog avatar), Tarleton's song borrows the melody of "Big Rock Candy Mountain" to lampoon an older generation of baby boomers for their hypocrisy, greed, and lip service to progressive ideals.[80] The alt-right thrives on the snide unmasking of such hypocrisy—Anglin's *Daily Stormer* style guide noting that "one of our greatest strengths has been exposing and mocking the obvious internal contradictions of the mainstream narrative." Although written from an opposing standpoint, Ochs's "Love Me, I'm a Liberal" has a strikingly similar message. In a live recording, Ochs prefaces the song by depicting liberals as "an outspoken group on many subjects, ten degrees to the left of center in good times, ten degrees to the right of center if it affects them personally."[81] His lyrical protagonist is a hypocrite par excellence who attends civil rights rallies and professes to "love Puerto Ricans and Negroes"—just "as long as they don't move next door." Curiously, both songs contain an almost verbatim line: "might as well be a Jew" (Tarleton) and "I feel like I'm almost a Jew" (Ochs). In liberal centrists, both the alt-right and the radical left of the 1960s share a common target—symptoms of a complacent establishment who, for Ochs, found kindred spirits in Harry Golden and Max Lerner; or who, for Tarleton, embrace cosmopolitan ideals. What links these two starkly contrasting singer-songwriters is this act of protesting against a duplicitous "system," a tradition that produces uncomfortable bedfellows.[82] With one crucial difference: Ochs was himself Jewish, and his use of the word "almost" here is laden with ridicule—ventriloquized, much like in Dylan's "Talkin' John Birch Paranoid Blues," as an indirect admonition. Tarleton's line, by way of contrast, is one-dimensional, an act of puerile soapbox racism.

To see Tarleton as inauthentic or an imposter, however, is to make a political point about the meaning of the folk. Although the majority of folk revivalism is synonymous with the left, the alt-right's interpretation of folk song is in many ways far more consistent with the anti-Enlightenment tradition from which it emerged.[83] As Anderson points out, nationalism and the very concept of nationhood have proved to be "an uncomfortable *anomaly* for Marxist theory"—and, for that reason, elided.[84] Such contradictions endlessly plague folk revivalism on the left, its songs and dances endeavoring to reconcile the conflicting pull of human unity and ethnic particularity, insider and outsider, the local and the global. In modernity, folk songs have always been employed as weapons of cultural defiance: we should not be surprised to find that such weapons afford a variety of uses in support of irreconcilable ideals.

As I mentioned at the start of this book, the folk have bestowed upon us a double-edged sword. Claiming an equal right to folk heritage, Woody Guthrie and Paddy Tarleton are prime examples of this ideological polarity—one carrying a guitar emblazoned with the well-known slogan "THIS MACHINE KILLS FASCISTS," one penning fascist lyrics in defense of race and nation. Yet both indulge in a form of dissident, anti-capitalist longing predicated on forging authentic connections between a people and a place—on one hand, a nativist utopia; on the other, the radical promise of a new world in which all are welcome as equals under an endless sky.[85] Another example of this strange overlapping of political vision would be the left's enduring anti-Semitism. What unites these balladeers on opposing ends of a political spectrum is the "restorative nostalgia" that we encountered at the end of chapter 3.

Restorative nostalgia, as Svetlana Boym contends, encompasses two interwoven narratives: the restoration of origins and, when pushed to an extreme, the conspiracy theory. Whereas we could align Guthrie's "This Land Is Your Land" with the former, Tarleton's work epitomizes the latter. This conspiratorial worldview, she writes, invests in "a transcendental cosmology" and "single transhistorical plot" driven by "a Manichean battle of good and evil and the inevitable scapegoating of the mythical enemy": historical complexity and ambivalences are erased in order to sustain the idea that modern nationalism is "a fulfillment of ancient prophecy."[86] In this worldview, a homeland "is forever under siege, requiring defense against the plotting enemy"—in the case of the alt-right, international Jewry, communists, leftists of every stripe, "cucks," liberals, neoliberals, migrants, Blacks, Muslims, Mexicans, homosexuals, transsexuals, women, feminists, "NPCs," "SJWs," the mainstream media, fake news, multiculturalists, globalists, the state, the deep state, and so on ad nauseam.[87] It is a "red pill" world of memes and malicious in-jokes, furtive symbols and runic occultism, reframed leftism and ironic bait—this "red pill" borrowed from the 1999 cyberpunk classic *The Matrix* to indicate access to a higher realm of truth supposedly hidden from the mindless masses. Such a "paranoiac reconstruction of home," Boym writes, "is predicated on the fantasy of persecution . . . a psychotic substitution of actual experiences with a dark

FIGURE 25. Woody Guthrie, March 1943. Photograph by Al Aumuller.

conspiratorial vision."[88] Such conspiracy theorists, in other words, tend to take on and replicate characteristics of the very conspiracies they dread, performatively bringing their own worst fears to life that in turn justify the use of extreme countermeasures. In response, tradition "is to be restored with a nearly apocalyptic vengeance"—a reprisal that, in the case of European fascism, found its most catastrophic form in the Holocaust.[89]

We have not tended to think of folk song in relation to conspiracy theory or the political terrors of the past century, yet via the strange and foreboding world of the alt-right these connections are brought to the fore with disturbing clarity. It is only through a folkloric imagination that a white nationalist singer such as Tarleton can make the kinds of claims he does—claims binding melodies to territories, blood to soil, race to homeland, a folk to past glories, and an inheritance to a culture under threat from outsiders. Folk song and its political imaginaries have empowered us to tell these stories of belonging, narratives of identification uttered in aesthetic form. But such stories are always partial tales underwritten by cultural amnesia and omission, neglectful of the deeper and more profound interlacing of human history across time and geographical space. Just as our own biographies are never solitary, so nations and ethnicities are rhizomes connecting lives to myriad plateaus of difference. Whenever folkloric thinking rears its many heads, we should ask ourselves to what extent its fantasies of purity and community resonate not only with solidarity and lost unity, but also with a politics of division, exclusion, and *Volksgemeinschaft*—that ever-present specter hiding behind the bright and cheerful enactment of folk heritage, the revenant of a troubled and still unquiet European past. The alt-right's embrace of folk song yields a glimpse of such retrotopian thinking at its most impassioned and irrational, laying bare beliefs that drift beneath the surface and refuse to dissipate.

# Notes

PREFACE

1. Henry David Thoreau, *A Week on the Concord and Merrimack Rivers* (New York: Penguin, 1998), 79.

2. See *I to Myself: An Annotated Selection from the Journal of Henry D. Thoreau*, ed. Jeffrey S. Cramer (New Haven, CT: Yale University Press, 2007), 207.

3. Thoreau, *A Week on the Concord and Merrimack Rivers*, 45.

4. Thoreau, 46. On the Ossian legend, held dear by the Romantic generation, see Matthew Gelbart, *The Invention of "Folk Music" and "Art Music": Emerging Concepts from Ossian to Wagner* (Cambridge: Cambridge University Press, 2007); and Maureen N. McLane, *Balladeering, Minstrelsy, and the Making of British Romantic Poetry* (Cambridge: Cambridge University Press, 2008).

5. Hannah Arendt, *The Origins of Totalitarianism* (London: Penguin, 2017), xi–xii.

6. Arendt, x.

INTRODUCTION

1. Excerpt from John Keats, "Ode on a Grecian Urn," in *Romantic Poetry: An Annotated Anthology*, ed. Michael O'Neill and Charles Mahoney (Malden, MA: Blackwell, 2008), 449.

2. See Keir Keightley, "Tin Pan Allegory," *Modernism/Modernity* 19/4 (2012): 717–36.

3. Bob Dylan, New York 1985, quoted in Christian Williams, *Bob Dylan: In His Own Words* (London: Omnibus Press, 1993), 30.

4. Bob Dylan, *Chronicles: Volume One* (London: Simon & Schuster, 2004), 18. See also James Dunlap, "Through the Eyes of Tom Joad: Patterns of American Idealism, Bob Dylan, and the Folk Protest Movement," *Popular Music and Society* 29/5 (2006): 549–73. More broadly, see Timothy Hampton, *Bob Dylan's Poetics: How the Songs Work* (New York: Zone Books, 2019).

5. Dylan, *Chronicles*, 19–20. On this history, see Robert Cantwell, *When We Were Good: The Folk Revival* (Cambridge, MA: Harvard University Press, 1996); Benjamin Filene, *Romancing the Folk: Public Memory and American Roots Music* (Chapel Hill: University of North Carolina Press, 2000); and Ronald D. Cohen, *Rainbow Quest: The Folk Music Revival and American Society, 1940–1970* (Amherst: University of Massachusetts Press, 2002).

6. See Maureen N. McLane, *Balladeering, Minstrelsy, and the Making of British Romantic Poetry* (Cambridge: Cambridge University Press, 2008); Matthew Gelbart, *The Invention of "Folk Music" and "Art Music": Emerging Concepts from Ossian to Wagner* (Cambridge: Cambridge University Press, 2007); and Nick Groom, *The Making of Percy's "Reliques"* (Oxford: Oxford University Press, 1999).

7. On field recording during this era in a global context, see Tom Western, "'The Age of the Golden Ear': *The Columbia World Library* and Sounding Out Post-war Field Recording," *Twentieth-Century Music* 11/2 (2014): 275–300. See also Mark Katz, *Capturing Sound: How Technology Has Changed Music* (Berkeley: University of California Press, 2010).

8. Milan Kundera, *The Joke*, trans. Michael Henry Heim (London: Faber and Faber, 1992), 133.

9. See A. Kemp-Welch, *Poland under Communism: A Cold War History* (Cambridge: Cambridge University Press, 2008); Katherine Lebow, *Unfinished Utopia: Nowa Huta, Stalinism, and Polish Society, 1949–56* (Ithaca, NY: Cornell University Press, 2013); and Hugo Service, *Germans to Poles: Communism, Nationalism and Ethnic Cleansing after the Second World War* (Cambridge: Cambridge University Press, 2013).

10. On socialist realism, see: Brandon Taylor, "Socialist Realism: 'To Depict Reality in Its Revolutionary Development,'" in *A Concise Companion to Realism*, ed. Matthew Beaumont (Oxford: Wiley-Blackwell, 2010), 160–75; Petre Petrov, "The Industry of Truing: Socialist Realism, Reality, Realization," *Slavic Review* 70 (2011): 873–92; Boris Groys, *The Total Art of Stalinism: Avant-Garde, Aesthetic Dictatorship, and Beyond*, trans. Charles Rougle (Princeton, NJ: Princeton University Press, 1992); and Evgeny Dobrenko, *Political Economy of Socialist Realism*, trans. Jesse M. Savage (New Haven, CT: Yale University Press, 2007). I address similar issues in relation to postwar British folk music and the work of Ewan MacColl in Ross Cole, "Industrial Balladry, Mass Culture, and the Politics of Realism in Cold War Britain," *Journal of Musicology* 34/3 (2017): 354–90.

11. Kundera, *The Joke*, 138, 141.

12. Kundera, 139.

13. Walter Benjamin, "Theses on the Philosophy of History," in *Illuminations*, trans. Harry Zorn (London: Pimlico, 1999), 249.

14. Paul Gilroy, *The Black Atlantic: Modernity and Double Consciousness* (London: Verso, 1993), 15.

15. Gilroy, 15. A similar pattern is traced in Joseph Roach, *Cities of the Dead: Circum-Atlantic Performance* (New York: Columbia University Press, 1996).

16. Charles Keil, "Who Needs 'the Folk'?," *Journal of the Folklore Institute* 15/3 (1978): 263–65. Keil was ahead of the curve in many important ways when it came to criticizing folk ideology: see, for instance, his pioneering *Urban Blues* (Chicago: University of Chicago Press, 1966).

17. Keil, "Who Needs 'the Folk'?," 263. This point is developed at length in Gelbart, *The Invention of "Folk Music" and "Art Music."*

18. See Richard Middleton, "Musical Belongings: Western Music and Its Low-Other," in *Western Music and Its Others: Difference, Representation, and Appropriation in Music*, ed. Georgina Born and David Hesmondhalgh (Berkeley: University of California Press, 2000), 59–85.

19. Dave Harker, *Fakesong: The Manufacture of British "Folksong," 1700 to the Present Day* (Milton Keynes: Open University Press, 1985). Harker's work has aroused a certain degree of ire among more conservative scholars: see, for instance, C. J. Bearman, "Cecil Sharp in Somerset: Some Reflections on the Work of David Harker," *Folklore* 113/1 (2002): 11–34, and David Gregory, "Fakesong in an Imagined Village? A Critique of the Harker-Boyes Thesis," *Musique Folklorique Canadienne* 43/3 (2009): 18–26. I discuss this dissensus in Ross Cole, "On the Politics of Folk Song Theory in Edwardian England," *Ethnomusicology* 63/1 (2019): 19–42. Gregory's work also includes *Victorian Songhunters: The Recovery and Editing of English Vernacular Ballads and Folk Lyrics, 1820–1883* (Lanham, MD: Scarecrow Press, 2006) and *The Late Victorian Folksong Revival: The Persistence of English Melody, 1878–1903* (Lanham, MD: Scarecrow Press, 2010).

20. Harker, *Fakesong*, xii, xvi.

21. Georgina Boyes, *The Imagined Village: Culture, Ideology and the English Folk Revival*, rev. ed. (Leeds: No Masters Co-operative, 2010), ix. Boyes is drawing here on Eric Hobsbawm and Terence Ranger, ed., *The Invention of Tradition* (Cambridge: Cambridge University Press, 1983). For a more recent introduction to the topic, see Steve Roud, *Folk Song in England* (London: Faber & Faber, 2017).

22. E. P. Thompson, *The Making of the English Working Class* (London: Gollancz, 1963), 12. Such arguments also echo Gayatri Chakravorty Spivak's well-known essay "Can the Subaltern Speak?," in *Marxism and the Interpretation of Culture*, ed. Cary Nelson and Lawrence Grossberg (Urbana: University of Illinois Press, 1988), 271–313.

23. Harker, *Fakesong*, 175; Boyes, *The Imagined Village*, 159.

24. See Zeev Sternhell, *The Anti-Enlightenment Tradition*, trans. David Maisel (New Haven, CT: Yale University Press, 2010); and Hannah Arendt, *The Origins of Totalitarianism* (London: Penguin, 2017).

25. Philip V. Bohlman, *Focus: Music, Nationalism, and the Making of the New Europe*, 2nd ed. (New York: Routledge, 2011), xx; see also Philip V. Bohlman, *The Study of Folk Music in the Modern World* (Bloomington: Indiana University Press, 1988).

26. See Johann Gottfried Herder and Philip V. Bohlman, *Song Loves the Masses: Herder on Music and Nationalism* (Oakland: University of California Press, 2017) and Hans Adler and Wulf Koepke, ed., *A Companion to the Works of Johann Gottfried Herder* (Rochester, NY: Camden House, 2009).

27. See Gelbart, *The Invention of "Folk Music" and "Art Music,"* 105–7. The sources in these two paragraphs suggest that the term *folk-song* was in use well before the date Gelbart gives (260–61); more research is needed to establish exactly when and how this term enters British discourse.

28. Ambrose Merton [William Thoms], "Folk-Lore," *The Athenaeum*, 22 August 1846, 862.

29. On these two societies, see Chris Wingfield and Chris Gosden, "An Imperialist Folklore? Establishing the Folk-Lore Society in London," in *Folklore and Nationalism in Europe during the Long Nineteenth Century*, ed. Timothy Baycroft and David M. Hopkin (Leiden: Brill, 2012): 255–74; and C. J. Bearman, "Kate Lee and the Foundation of the Folk-Song Society," *Folk Music Journal* 7/5 (1999): 627–43. For a broad overview of this era, see K. Theodore Hoppen, *The Mid-Victorian Generation, 1846–1886* (Oxford: Oxford University Press, 1998) and G. R. Searle, *A New England? Peace and War, 1886–1918* (Oxford: Oxford University Press, 2004).

30. "ART.—II. Hymns and Lays of Ancient Germany," *Foreign and Colonial Quarterly Review*, January 1843, 94. This passage, from a substantial review featuring a book entitled *Ueber die Lais, Sequenzen und Leiche* (Heidelberg, 1841) by Von F. Wolf is as follows: "Herr Wolf has dedicated his thick octavo to Ludwig Uhland, Francisque Michel, and our countryman the distinguished Thomas Wright. A perusal of his pages will also convince us, that he has almost exhausted the lay and sequence literature of the three nations of which those gentlemen are the representatives. The lais, as folk song, as epic song, and as historic song, the lyric lais, and the German leiche, the church sequence, and the cloister prosæ and cantilenæ, are all most abundantly discussed, identified, and illustrated in his very instructive paragraphs."

31. Further evidence for this dating can be found in an article published in London in *Howitt's Journal of Literature and Popular Progress* 1 (1847): 212, entitled "The Three Little Roses: A German Folk's Song" that makes explicit reference to "the German Volkslieder, or people's songs."

32. Andrew Lang, "The Folk-Lore of France," *The Folk-Lore Record* 1 (1878): 109; James Napier, "Old Ballad Folk-Lore," *The Folk-Lore Record* 2 (1879): 92. See also William A. E. Axon, *Folk Song and Folk-Speech of Lancashire: On the Ballads and Songs of the County Palatine* (Manchester: Tubbs & Brook, 1870).

33. See Stuart Hall, "Notes on Deconstructing 'the Popular,'" in *People's History and Socialist Theory*, ed. Raphael Samuel (London: Routledge & Kegan Paul, 1981): 277–39. I develop this point more fully in Ross Cole, "Notes on Troubling 'the Popular,'" *Popular Music* 37/3 (2018): 392–414.

34. Geza Vermes, *Jesus: Nativity—Passion—Resurrection* (London: Penguin, 2010), 5. On imagination, see also Gaston Bachelard, *The Poetics of Space*, trans. Maria Jolas (New York: Penguin, 2014).

35. On this point, see Neil V. Rosenberg, ed., *Transforming Tradition: Folk Music Revivals Examined* (Urbana: University of Illinois Press, 1993);

Tamara E. Livingston, "Music Revivals: Toward a General Theory," *Ethnomusicology* 43/1 (1999): 66–85; Ian Russell and David Atkinson, ed., *Folk Song: Tradition, Revival, and Re-Creation* (Aberdeen: University of Aberdeen Press, 2004); Kay Kaufman Shelemay, "Musical Communities: Rethinking the Collective in Music," *Journal of the American Musicological Society* 64/2 (2011): 349–90; and Caroline Bithell and Juniper Hill, ed., *The Oxford Handbook of Music Revival* (Oxford: Oxford University Press, 2014).

36. Slavoj Žižek, *The Sublime Object of Ideology* (London: Verso, 2008), 105; see also Saul A. Kripke, *Naming and Necessity* (Cambridge, MA: Harvard University Press, 1980).

37. Žižek, *The Sublime Object of Ideology*, 104. For Žižek, this is the Lacanian *objet petit a*; see Dylan Evans, *An Introductory Dictionary of Lacanian Psychoanalysis* (London: Routledge, 1996). Related themes are explored in J. P. E. Harper-Scott, *The Quilting Points of Musical Modernism: Revolution, Reaction, and William Walton* (Cambridge: Cambridge University Press, 2012); and Richard Middleton, *Voicing the Popular: On the Subjects of Popular Music* (London: Routledge, 2006).

38. See, for instance, Edward W. Said, *Culture and Imperialism* (London: Vintage, 1994); Homi K. Bhabha, *The Location of Culture* (London: Routledge, 2004); and Gilroy, *The Black Atlantic*.

39. See Michel de Certeau, *The Mystic Fable, Vol.1: The Sixteenth and Seventeenth Centuries*, trans. Michael B. Smith (Chicago: University of Chicago Press, 1992) and Michel de Certeau, *The Possession at Loudun*, trans. Michael B. Smith (Chicago: University of Chicago Press, 2000).

40. See Michel de Certeau, *The Writing of History*, trans. Tom Conley (New York: Columbia University Press, 1988); in relation to this theme, see also Hayden White, *The Content of the Form: Narrative Discourse and Historical Representation* (Baltimore: Johns Hopkins University Press, 1987).

41. Certeau, *The Writing of History*, 85.

42. Michel de Certeau, *The Practice of Everyday Life*, trans. Steven Rendall (Berkeley: University of California Press, 1984), 159.

43. Certeau, *The Writing of History*, 226, 227.

44. Certeau, *The Practice of Everyday Life*, 20.

45. See Gayatri Chakravorty Spivak, preface to Jacques Derrida, *Of Grammatology*, trans. Gayatri Chakravorty Spivak (Baltimore: Johns Hopkins University Press, 1997), xiii–xx.

46. Certeau, *The Practice of Everyday Life*, 160.

47. Michel de Certeau, *Culture in the Plural*, trans. Tom Conley (Minneapolis: University of Minnesota Press, 1994), 138–39.

48. J. S. Stuart Glennie, "The Principles of the Classification of Folk-Lore," *The Folk-Lore Journal* 4/1 (1886): 79.

49. G. L. Gomme, "Folk-Lore Terminology," *The Folk-Lore Journal* 2/9 (1884): 285.

50. See Maud Karpeles, "The International Folk Music Council," *Journal of the Folklore Institute* 2/3 (1965): 308–13; and International Council for Traditional Music (ICTM) website: http://ictmusic.org/general-information (accessed 2 August 2020).

51. Johannes Fabian, *Time and the Other: How Anthropology Makes Its Object* (New York: Columbia University Press, 2014), 17. Classic texts dealing with this theme include Tim Ingold, *Evolution and Social Life*, 2nd ed. (Abingdon: Routledge, 2016) and Adam Kuper, *The Reinvention of Primitive Society: Transformations of a Myth*, 3rd ed. (Abingdon: Routledge, 2017). See also Rachel Mundy, "Evolutionary Categories and Musical Style from Adler to America," *Journal of the American Musicological Society* 67/3 (2014): 735–67; Bennett Zon, *Representing Non-Western Music in Nineteenth-Century Britain* (Rochester, NY: University of Rochester Press, 2007); and Bennett Zon, *Evolution and Victorian Musical Culture* (Cambridge: Cambridge University Press, 2017).

52. Certeau, *The Writing of History*, 209.

53. Fabian, *Time and the Other*, 18.

54. See Robin D. G. Kelley, "Notes on Deconstructing 'The Folk,'" *American Historical Review* 97/5 (1992): 1400–1408; Regina Bendix, *In Search of Authenticity: The Formation of Folklore Studies* (Madison: University of Wisconsin Press, 1997); and Gelbart, *The Invention of "Folk Music" and "Art Music."*

55. Kelley, "Notes on Deconstructing 'The Folk,'" 1402; see also Claude Lévi-Strauss, *The Savage Mind*, trans. Sybil Wolfram (London: Weidenfeld and Nicolson, 1966).

56. Julian Johnson, *Out of Time: Music and the Making of Modernity* (New York: Oxford University Press, 2015), 37.

57. Raymond Williams, *The Country and the City* (London: Chatto & Windus, 1973), 43. This idea is developed further in Roach, *Cities of the Dead.*

58. See Certeau, *The Writing of History*, 209.

59. On the problems of this essay, see Sidonie Kellerer, "Rewording the Past: The Postwar Publication of a 1938 Lecture by Martin Heidegger," *Modern Intellectual History*, 11/3 (2014): 575–602. This 1938 talk was originally entitled "*Die Begründung des neuzeitlichen Weltbildes durch die Metaphysik*," but was retitled (and revised) in 1950 as "*Die Zeit des Weltbildes*," which is the text I quote from here.

60. Martin Heidegger, "The Age of the World Picture," in *Off the Beaten Track*, trans. Julian Young and Kenneth Haynes (Cambridge: Cambridge University Press, 2002): 57–58. On this theme, see also Jacques Rancière, *The Future of the Image*, trans. Gregory Elliott (London: Verso, 2007) and Jacques Rancière, *The Emancipated Spectator*, trans. Gregory Elliott (London: Verso, 2009).

61. Heidegger, "The Age of the World Picture," 64. On this point about technocracy, see also Jean-François Lyotard, *The Postmodern Condition: A Report on Knowledge*, trans. Geoff Bennington and Brian Massumi (Minneapolis: University of Minnesota Press, 1984).

62. Heidegger, "The Age of the World Picture," 66.

63. Heidegger, 67–8.

64. Heidegger, 69.

65. Heidegger, 71.

66. Heidegger, 66.

67. Heidegger, 72.

68. Theodor W. Adorno and Max Horkheimer, *Dialectic of Enlightenment*, trans. John Cumming (London: Verso, 1997), xiii. For a more recent iteration of this argument, see Justin E. H. Smith, *Irrationality: A History of the Dark Side of Reason* (Princeton, NJ: Princeton University Press, 2019).

69. Bruno Latour, *We Have Never Been Modern*, trans. Catherine Porter (Cambridge, MA: Harvard University Press, 1993), 65–67.

70. Latour, 35.

71. See, for instance, Tim Flannery, *Europe: The First 100 Million Years* (London: Penguin, 2019).

72. Latour, *We Have Never Been Modern*, 47.

73. Latour, 76. Latour even goes as far as to suggest that if we were to "look for the origins of the modern myths" we would "almost always find them among those who claim to be countering modernism with the impenetrable barrier of the spirit, of emotion, the subject, or the margins" (124).

74. See Arendt, *The Origins of Totalitarianism.*

75. Zygmunt Bauman, *Retrotopia* (Cambridge: Polity Press, 2017), 5, 9. Related themes are explored in Svetlana Boym, *The Future of Nostalgia* (New York: Basic Books, 2001) and David Lowenthal, *The Heritage Crusade and the Spoils of History* (Cambridge: Cambridge University Press, 1998).

## CHAPTER 1. COLLECTING CULTURE

1. "The Profit of Collecting," *The Art Amateur* 3/1 (June 1880): 16.

2. There is an extensive literature on this subject: see, for instance, Carla Yanni, *Nature's Museums: Victorian Science and the Architecture of Display* (Baltimore, MD: Johns Hopkins University Press, 1999); Tim Barringer and Tom Flynn, eds., *Colonialism and the Object: Empire, Material Culture and the Museum* (London: Routledge, 1998); and, more recently, Carin Berkowitz and Bernard Lightman, *Science Museums in Transition: Cultures of Display in Nineteenth-Century Britain and America* (Pittsburgh, PA: University of Pittsburgh Press, 2017).

3. Jean Baudrillard, "The System of Collecting," in *The Cultures of Collecting*, ed. John Elsner and Roger Cardinal (London: Reaktion Books, 1994): 7.

4. Baudrillard, 8. See also Jean Baudrillard, *The System of Objects*, trans. James Benedict (London: Verso, 1996), 85–106.

5. Cecil Sharp, Unpublished diary 23 November 1917, Vaughan Williams Memorial Library, https://www.vwml.org/record/SharpDiary1917/1917/p335, accessed 12 July 2019.

6. Orhan Pamuk, *The Museum of Innocence*, trans. Maureen Freely (London: Faber and Faber, 2009), 685; see also Orhan Pamuk, *The Innocence of Objects: The Museum of Innocence, Istanbul*, trans. Ekin Oklap (New York: Abrams, 2012).

7. Cecil J. Sharp, *English Folk-Song: Some Conclusions* (London: Simpkin & Co., 1907), vii–viii.

8. J. H. Slater, *The Romance of Book-Collecting* (London: Elliot Stock, 1898), 32.

9. Slater, 32.

10. Sharp, *English Folk-Song*, 127, vii.

11. Sharp, 137.

12. Percy Fitzgerald, *The Book Fancier; or, The Romance of Book Collecting*, rev. ed. (London: Sampson Low, Marston, Searle, & Rivington, 1887), v.

13. Sharp, *English Folk-Song*, 137.

14. See Barry J. Faulk, *Music Hall and Modernity: The Late-Victorian Discovery of Popular Culture* (Athens: Ohio University Press, 2004) and Derek B. Scott, *Sounds of the Metropolis: The Nineteenth-Century Popular Music Revolution in London, New York, Paris, and Vienna* (New York: Oxford University Press, 2008).

15. Sharp, *English Folk-Song*, 137.

16. John Elsner and Roger Cardinal, introduction to *The Cultures of Collecting*, 1.

17. Elsner and Cardinal, 1.

18. Elsner and Cardinal, 1; Sharp, *English Folk-Song*, viii.

19. F. J. Child, letter of 25 August 1872, quoted in Roy Palmer, "'Veritable Dunghills': Professor Child and the Broadside," *Folk Music Journal* 7/2 (1996): 157. See also Mary Ellen Brown, *Child's Unfinished Masterpiece: The English and Scottish Popular Ballads* (Urbana: University of Illinois Press, 2011) and David Atkinson, "The English Revival Canon: Child Ballads and the Invention of Tradition," *Journal of American Folklore* 114/453 (2001): 370–80.

20. Frank Kidson, *Traditional Tunes: A Collection of Ballad Airs, Chiefly Obtained in Yorkshire and the South of Scotland; Together with Their Appropriate Words from Broadsides and from Oral Tradition* (Oxford: Chas. Taphouse & Son, 1891), v, xii. Emphasis in original. On Kidson, see John Francmanis, "The Roving Artist: Frank Kidson, Pioneer Song Collector," *Folk Music Journal* 8/1 (2001): 41–66.

21. Kidson, *Traditional Tunes*, v.

22. Kidson, xii.

23. I address this point further in Ross Cole, "Notes on Troubling 'the Popular,'" *Popular Music* 37/3 (2018): 392–414.

24. William Chappell, *The Ballad Literature and Popular Music of the Olden Time: A History of the Ancient Songs, Ballads, and of the Dance Tunes of England, with Numerous Anecdotes and Entire Ballads* (London: Chappell and Co., 1855), vi.

25. Susan M. Pearce, *On Collecting: An Investigation into Collecting in the European Tradition* (London: Routledge, 1995), 27.

26. Sharp, *English Folk-Song*, vii.

27. Sharp, viii.

28. Sharp, 138.

29. Sharp, viii.

30. William Whewell, *The Philosophy of the Inductive Sciences, Founded upon Their History*, new ed., vol. 1 (London: John W. Parker, 1847), 2. See Richard Yeo, *Defining Science: William Whewell, Natural Knowledge, and Public Debate in Early Victorian Britain* (Cambridge: Cambridge University Press, 1993) and, more broadly, *Geographies of Nineteenth-Century Science*,

ed. David N. Livingstone and Charles W. J. Withers (Chicago: University of Chicago Press, 2011).

31. Whewell, *The Philosophy of the Inductive Sciences*, 3.

32. Whewell, 3.

33. Sharp, *English Folk-Song*, ix.

34. Sharp, ix.

35. Kidson, *Traditional Tunes*, xv, xiv. On this point, see Oskar Cox Jensen, "The *Travels* of John Magee: Tracing the Geographies of Britain's Itinerant Print-Sellers, 1789–1815," *Cultural and Social History* 11/2 (2014): 195–216.

36. Sharp, *English Folk-Song*, xiii. See also Gregory Claeys, "The 'Survival of the Fittest' and the Origins of Social Darwinism," *Journal of the History of Ideas* 61/2 (2000): 223–40; Mike Hawkins, *Social Darwinism in European and American Thought, 1860–1945: Nature as Model and Nature as Threat* (Cambridge: Cambridge University Press, 1997); and Bernard Lightman and Bennett Zon, eds., *Evolution and Victorian Culture* (Cambridge: Cambridge University Press, 2014).

37. Sharp, *English Folk-Song*, 15. Later, Sharp expands on this terse definition, pointing out that what he means by "communal authorship" is in fact "communal choice" made over time (31). On the history of race thinking, see Hannah Arendt, *The Origins of Totalitarianism* (London: Penguin, 2017).

38. Sharp, *English Folk-Song*, 34.

39. Sharp, 34.

40. Sharp, 34. On this point, see Johannes Fabian, *Time and the Other: How Anthropology Makes Its Object* (New York: Columbia University Press, 2014).

41. Sharp, *English Folk-Song*, 11.

42. Sharp, 8. For Sharp's list of seven "technical qualities" that tend to mark out a folk song, see 88.

43. Henry David Thoreau, *A Week on the Concord and Merrimack Rivers* (New York: Penguin Books, 1998), 255.

44. Thoreau, 79.

45. Thoreau, 264.

46. Whewell, *The Philosophy of the Inductive Sciences*, 2:48–49.

47. Whewell, 49. For the debates around induction, see Peter Achinstein, ed., *Science Rules: A Historical Introduction to Scientific Methods* (Baltimore: Johns Hopkins University Press, 2004).

48. See Thomas Nagel, *The View from Nowhere* (New York: Oxford University Press, 1986).

49. Sharp, *English Folk-Song*, 124.

50. Sharp, 124.

51. Sharp, 3, 35, 72.

52. Sharp, 89, 103.

53. Sharp, 125.

54. William Whitman Bailey, *Botanizing: A Guide to Field-Collecting and Herbarium Work* (Providence, RI: Preston and Rounds Co., 1899), 2. On this subject's history in Europe, see Sarah Easterby-Smith, *Cultivating Commerce: Cultures of Botany in Britain and France, 1760–1815* (Cambridge: Cambridge University Press, 2018).

55. Bailey, *Botanizing*, 2, 3–4.

56. Sharp, *English Folk-Song*, 105.

57. Bailey, *Botanizing*, 4.

58. Bailey, 5.

59. Sharp, *English Folk-Song*, 72. More broadly on early sound recording, see William Howland Kenney, *Recorded Music in American Life: The Phonograph and Popular Memory, 1890–1945* (Oxford: Oxford University Press, 1999) and Karl Hagstrom Miller, *Segregating Sound: Inventing Folk and Pop Music in the Age of Jim Crow* (Durham, NC: Duke University Press, 2010).

60. Walter Benjamin, "The Work of Art in the Age of Mechanical Reproduction," in *Illuminations*, trans. Harry Zorn (London: Pimlico, 1999): 214.

61. Benjamin, 217, 215.

62. Benjamin, 244.

63. Quoted in the "Discussion" following Lucy E. Broadwood, "On the Collecting of English Folk-Song," *Proceedings of the Musical Association* 31 (1904–05): 107.

64. J. A. Fuller Maitland quoted in the "Discussion" following Broadwood, 108.

65. "Folk Song and National Song," *Musical Herald* 706 (January 1907), 20–21; the meeting had taken place in early December 1906 at the Royal Academy of Music in London.

66. "Folk Song and National Song," 20.

67. "Folk Song and National Song," 21.

68. Percy Grainger, "Collecting with the Phonograph," *Journal of the Folk-Song Society* 3/12 (1908): 148. There has been some degree of contention surrounding this article: see Michael Yates, "Percy Grainger and the Impact of the Phonograph," *Folk Music Journal* 4/3 (1982): 265–75 and C. J. Bearman, "Percy Grainger, the Phonograph, and the Folk Song Society," *Music & Letters* 84/3 (2003): 434–55. A useful perspective is provided by Suzanne Robinson and Kay Dreyfus, eds., *Grainger the Modernist* (Abingdon: Routledge, 2016). See also John Bird, *Percy Grainger* (Oxford: Oxford University Press, 1999).

69. See *Journal of the Folk-Song Society* 3/12 (1908), 205.

70. Charles S. Myers, "A Study of Rhythm in Primitive Music," *British Journal of Psychology* 1/4 (1905): 397.

71. Meyers, 398.

72. This idea is explored in a different context by Michel Foucault in *The Will to Knowledge: The History of Sexuality Volume I*, trans. Robert Hurley (London: Penguin Books, 1998).

73. Myers, "A Study of Rhythm in Primitive Music," 401.

74. Richard Wallaschek, *Primitive Music: An Inquiry into the Origin and Development of Music, Songs, Instruments, Dances, and Pantomimes of Savage Races* (London: Longmans, Green, and Co., 1893), 291, 294.

75. Wallaschek, 230. For further discussion of such ideas, see Alexander Rehding, "The Quest for the Origins of Music in Germany Circa 1900," *Journal of the American Musicological Society* 53/2 (2000): 345–85; Rachel Mundy, "Evolutionary Categories and Musical Style from Adler to America," *Journal of the American Musicological Society* 67/3 (2014): 735–67; and Carl Stumpf,

*The Origins of Music*, trans. David Trippett (Oxford: Oxford University Press, 2012).

76. Fabian, *Time and the Other*, 31.

77. Myers, "A Study of Rhythm in Primitive Music," 402; see also Catherine Tackley, *The Evolution of Jazz in Britain, 1880–1935* (Aldershot: Ashgate, 2005).

78. Myers, "A Study of Rhythm in Primitive Music," 402.

79. Myers, 405.

80. For extended discussions of this issue, see Kofi Agawu, *Representing African Music: Postcolonial Notes, Queries, Positions* (New York: Routledge, 2003) and Ronald Radano and Tejumola Olaniyan, eds., *Audible Empire: Music, Global Politics, Critique* (Durham, NC: Duke University Press, 2015).

81. Myers, "A Study of Rhythm in Primitive Music," 406.

82. See Matthew Gelbart, *The Invention of "Folk Music" and "Art Music": Emerging Concepts from Ossian to Wagner* (Cambridge: Cambridge University Press, 2007).

83. Grainger, "Collecting with the Phonograph," 150. Emphasis in original.

84. See Percy Grainger, "The Impress of Personality in Traditional Singing," *Journal of the Folk-Song Society* 3/12 (1908): 163–66; Grainger, "Collecting with the Phonograph," 151.

85. Grainger, "Collecting with the Phonograph," 154, 155.

86. Grainger, 150.

87. Grainger, 150.

88. See Robert Cantwell, *Ethnomimesis: Folklife and the Representation of Culture* (Chapel Hill: University of North Carolina Press, 1993); "Folk Song and National Song," 21. See also Michael Taussig, *Mimesis and Alterity: A Particular History of the Senses* (Abingdon: Routledge, 2018).

89. Cantwell, *Ethnomimesis*, 6.

90. Grainger, "The Impress of Personality," 164–65.

91. See, for example, Eléanor M. Hight and Gary D. Sampson, eds., *Colonialist Photography: Imag(in)ing Race and Place* (New York: Routledge, 2002) and Christopher Pinny and Nicolas Peterson, eds., *Photography's Other Histories* (Durham, NC: Duke University Press, 2003).

92. Cecil Sharp, Unpublished diary 13 October 1918, Vaughan Williams Memorial Library, https://www.vwml.org/record/SharpDiary1918/1918/p289, accessed 19 July 2019.

93. Cecil Sharp, Unpublished diary 16 October 1918, Vaughan Williams Memorial Library, https://www.vwml.org/record/SharpDiary1918/1918/p292, accessed 19 July 2019.

94. See, for instance, Maud Karpeles, *Cecil Sharp: His Life and Work* (London: Faber and Faber, 2008), 160.

95. See Jonathan Harris, *Federal Art and National Culture: The Politics of Identity in New Deal America* (Cambridge: Cambridge University Press, 1995) and Stuart Cohen, *The Likes of Us: Photography and the Farm Security Administration* (Boston, MA: David R. Godine, 2009).

96. Erika Brady, *A Spiral Way: How the Phonograph Changed Ethnography* (Jackson: University Press of Mississippi, 1999), 2.

97. J. H. Yoxall, *The ABC about Collecting* (London: London Opinion Curio Club, 1908), 127.

98. Charles William Taussig and Theodore Arthur Meyer, *The Book of Hobbies, or A Guide to Happiness* (New York: A. L. Burt Company, 1924), 279.

99. Tausssig and Meyer, 280–81.

100. I borrow the terms *studium* and *punctum* here from Roland Barthes, *Camera Lucida: Reflections on Photography*, trans. Richard Howard (London: Vintage, 2000).

101. John Ruskin, *The Seven Lamps of Architecture*, 6th ed. (Sunnyside, Orpington: George Allen, 1889), 150.

102. Ruskin, 151.

103. Barthes, *Camera Lucida*, 4.

104. Walter Johnson, *Folk-Memory; or The Continuity of British Archaeology* (Oxford: Clarendon Press, 1908), 11.

105. Johnson, 7, 11.

106. Johnson, 23, 12

107. Johnson, 13, 15.

108. Johnson, 13.

109. Johnson, 15.

110. Johnson, 18.

111. John A. Lomax, *Cowboy Songs and Other Frontier Ballads* (New York: Sturgis & Walton Company, 1910), unnumbered p. vii.

112. Lomax, unnumbered pp. vii–viii.

113. See Regina Bendix, *In Search of Authenticity: The Formation of Folklore Studies* (Madison: University of Wisconsin Press, 1997) and Roger D. Abrahams, "Mr Lomax Meets Professor Kittredge," *Journal of Folklore Research* 37/2–3 (2000): 99–118.

114. Lomax, *Cowboy Songs*, xxii.

115. John A. Lomax, "Cowboy Songs of the Mexican Border," *The Sewanee Review* 19/1 (1911): 1, 15. The song "Home on the Range," for example, had been composed by a Kansas doctor and published in 1873; see Nolan Porterfield, *Last Cavalier: The Life and Times of John A. Lomax, 1867–1948* (Urbana: University of Illinois Press, 1996), 297.

116. F. Scott Fitzgerald, *The Great Gatsby* (London: Penguin, 2000), 171–72.

117. Roland Barthes, *Roland Barthes*, translated by Richard Howard (New York: Hill and Wang, 2010), 61.

118. Pamuk, *The Innocence of Objects*, 51–52.

119. Orhan Pamuk, "A Modest Manifesto for Museums," in *The Innocence of Objects*, 55.

120. Pahmuk, 56. On this theme, see John Brewer, "Microhistory and the Histories of Everyday Life," *Cultural and Social History* 7/1 (2010): 87–109.

121. Susan Sontag, *On Photography* (London: Penguin, 1977), 4.

122. Sontag, 14.

123. See Michel Foucault, *Discipline and Punish: The Birth of the Prison*, trans. Alan Sheridan (London: Penguin Books, 1991), 27. This is what Michel de Certeau would describe as "the circularity between the production of the

Other and the production of the text"; see Michel de Certeau, "Montaigne's 'Of Cannibals': The Savage 'I,'" in *Heterologies: Discourse on the Other* (Minneapolis: University of Minnesota Press, 1986): 68.

124. See Foucault, *The Will to Knowledge* and Friedrich Nietzsche, *Beyond Good and Evil: Prelude to a Philosophy of the Future*, trans. Judith Norman (Cambridge: Cambridge University Press, 2002).

125. Foucault, *The Will to Knowledge*, 92.

126. John A. Lomax and Alan Lomax, *Negro Folk Songs as Sung by Lead Belly* (New York: Macmillan, 1936), xiii. For a history of this encounter, see Benjamin Filene, *Romancing the Folk: Public Memory and American Roots Music* (Chapel Hill: University of North Carolina Press, 2000).

## CHAPTER 2. A GEOGRAPHY OF THE FORGOTTEN

1. On this society, see Chris Wingfield and Chris Gosden, "An Imperialist Folklore? Establishing the Folk-Lore Society in London," in *Folklore and Nationalism in Europe during the Long Nineteenth Century*, ed. Timothy Baycroft and David M. Hopkin (Leiden: Brill, 2012): 255–74.

2. Joseph Jacobs, "The Folk," *Folklore* 4/2 (1893): 233. See also Anne J. Kershen, "Jacobs, Joseph (1854–1916)," *Oxford Dictionary of National Biography* (Oxford: Oxford University Press, 2004), http://www.oxforddnb.com/view/article/51106, accessed 1 June 2016.

3. Jacobs, "The Folk," 235–36.

4. Jacobs, 234.

5. Michel de Certeau, "The Beauty of the Dead: Nisard" (Written in collaboration with Dominique Julia and Jacques Revel), in *Heterologies: Discourse on the Other*, trans. Brian Massumi (Minneapolis: University of Minnesota Press, 1986): 131. I discuss this point further in Ross Cole, "Vernacular Song and the Folkloric Imagination at the *Fin de Siècle*," *19th-Century Music*, 42/2 (2018): 73–95.

6. Here, I'm drawing on Benedict Anderson's seminal *Imagined Communities: Reflections on the Origins and Spread of Nationalism*, rev. ed. (London: Verso, 2006) as well as extending ideas sketched out by Georgina Boyes in *The Imagined Village: Culture, Ideology and the English Folk Revival* (Manchester: Manchester University Press, 1993). The term resonates in significant ways with what Radano and Bohlman have called the "racial imagination": see Ronald Radano and Philip V. Bohlman, *Music and the Racial Imagination* (Chicago: University of Chicago Press, 2000).

7. "Our London Correspondence," *Manchester Guardian*, 28 January 1898: 5.

8. "Our London Correspondence," 5.

9. William Morris, Letter to the *Athenaeum*, 10 March 1877, in *News from Nowhere and Other Writings*, ed. Clive Wilmer (London: Penguin Books, 2004), 401–2. See also Chris Miele, ed., *From William Morris: Building Conservation and the Arts and Crafts Cult of Authenticity, 1877–1939* (New Haven, CT: Yale University Press, 2005).

10. J. E. B. "Comments on Events," *Musical News* 14/362 (1898): 129.

11. *Journal of the Folk-Song Society* 1/1 (1899), i–viii.

12. "The Late Honorary Secretary," *Journal of the Folk-Song Society* 2/6 (1905): 67. See also C. J. Bearman, "Kate Lee and the Foundation of the Folk-Song Society," *Folk Music Journal* 7/5 (1999): 627–43.

13. See "Musical Matters at the International Congress of Women," *School Music Review* 8/87 (1899): 45–46. More broadly, see Gillian Sutherland, *In Search of the New Woman: Middle-Class Women and Work in Britain 1870–1914* (Cambridge: Cambridge University Press, 2015).

14. "Experiences of a Folk-Song Collector," *Musical Herald* 612 (March 1899): 71.

15. Kate Lee, "Some Experiences of a Folk-Song Collector," *Journal of the Folk-Song Society* 1/1 (1899): 10.

16. Lee, 8.

17. Lee, 9.

18. Lee, 10–11.

19. Lee, 11.

20. Lee, 12.

21. Bob Copper, *A Song for Every Season: A Hundred Years of a Sussex Farming Family* (London: Heinemann, 1971), 12. There are some minor discrepancies between Lee's account and that of Bob Copper; for clarification, see Vic Gammon, "Copper family (*per.* 1845–2000)," *Oxford Dictionary of National Biography* (Oxford: Oxford University Press, 2004), http://www.oxforddnb.com/view/article/76466, accessed 20 June 2016.

22. Copper, *A Song for Every Season*, 11.

23. "The Folk-Lore Society: Rules," *The Folk-Lore Record* 1 (1878): viii.

24. See Nick Groom, *The Making of Percy's "Reliques"* (Oxford: Oxford University Press, 1999).

25. Lucy E. Broadwood, "On the Collecting of English Folk-Song," *Proceedings of the Musical Association* 31 (1904–05): 101.

26. Michel de Certeau, *The Writing of History*, trans. Tom Conley (New York: Columbia University Press, 1988), 73.

27. This idea is explored, for instance, in Alun Munslow, "Why Should Historians Write about the Nature of History (Rather Than Just Do It)?" *Rethinking History* 11/4 (2007): 613–25.

28. "A Folk-Song Function," *Musical Times* 40/673 (1899): 168–69; see also Vanessa Curney, "Beer [*née* Sassoon], Rachel (1858–1927)," *Oxford Dictionary of National Biography* (Oxford: Oxford University Press, 2004) http://www.oxforddnb.com/view/article/48270, accessed 20 June 2016.

29. "The Folk-Song Society," *Musical Standard* 11/267 (February 1899): 81.

30. Kay Kaufman Shelemay, "Musical Communities: Rethinking the Collective in Music," *Journal of the American Musicological Society* 64/2 (2011): 349–90, 367.

31. Maud Karpeles, *Cecil Sharp: His Life and Work* (London: Faber & Faber, 2008), 39.

32. Henry Burstow, *Reminiscences of Horsham: Recollections of Henry Burstow, the Celebrated Bellringer and Songsinger*, ed. William Albery (Norwood, PA: Norwood Editions, 1975), 108–9. Albery was a local saddle-maker,

socialist, and amateur historian who recorded Burstow's dictated recollections; all proceeds from the book went to Burstow himself.

33. A. E. Green and Tony Wales, "Foreword" to Burstow, *Reminiscences of Horsham*. For a detailed exploration of Burstow's repertoire, see Vic Gammon, "'Not Appreciated in Worthing?' Class Expression and Popular Song Texts in Mid-Nineteenth-Century Britain," *Popular Music* 4 (1984): 5–24. See also Vic Gammon, "Folk Song Collecting in Sussex and Surry, 1843–1914," *History Workshop Journal* 10 (1980): 61–89.

34. Burstow, *Reminiscences of Horsham*, 107.

35. "News from All Parts," *Musical Herald* 816 (March 1916): 113.

36. Burstow, *Reminiscences of Horsham*, 109.

37. "News from All Parts," *Musical Herald* 721 (April 1908): 109.

38. Burstow, *Reminiscences of Horsham*, 108.

39. Burstow, 109.

40. Burstow, 107–8.

41. Burstow, 25, 55, 64, and 108.

42. Literature on these figures is unfortunately sparse, with the notable exception of Oskar Cox Jensen, David Kennerley, and Ian Newman, eds., *Charles Dibdin and Late Georgian Culture* (Oxford: Oxford University Press, 2018) and Ken Emerson, *Doo-dah! Stephen Foster and the Rise of American Popular Culture* (New York: Simon & Schuster, 1997).

43. Burstow's songs appear in catalogs for the printers H. P. Such, William Fortey, and Pearson of Manchester. See Gammon, "'Not Appreciated in Worthing?'" More broadly, see also Derek B. Scott, *Sounds of the Metropolis: The Nineteenth-Century Popular Music Revolution in London, New York, Paris, and Vienna* (New York: Oxford University Press, 2008) and David Atkinson and Steve Roud, eds., *Street Ballads in Nineteenth-Century Britain, Ireland, and North America: The Interface between Print and Oral Traditions* (London: Routledge, 2016).

44. Burstow, *Reminiscences of Horsham*, 110.

45. Burstow, 110.

46. See, for instance, Christopher Marsh, *Music and Society in Early Modern England* (Cambridge: Cambridge University Press, 2010) and Adam Fox, *Oral and Literate Culture in England, 1500–1700* (Oxford: Oxford University Press, 2000).

47. For biographical information, see Dorothy de Val, *In Search of Song: The Life and Times of Lucy Broadwood* (Farnham, UK: Ashgate, 2011) and David Gregory, "Before the Folk-Song Society: Lucy Broadwood and English Folk Song, 1884–97," *Folk Music Journal* 9/3 (2008): 372–414.

48. Lucy E. Broadwood and J. A. Fuller Maitland, eds., *English County Songs* (London: The Leadenhall Press, 1893), iv.

49. Broadwood and Maitland, v.

50. Broadwood and Maitland, v.

51. "Au Courant," *Magazine of Music* 10/3 (March 1893): 50.

52. "Au Courant," 50.

53. E. B. Tylor, "On the Survival of Savage Thought in Modern Civilization," *Appletons' Journal of Literature, Science and Art* 18–19 (1869): 566.

54. Tylor, 598.
55. Tylor, 598.
56. Tylor, 598.
57. Tylor, 598. More broadly on this topic, see Bennett Zon, *Representing Non-Western Music in Nineteenth-Century Britain* (Rochester, NY: University of Rochester Press, 2007).
58. "Publications and Proceedings of Archaeological Societies," *The Antiquary* 27 (April 1893): 172.
59. Sabine Baring-Gould, *Strange Survivals: Some Chapters in the History of Man* (London: Methuen & Co., 1892), 127, 143–44, 61.
60. Baring-Gould, 219.
61. Hubert Parry, "Inaugural Address," *Journal of the Folk-Song Society* 1/1 (1899): 1. For biographical information, see Jeremy Dibble, *C. Hubert H. Parry: His Life and Music* (Oxford: Clarendon Press, 1992).
62. Parry, "Inaugural Address," 1.
63. Parry, 1.
64. Parry, 1–2.
65. Parry, 2.
66. Parry, 2.
67. Parry, 2.
68. Parry, 2–3. See Meirion Hughes and Robert Stradling, *The English Musical Renaissance, 1840–1940: Constructing a National Music* (Manchester: Manchester University Press, 2001).
69. Parry, "Inaugural Address," 3.
70. Parry, 3.
71. On this topic, see Leela Gandhi, *Affective Communities: Anticolonial Thought, Fin-de-Siècle Radicalism, and the Politics of Friendship* (Durham, NC: Duke University Press, 2006).
72. Oscar Wilde, "The Soul of Man under Socialism" [1891], in *The Soul of Man Under Socialism and Selected Critical Prose*, ed. Linda Dowling (London: Penguin, 2001), 128, 146.
73. Dorothea Ponsonby, "Hubert Parry," *Musical Times* 97/1359 (1956): 263. See also Caroline Arscott, *William Morris and Edward Burne-Jones: Interlacings* (New Haven, CT: Yale University Press, 2008).
74. William Morris, *How I Became a Socialist* (London: Twentieth Century Press, 1896), 9.
75. Morris, 12.
76. Parry, "Inaugural Address," 1.
77. William Wordsworth, *The Major Works*, ed. Stephen Gill (Oxford: Oxford University Press, 2008), 488–89. "Complacency" here means "tranquil satisfaction" (733). On the history of this intersection, see Maureen N. McLane, *Balladeering, Minstrelsy, and the Making of British Romantic Poetry* (Cambridge: Cambridge University Press, 2008). On Wordsworth's politics, see Nicholas Roe, *Wordsworth and Coleridge: The Radical Years*, 2nd ed. (Oxford: Oxford University Press, 2018).
78. See Dibble, *C. Hubert H. Parry*, 227.
79. Walt Whitman, *Leaves of Grass* (Brooklyn, NY: 1855), v.

80. Whitman, v.

81. Whitman, v.

82. Whitman, vi. Such themes are explored in John E. Seery, ed., *A Political Companion to Walt Whitman* (Lexington: University Press of Kentucky, 2011) and Christian P. Haines, *A Desire Called America: Biopolitics, Utopia, and the Literary Commons* (New York: Fordham University Press, 2019).

83. Henry David Thoreau, *Walden; or, Life in the Woods*, ed. Jeffry S. Cramer (New Haven, CT: Yale University Press, 2004), 5.

84. Ralph Waldo Emerson, "Nature" (1836), in *Nature and Selected Essays*, ed. Larzer Ziff (New York: Penguin, 2003), 38.

85. Emerson, 47, 51.

86. Morris, *How I Became a Socialist*, 12.

87. From a paragraph statement above the table of contents of *The Century Guild Hobby Horse* 2/10 (1888), unpaged. The magazine was edited by Herbert Horne.

88. Hubert Parry, "The Present Condition of English Song-Writing," *The Century Guild Hobby Horse* 2/10 (1888): 69.

89. Parry, 69.

90. Parry, 69.

91. On mobs and masses, see Hannah Arendt, *The Origins of Totalitarianism* (London: Penguin, 2017).

92. Such ideas are explored in greater detail in Rachel Mundy, "Evolutionary Categories and Musical Style from Adler to America," *Journal of the American Musicological Society* 67/3 (2014): 735–67 and Bernard Lightman and Bennett Zon, eds., *Evolution and Victorian Culture* (Cambridge: Cambridge University Press, 2014). See also Gregory Claeys, "The 'Survival of the Fittest' and the Origins of Social Darwinism," *Journal of the History of Ideas* 61/2 (2000): 223–40; Mike Hawkins, *Social Darwinism in European and American Thought, 1860–1945: Nature as Model and Nature as Threat* (Cambridge: Cambridge University Press, 1997); and Johannes Fabian, *Time and the Other: How Anthropology Makes Its Object* (New York: Columbia University Press, 2014).

93. Hubert Parry, *The Evolution of the Art of Music* (London: K. Paul, Trench, Trübner, 1896), 48.

94. Parry, 80.

95. W. Stanley Jevons, "Methods of Social Reform: I—Amusements of the People," *Contemporary Review* 33 (1878): 500. I explore such ideas at greater length in Ross Cole, "Notes on Troubling 'The Popular,'" *Popular Music* 37/3 (2018): 392–414.

96. Jevons, "Methods of Social Reform," 500.

97. Jevons, 513. A useful resource here is Peter Bailey's classic study *Leisure and Class in Victorian England: Rational Recreation and the Contest for Control, 1830–1885* (London: Routledge & Kegan Paul, 1978). See also Peter Bailey, *Popular Culture and Performance in the Victorian City* (Cambridge: Cambridge University Press, 1998); James Garratt, *Music, Culture and Social Reform in the Age of Wagner* (Cambridge: Cambridge University Press, 2010); and Dave Russell, *Popular Music in England, 1840–1914*, 2nd ed. (Manchester: Manchester University Press, 1997).

98. J. Spencer Curwen, "The Progress of Popular Music," *Contemporary Review* 52 (1887): 245.

99. Wilde, "The Soul of Man under Socialism," 154.

100. See Curwen, "The Progress of Popular Music," 247–48.

101. Hubert Parry, *Style in Musical Art* (London: Macmillan, 1911), 112.

102. John Carey, *The Intellectuals and the Masses: Pride and Prejudice among the Literary Intelligentsia, 1880–1939* (London: Faber and Faber, 1992), 15. See also Andreas Huyssen, *After the Great Divide: Modernism, Mass Culture and Postmodernism* (Basingstoke, UK: Macmillan, 1988).

103. Herbert Spencer, "The Origin of Music," *Mind* 15/60 (1890): 465.

104. Parry, *Style in Musical Art*, 131.

105. Parry, 131–32.

106. Parry, "Inaugural Address," 1. Similar themes are explored in Julian Onderdonk, "The Composer and Society: Family, Politics, Nation," in *The Cambridge Companion to Vaughan Williams*, ed. Alain Frogley and Aiden J. Thompson (Cambridge: Cambridge University Press, 2013), 9–28.

107. This event organized by the Social Democratic Federation and the Irish National League (at which William Morris was present, along with a number of other prominent radicals) sent shockwaves through Victorian society and became known as "Bloody Sunday"; see Lisa Keller, *Triumph of Order: Democracy and Public Space in New York and London* (New York: Columbia University Press, 2009).

108. Sidney J. Low, "The Rise of the Suburbs: A Lesson of the Census," *Contemporary Review* 60 (October 1891): 546–47. See also Lara Baker Whelan, *Class, Culture and Suburban Anxieties in the Victorian Era* (New York: Routledge, 2010) and Richard Perren, *Agriculture in Depression, 1870–1940* (Cambridge: Cambridge University Press, 1995).

109. Low, "The Rise of the Suburbs," 547–48.

110. Low, 550.

111. Low, 550, 551.

112. Low, 552.

113. "Our London Correspondent," *Manchester Guardian*, 3 February 1899: 7.

114. "The Folk-Song Society."

115. Low, "The Rise of the Suburbs," 550–53.

116. See Mary S. Morgan, ed., *Charles Booth's London Poverty Maps* (London: Thames & Hudson, 2019) and the London School of Economics and Political Science, https://booth.lse.ac.uk, which hosts digital versions of Booth's maps and notebooks.

117. See Max Nordau, *Entartung* [Degeneration], ed. Karin Tebben (Berlin: De Gruyter, 2013).

118. "Degeneracy," *National Observer*, 18 June (1892): 115.

119. Isabel Foard, "The Power of Heredity," *Westminster Review* 151/5 (1899): 538.

120. Foard, 538.

121. Robert Donald, "Housing the Poor: Experiments and Problems," *Contemporary Review* 77 (March 1900): 323.

122. Donald, 333.

123. Low, "The Rise of the Suburbs," 553.

124. Low, 553.

125. See Huyssen, *After the Great Divide.*

126. Parry, "The Present Condition of English Song-Writing," 69.

127. Richard Middleton, *Voicing the Popular: On the Subjects of Popular Music* (Abingdon: Routledge, 2006), 23.

128. See, for instance, David Atkinson, "Folk Songs in Print: Text and Tradition," *Folk Music Journal* 8/4 (2004): 456–83, and Oskar Cox Jensen, "The *Travels* of John Magee: Tracing the Geographies of Britain's Itinerant Print-Sellers, 1789–1815," *Cultural and Social History* 11/2 (2014): 195–216.

129. Certeau, "The Beauty of the Dead," 129.

130. For biographical information, see Robert Cochran, *Louise Pound: Scholar, Athlete, Feminist Pioneer* (Lincoln: University of Nebraska Press, 2009).

131. See Louise Pound, "The Southwestern Cowboy Songs and the English and Scottish Popular Ballads," *Modern Philology* 11/2 (1913): 195–207, and Louise Pound, "The Pedigree of a 'Western' Song," *Modern Language Notes* 29/1 (1914): 30–31.

132. Louise Pound, *Poetic Origins and the Ballad* (New York: Macmillan, 1921), vii.

133. Letter from Mendel G. Frampton (16 February 1922) quoted in Esther K. Birdsall, "Some Notes on the Role of George Lyman Kittredge in American Folklore Studies," *Journal of the Folklore Institute* 10/1–2 (1973): 59–60. Kittredge himself, however, was unconvinced by Pound's critique.

134. Pound, *Poetic Origins and the Ballad*, 35, 34.

135. Pound, 91, 106.

136. Pound, 120.

137. Louise Pound, "The Term 'Communal,'" *PMLA* 39/2 (1924): 444.

138. Pound, 445–46.

139. Certeau, *The Practice of Everyday Life*, 41.

140. Mary Ellen Brown, "Placed, Replaced, or Misplaced? The Ballads' Progress," *The Eighteenth Century* 47/2 (2006): 123.

141. Pound, "The Term 'Communal'" 444.

## CHAPTER 3. UTOPIAN COMMUNITY

1. William Morris, "How I Became a Socialist" (1894), in *News from Nowhere and Other Writings*, ed. Clive Wilmer (London: Penguin Books, 2004), 380.

2. Morris, 380.

3. Karl Marx and Frederick Engels, *The German Ideology*, ed. C. J. Arthur (New York: International Publishers, 1970), 82.

4. Marx and Engels, 82.

5. Lawrence Kramer, *Music as Cultural Practice, 1800–1900* (Berkeley: University of California Press, 1990), 9.

6. Lawrence Kramer, *Interpreting Music* (Berkeley: University of California Press, 2011), 27; see 7–11.

7. "The Best Hundred Books," *Pall Mall Gazette*, 19 January 1886 (Issue 6504), 1.

8. "The Best Hundred Books—V," *Pall Mall Gazette*, 2 February 1886 (Issue 6516), 1.

9. "The Best Hundred Books—V," 2.

10. "The Best Hundred Books—V," 2 (emphasis in original).

11. Jacob Grimm, *Teutonic Mythology*, trans. James Steven Stallybrass (Cambridge: Cambridge University Press, 2012), 11.

12. On this nexus, see Leela Gandhi, *Affective Communities: Anticolonial Thought, Fin-de-Siècle Radicalism, and the Politics of Friendship* (Durham, NC: Duke University Press, 2006).

13. William Morris, "Foreword to *Utopia* by Sir Thomas More" (1893), in *News from Nowhere and Other Writings*, 373.

14. Morris, 374.

15. Morris, 375.

16. Most notably, Theodor W. Adorno [with the assistance of George Simpson], "On Popular Music," in *Essays on Music*, ed. Richard Leppert (Berkeley: University of California Press, 2002): 437–69. See also Richard Middleton, *Studying Popular Music* (Milton Keynes, UK: Open University Press, 1990) and Max Paddison, *Adorno's Aesthetics of Music* (Cambridge: Cambridge University Press, 1993).

17. William Morris, "'Looking Backward': A Review of *Looking Backward* by Edward Bellamy" (1889), in *News from Nowhere and Other Writings*, 355.

18. Morris, 355.

19. For an exploration of this portentous flip side of Bellamy's utopianism, see Gregory Claeys, *Dystopia: A Natural History* (Oxford: Oxford University Press, 2017).

20. Morris, "'Looking Backward,'" 356.

21. Morris, 357.

22. Morris, 357

23. Morris, 358.

24. Edward Bellamy, *Looking Backward: 2000–1887* (Oxford: Oxford University Press, 2007), 29, 57.

25. "New Publications: A Modern Utopia," *New York Times*, 29 December 1890, 3.

26. "New Publications," 3.

27. "News from Nowhere," *The Critic*, 30 May 1891, 285. For discussions of this genre, see Michael Robertson, *The Last Utopians: Four Late 19th-Century Visionaries and their Legacy* (Princeton, NJ: Princeton University Press, 2018) and Matthew Beaumont, *Utopia Ltd.: Ideologies of Social Dreaming in England, 1870–1900* (Leiden: Brill, 2005). Utopian studies has grown to become a major field of inquiry; particularly important texts are Ruth Levitas, *The Concept of Utopia* (Hemel Hempstead, UK: Philip Allan, 1990) and Fredric Jameson, *Archaeologies of the Future: The Desire Called Utopia and Other Science Fictions* (London: Verso, 2005). See also Gregory Claeys, ed., *The Cambridge Companion to Utopian Literature* (Cambridge: Cambridge University Press, 2010).

28. "A Poet's Paradise," *The Speaker*, 9 May 1891, 561.

29. Lionel Johnson, "*News from Nowhere* by William Morris," *The Academy*, 23 May 1891, 483–84.

30. Johnson, 483.

31. Johnson, 483; Walt Whitman, "Give Me the Splendid Silent Sun," in *Leaves of Grass* (New York: Wm. E. Chapin & Co, 1867), 47.

32. William Graham, "*News from Nowhere* by William Morris," *The Economic Journal* 1/3 (1891): 591.

33. Graham,, 593.

34. See "A Poet's Vision of a Socialist Millennium," *The Review of Reviews* 3/17 (1891): 509–13.

35. This issue is explored at greater length in Alastair Bonnett, *Left in the Past: Radicalism and the Politics of Nostalgia* (New York: Continuum, 2010).

36. "Two Utopias," *The Speaker*, 25 June 1904, 287.

37. "Two Utopias," 287.

38. "Two Utopias," 287.

39. This double meaning in Morris's title is discussed in Owen Holland, *William Morris's Utopianism: Propaganda, Politics, and Prefiguration* (Basingstoke, UK: Palgrave Macmillan, 2017).

40. Two Utopias," 287.

41. Bellamy, *Looking Backward*, 181.

42. Bellamy, 182–83.

43. Bellamy, 184.

44. Margaret Thatcher, "Interview for *Woman's Own*," 23 September 1987, https://www.margaretthatcher.org/document/106689, accessed 27 June 2019. Leading up to this statement, Thatcher made the following comments: "I think we have gone through a period when too many children and people have been given to understand 'I have a problem, it is the Government's job to cope with it!' or 'I have a problem, I will go and get a grant to cope with it!' 'I am homeless, the Government must house me!' and so they are casting their problems on society and who is society? There is no such thing! There are individual men and women and there are families and no government can do anything except through people and people look to themselves first." On this topic, see David Harvey, *A Brief History of Neoliberalism* (Oxford: Oxford University Press, 2005).

45. Bellamy, *Looking Backward*, 185.

46. William Morris, "Useful Work *versus* Useless Toil" (1884), in *News from Nowhere and Other Writings*, 289.

47. Morris, 291.

48. Morris, 292.

49. Hubert Parry, "Inaugural Address," *Journal of the Folk-Song Society* 1/1 (1899): 1–3.

50. Bellamy, *Looking Backward*, 189.

51. Morris, "Useful Work *versus* Useless Toil," 302.

52. Morris, 289.

53. Morris, 300–301. I discuss the contradictory meanings of the term *popular* during this period in Ross Cole, "Notes on Troubling 'The Popular,'" *Popular Music* 37/3 (2018): 392–414.

54. Constant Lambert, *Music Ho! A Study of Music in Decline* (New York: Charles Scribner's Sons, 1934), 174. See also Eric Saylor, *English Pastoral Music: From Arcadia to Utopia, 1900–1955* (Urbana, IL: University of Illinois Press, 2017).

55. George Bernard Shaw, "Belloc and Chesterton," *The New Age*, 15 February 1908, 310, 311.

56. "Precious, *adj.*, *adv.*, and *n.* §3," *Oxford English Dictionary*, https://www.oed.com/view/Entry/149623#eid28814579, accessed 28 June 2019.

57. Lambert, *Music Ho!*, 184, 186.

58. May Morris, "Introduction" to William Morris, *The Collected Works of William Morris, Volume 12: The Story of Sigurd the Volsung and the Fall of the Niblungs* (Cambridge: Cambridge University Press, 2012): ix.

59. Morris, ix.

60. Morris, x.

61. Elizabeth Helsinger, "Poem into Song," *New Literary History* 46/4 (2015): 685, 687.

62. Frederick Engels, *Socialism: Utopian and Scientific*, trans. Edward Aveling (London: Swan Sonnenschein & Co, 1892), 51.

63. Engels, 57.

64. Engels, 86–87.

65. Engels, 26–27. On British socialism, see Gregory Claeys, *Citizens and Saints: Politics and Anti-Politics in Early British Socialism* (Cambridge: Cambridge University Press, 1989) and Mark Bevir, *The Making of British Socialism* (Princeton, NJ: Princeton University Press, 2011); see also Jon Lawrence, *Speaking for the People: Party, Language, and Popular Politics in England, 1867–1914* (Cambridge: Cambridge University Press, 1998).

66. Engels, *Socialism*, 12. This point is also made in Karl Marx and Friedrich Engels, *The Communist Manifesto* (London: Penguin Books, 2002). Of course, such a scheme was itself a classic instance of ideology: see Hannah Arendt, *The Origins of Totalitarianism* (London: Penguin, 2017).

67. William Morris, *News from Nowhere; or, An Epoch of Rest, Being Some Chapters from a Utopian Romance* (1890), in *News from Nowhere and Other Writings*, 133.

68. Morris, 133–34.

69. Morris, 134.

70. Arendt, *The Origins of Totalitarianism*, 415. On this topic, see also David Cannadine, *Class in Britain* (London: Penguin, 2000).

71. Morris, *News from Nowhere*, 136.

72. See Lisa Keller, *Triumph of Order: Democracy and Public Space in New York and London* (New York: Columbia University Press, 2009) and E. P. Thompson's classic text *William Morris: Romantic to Revolutionary* (Oakland: PM Press, 2011). Thompson points out that this event acted as a catalyst for a parting of the ways between Fabians and revolutionary socialists in Britain.

73. Morris, *News from Nowhere*, 144–46.

74. Morris, 144.

75. See R. J. Rummel, *Death by Government* (New Brunswick, NJ: Transaction Publishers, 1994).

76. Morris, *News from Nowhere*, 148.

77. Noam Chomsky, "Notes on Anarchism," in *The Essential Chomsky*, ed. Anthony Arnove (New York: The New Press, 2008), 103.

78. Chomsky, 98.

79. Chomsky, 101. The academic literature on anarchism is fairly scant; a recent exception is Benjamin Franks, Nathan Jun, and Leonard Williams, eds., *Anarchism: A Conceptual Approach* (New York: Routledge, 2018). On "bureaucratic despotism," see also Arendt, *The Origins of Totalitarianism.*

80. Mikhail Bakunin, "Statism and Anarchy" (1873), in *Bakunin on Anarchy: Selected Works by the Activist-Founder of World Anarchism*, ed. Sam Dolgoff (New York: Vintage Books, 1971), 331.

81. Morris, *News from Nowhere*, 150.

82. Morris, 155.

83. Morris, 158.

84. Morris, 158.

85. Morris, 160.

86. Morris, 160 (emphasis added).

87. Morris, 160

88. See Raymond Williams, "Culture," in *Keywords: A Vocabulary of Culture and Society* (London: Fourth Estate, 2014), 84–90.

89. Karl Marx, *Capital: A Critique of Political Economy*, ed. Frederick Engels (New York: The Modern Library, 1906), 708. For further discussions of alienation in Marx, see Bertell Ollman, *Alienation: Marx's Conception of Man in a Capitalist Society*, 2nd ed. (Cambridge: Cambridge University Press, 1976); Amy E. Wendling, *Karl Marx on Technology and Alienation* (Basingstoke, UK: Palgrave Macmillan, 2009); and Jan Kandiyali, ed., *Reassessing Marx's Social and Political Philosophy: Freedom, Recognition, and Human Flourishing* (New York: Routledge, 2018).

90. Karl Marx, "Economic and Philosophic Manuscripts" (1844), in *Early Writings*, trans. Rodney Livingstone and Gregor Benton (London: Penguin Books, 1992): 322, 323.

91. Marx, 326.

92. Marx, 326.

93. Marx, 329.

94. Marx, 328. "Species-being" is a complex and rather under-theorized term in Marxist theory, yet one that is arguably central to Marx's vision of human well-being: see Thomas E. Wartenberg, "'Species-Being' and 'Human Nature' in Marx," *Human Studies* 5/2 (1982): 77–95; and James M. Czank, "On the Origin of Species-Being: Marx Redefined," *Rethinking Marxism* 24/2 (2012): 316–23.

95. Marx, "Economic and Philosophic Manuscripts," 333.

96. See John Ruskin, *Selected Writings*, ed. Dinah Birch (Oxford: Oxford University Press, 2004), 267.

97. Morris, "How I Became a Socialist," 381. A useful resource on Ruskin is Francis O'Gorman, ed., *The Cambridge Companion to John Ruskin* (Cambridge: Cambridge University Press, 2015).

98. John Ruskin, *The Stones of Venice, Volume the Second: The Sea-Stories* (London: Smith, Elder and Co., 1867), 155.

99. Ruskin, 161.

100. Ruskin, 162.

101. Ruskin, 162.

102. Ruskin, 172.

103. Ruskin, 165.

104. See Adorno, "On Popular Music," 441–44.

105. Ruskin, *The Stones of Venice*, 169.

106. Morris, "How I Became a Socialist," 379; Morris, *News from Nowhere*, 160.

107. John Ruskin, *The Seven Lamps of Architecture*, 6th ed. (Sunnyside, Orpington, UK: George Allen, 1889), 186–87.

108. Ruskin, 187.

109. John Ruskin, *Praeterita: Outlines of Scenes and Thoughts Perhaps Worthy of Memory in My Past Life*, Volume 1 (London: George Allen, 1907), 161.

110. Mark Frost, *The Lost Companions and John Ruskin's Guild of St George* (London: Anthem Press, 2014), 6.

111. William Wordsworth, *The Prelude* (1805), in *The Major Works*, ed. Stephen Gill (Oxford: Oxford University Press, 2011), 490. On Wordsworth's early politics, see Nicholas Roe, *Wordsworth and Coleridge: The Radical Years*, 2nd ed. (Oxford: Oxford University Press, 2018).

112. On the latter, see Jon Lawrence, "Popular Radicalism and the Socialist Revival in Britain," *Journal of British Studies* 31/2 (1992): 163–86.

113. Morris, *News from Nowhere*, 220.

114. Morris, 219.

115. H. G. Wells, *A Modern Utopia* (London: Penguin, 2005); see also Daniel J. Kevles, *In the Name of Eugenics: Genetics and the Uses of Human Heredity* (Cambridge, MA: Harvard University Press, 1995); Richard Soloway, *Demography and Degeneration: Eugenics and the Declining Birthrate in Twentieth-Century Britain* (Chapel Hill: University of North Carolina Press, 1995); and Alison Bashford and Philippa Levine, eds., *The Oxford Handbook of the History of Eugenics* (New York: Oxford University Press, 2010).

116. Morris, *News from Nowhere*, 132, 131, 104.

117. Morris, 199.

118. William Morris, "The Lesser Arts" (1882), in *News from Nowhere and Other Writings*, 244.

119. Morris, 246.

120. Morris, 254.

121. On Child, see Mary Ellen Brown, *Child's Unfinished Masterpiece: The English and Scottish Popular Ballads* (Urbana: University of Illinois Press, 2011) and David Atkinson, "The English Revival Canon: Child Ballads and the Invention of Tradition," *Journal of American Folklore* 114/453 (2001): 370–80.

122. Francis B. Gummere, "introduction" to *Old English Ballads*, ed. Francis B. Gummere (Boston: Ginn & Company, 1914), xvi.

123. Gummere, xiv.

124. Gummere, xvi.

125. George Lyman Kittredge, "introduction" to *English and Scottish Popular Ballads*, ed. George Lyman Kittredge and Helen Child Sargent (London: Harrap, 1904), xx, xxii. For more information, see Rosemary L. Zumwalt, *American Folklore Scholarship: A Dialogue of Dissent* (Bloomington: Indiana University Press, 1988) and Regina Bendix, *In Search of Authenticity: The Formation of Folklore Studies* (Madison: University of Wisconsin Press, 1997).

126. On this institution, see Joanna Bullivant, *Alan Bush, Modern Music, and the Cold War: The Cultural Left in Britain and the Communist Bloc* (Cambridge: Cambridge University Press, 2017).

127. A. L. Lloyd, *The Singing Englishman: An Introduction to Folksong* (London: Workers' Music Association, 1944), 70.

128. Lloyd, 4.

129. Lloyd, 12.

130. Lloyd, 45–46. Such ideas were indebted to A. L. Morton's *A People's History of England* (London: Victor Gollancz, 1938), which was available at the time through the Left Book Club. I discuss Lloyd's changing ideas and the postwar Marxist folk revival in Ross Cole, "Industrial Balladry, Mass Culture, and the Politics of Realism in Cold War Britain," *Journal of Musicology*, 34/3 (2017): 354–90.

131. See, for instance, Robbie Lieberman, "*My Song Is My Weapon': People's Songs, American Communism, and the Politics of Culture, 1930–50* (Urbana: University of Illinois Press, 1989) and William G. Roy, *Reds, Whites, and Blues: Social Movements, Folk Music, and Race in the United States* (Princeton, NJ: Princeton University Press, 2010).

132. Svetlana Boym, *The Future of Nostalgia* (New York: Basic Books, 2001), xvi.

133. Boym, xvii.

134. Boym, xvi.

135. See Eric Hobsbawm and Terence Ranger, eds., *The Invention of Tradition* (Cambridge: Cambridge University Press, 1983).

136. Boym, *The Future of Nostalgia*, xviii.

137. Boym, 41.

138. Boym, xviii.

139. Boym, 41.

140. Boym, xvi.

141. Boym, xvii.

142. Raymond Williams, *Culture and Society, 1780–1950* (London: Chatto & Windus, 1958), 335–36.

## CHAPTER 4. DIFFERENCE AND BELONGING

1. Maud Karpeles, *Cecil Sharp: His Life and Work* (London: Faber and Faber, 2008), 32.

2. It is, in fact, too good to be true: if we follow Sharp's own account quoted at the beginning of chapter 1, then he began collecting songs in 1899, eight years before the publication of his 1907 book.

3. Karpeles, *Cecil Sharp*, 32. For further information, see Derek Schofield, "Sowing the Seeds: Cecil Sharp and Charles Marson in Somerset in 1903," *Folk Music Journal* 8/4 (2004): 484–512.

4. See, for example, Dave Harker, "Cecil Sharp in Somerset: Some Conclusions," *Folk Music Journal* 2/3 (1972): 220–40, and Dave Harker, *Fakesong: The Manufacture of British "folksong" 1700 to the Present Day* (Milton Keynes, UK: Open University Press, 1985).

5. I'm drawing here on two seminal ideas respectively developed by the sociologist Erving Goffman in *Frame Analysis: An Essay on the Organization of Experience* (Cambridge, MA: Harvard University Press, 1974) and the psychologist James J. Gibson in *The Ecological Approach to Visual Perception* (Boston: Houghton Mifflin, 1979).

6. Houston A. Baker Jr., *Modernism and the Harlem Renaissance* (Chicago: University of Chicago Press, 1987), 58.

7. Joe R. Feagin, *The White Racial Frame: Centuries of Racial Framing and Counter-Framing*, 2nd ed. (New York: Routledge, 2013); see also Ronald Radano and Philip V. Bohlman, eds., *Music and the Racial Imagination* (Chicago: University of Chicago Press, 2000).

8. Feagin, *The White Racial Frame*, 3 (emphasis in original).

9. John A. Lomax, "A Quest for American Ballads," *New York Times*, 14 May 1910, BR12.

10. Lomax, BR12. On the representation of Native American culture in such contexts, see Jill Terry Rudy, "American Folklore Scholarship: Tales of the North American Indians, and Relational Communities," *Journal of American Folklore* 126/499 (2013): 3–30, and Derek B. Scott, *From the Erotic to the Demonic: On Critical Musicology* (Oxford: Oxford University Press, 2003).

11. Lomax, "A Quest for American Ballads."

12. John A. Lomax, "Some Types of American Folk-Song," *Journal of American Folklore* 28/107 (1915): 1–17, 15. On African American mythology, see Lawrence W. Levine, *Black Culture and Black Consciousness: Afro-American Folk Thought from Slavery to Freedom*, 30th anniversary ed. (New York: Oxford University Press, 2007) and Henry Louis Gates Jr., *The Signifying Monkey: A Theory of African-American Literary Criticism*, 25th anniversary ed. (New York: Oxford University Press, 2014). On music and dance under slavery, see also Samuel A. Floyd Jr., *The Power of Black Music: Interpreting its History from Africa to the United States* (New York: Oxford University Press, 1995); Ronald Radano, *Lying up a Nation: Race and Black Music* (Chicago: University of Chicago Press, 2003); and Katrina Dyonne Thompson, *Ring Shout, Wheel About: The Racial Politics of Music and Dance in North American Slavery* (Urbana: University of Illinois Press, 2014).

13. Joel Chandler Harris, *Uncle Remus, His Songs and His Sayings: The Folk-Lore of the Old Plantation* (New York: D. Appleton and Company, 1881), 3.

14. Harris, 4. Harris is referring to Stowe's hugely popular 1852 novel *Uncle Tom's Cabin; or, Life Among the Lowly*. On blackface caricature, see Eric Lott, *Love and Theft: Blackface Minstrelsy and the American Working Class*, 20th

anniversary ed. (New York: Oxford University Press, 2013); W. T. Lhamon Jr., *Raising Cain: Blackface Performance from Jim Crow to Hip Hop* (Cambridge, MA: Harvard University Press, 1998); and Karen Sotiropoulos, *Staging Race: Black Performers in Turn of the Century America* (Cambridge, MA: Harvard University Press, 2006). On the British context, see Michael Pickering, *Blackface Minstrelsy in Britain* (Aldershot, UK: Ashgate, 2008).

15. Harris, *Uncle Remus*, 12.

16. Matthew D. Morrison, "Race, Blacksound, and the (Re)Making of Musicological Discourse," *Journal of the American Musicological Society* 72/3 (2019): 781–823.

17. Lomax, "Some Types of American Folk-Song," 1–2.

18. Field diary August 1933, quoted in: John A. Lomax, *Adventures of a Ballad Hunter* (New York: Macmillan, 1947), 125.

19. See Nolan Porterfield, *Last Cavalier: The Life and Times of John A. Lomax, 1867–1948* (Urbana: University of Illinois Press, 1996).

20. John A. Lomax, "'Sinful Songs' of the Southern Negro," *Musical Quarterly* 20/2 (1934): 177–87, 181.

21. Lomax, 181.

22. Lomax, 181.

23. Dorothy Scarborough, "American Ballads and Folksongs: The Lomax Collection Brings Together Chanteys, Spirituals, Mountain 'Lonesomes' and Desperado Ballads," *New York Times*, 11 November 1934, 2. Alan Lomax would go on to become a major figure in the postwar folk revival: see, for instance, Ronald D. Cohen and Rachel Clare Donaldson, *Roots of the Revival: American and British Folk Music in the 1950s* (Urbana: University of Illinois Press, 2014); David Gregory, "Lomax in London: Alan Lomax, the BBC and the Folk-Song Revival in England, 1950–58," *Folk Music Journal* 8/2 (2002): 136–69; and Tom Western, "'The Age of the Golden Ear': *The Columbia World Library* and Sounding out Post-war Field Recording," *Twentieth-Century Music* 11/2 (2014): 275–300.

24. A valuable corrective to Lomax's fieldwork is Dena J. Epstein, *Sinful Tunes and Spirituals: Black Folk Music to the Civil War* (Urbana: University of Illinois Press, 1977).

25. Roland Barthes, *Mythologies* (London: Vintage Books, 2009), 139, 149.

26. Barthes, 169. I deal with this process at greater length in Ross Cole, "Mastery and Masquerade in the Transatlantic Blues Revival," *Journal of the Royal Musical Association* 143/1 (2018): 173–210.

27. Lomax, "'Sinful Songs,'" 182.

28. Lomax, 183–84.

29. For further discussions of this history, see Kofi Agawu, *Representing African Music: Postcolonial Notes, Queries, Positions* (New York: Routledge, 2003) and Ronald Radano and Tejumola Olaniyan eds., *Audible Empire: Music, Global Politics, Critique* (Durham, NC: Duke University Press, 2015).

30. Lomax, "'Sinful Songs,'" 184.

31. Lomax, 184.

32. Lomax, 185. On this trope, see Michael Taussig, *Mimesis and Alterity: A Particular History of the Senses* (Abingdon, UK: Routledge, 2018).

33. See, for instance, Samuel B. Charters, *The Country Blues* (New York: Rinehart, 1959) and Paul Oliver, *Blues Fell This Morning: The Meaning of the Blues* (London: Cassell, 1960). This way of conceiving the blues has been repeatedly challenged: see Charles Keil, *Urban Blues* (Chicago: University of Chicago Press, 1966); Elijah Wald, *Escaping the Delta: Robert Johnson and the Invention of the Blues* (New York: Amistad, 2004); Marybeth Hamilton, *In Search of the Blues: Black Voices, White Visions* (London: Jonathan Cape, 2007); Ulrich Adelt, *Blues Music in the Sixties: A Story in Black and White* (New Brunswick, NJ: Rutgers University Press, 2010); and Paige A. McGinley, *Staging the Blues: From Tent Shows to Tourism* (Durham, NC: Duke University Press, 2014).

34. This idea is explored at greater length in Karl Hagstrom Miller, *Segregating Sound: Inventing Folk and Pop Music in the Age of Jim Crow* (Durham, NC: Duke University Press, 2010).

35. Lomax, "'Sinful Songs,'" 182.

36. See Jerrold Hirsch, "Modernity, Nostalgia, and Southern Folklore Studies: The Case of John Lomax," *Journal of American Folklore* 105/416 (1992): 183–207 and Patrick B. Mullen, "The Dilemma of Representation in Folklore Studies: The Case of Henry Truvillion and John Lomax," *Journal of Folklore Research* 37/2–3 (2000): 155–74.

37. Lomax, *Adventures of a Ballad Hunter*, 299. This is a significant point, attesting to the different visions of Black modernity expressed by Booker T. Washington (associated with Tuskegee University) and W. E. B. Du Bois (associated with Fisk University). Notably, the word "folk" is absent from Washington's *Up From Slavery: An Autobiography* (New York: Doubleday & Company, 1901).

38. Ralph Ellison, *Invisible Man* (London: Penguin, 2001), 47. On this topic, see also Lawrence Schenbeck, *Racial Uplift and American Music, 1878–1943* (Jackson: University Press of Mississippi, 2012).

39. See Steven Garabedian, "Reds, Whites, and the Blues: Lawrence Gellert, "Negro Songs of Protest," and the Left-Wing Folk-Song Revival of the 1930s and 1940s," *American Quarterly* 57/1 (2005): 179–206.

40. Bentley Ball, *The Song-A-Logue of America* (Detroit, MI: Geo. A. Drake & Co. Press, 1922), 2.

41. Ball, 2.

42. Ball, 39.

43. Henry Edward Krehbiel, *Afro-American Folksongs: A Study in Racial and National Music* (New York: G. Schirmer, 1914), v.

44. Krehbiel, v. See Sotiropoulos, *Staging Race*; Edward A. Berlin, *Ragtime: A Musical and Cultural History* (Berkeley: University of California Press, 1980); John Baxendale, "'. . . into another kind of life in which anything might happen. . .': Popular Music and Late Modernity, 1910–1930," *Popular Music* 14/2 (1995): 137–54; and Patricia R. Schroeder, "Passing for Black: Coon Songs and the Performance of Race," *Journal of American Culture* 33/2 (2010): 139–53.

45. Krehbiel, *Afro-American Folksongs*, 92–3, 68.

46. Krehbiel, 3.

47. Krehbiel, 112, 114, 103.

48. Krehbiel, 73. See Rachel Mundy, "Evolutionary Categories and Musical Style from Adler to America," *Journal of the American Musicological Society* 67/3 (2014): 735–67.

49. Krehbiel, *Afro-American Folksongs*, 84. A useful resource here is Gerhard Kubik, *Africa and the Blues* (Jackson: University Press of Mississippi, 1999).

50. Krehbiel, *Afro-American Folksongs*, 3.

51. Natalie Curtis Burlin, *Negro Folk-Songs, in Four Books*, Book I (New York: G. Schirmer, 1918), 5, 4.

52. Burlin, 3.

53. Burlin, 5.

54. See Lott, *Love and Theft.*

55. Percy Grainger, "Mrs. Burlin's Study of Negro Folk-Music," *New York Times*, 14 April 1918, BR5.

56. Grainger, BR5.

57. Grainger, BR5.

58. See Raymond Williams, *Culture and Society, 1780–1950* (London: Chatto & Windus, 1958), 335 and Raymond Williams, "Culture," in *Keywords: A Vocabulary of Culture and Society* (London: Fourth Estate, 2014), 84–90. I expand on this idea in Ross Cole, "Towards an Ecological History of Music," in *Remixing Music Studies: Essays in Honour of Nicholas Cook*, ed. Ananay Aguilar, Ross Cole, Matthew Pritchard, and Eric Clarke (Abingdon, UK: Routledge, 2020): 194–209.

59. On this term, see Steven Feld, "Acoustemology," in *Keywords in Sound*, ed. David Novak and Matt Sakakeeny (Durham, NC: Duke University Press): 12–21.

60. John Wesley Work, *Folk Song of the American Negro* (Nashville, TN: Press of Fisk University, 1915), 123.

61. I'm borrowing this phrase from Ralph Ellison, *Shadow and Act* (New York: Vintage International, 1995), 45–59.

62. Work, *Folk Song*, 123.

63. Frantz Fanon, *Black Skin, White Masks*, trans. Charles Lam Markmann (London: Pluto Press, 2008), 6.

64. Work, *Folk Song*, 20.

65. Work, 7, 22.

66. Work, 23.

67. Work, 119–20.

68. Work, 107, 106.

69. Work, 106. For more detail, see Toni P. Anderson, *"Tell Them We Are Singing for Jesus": The Original Fisk Jubilee Singers and Christian Reconstruction, 1871–1878* (Macon, GA: Mercer University Press, 2010) and K. Stephen Prince, *Stories of the South: Race and the Reconstruction of Southern Identity, 1865–1915* (Chapel Hill: University of North Carolina Press, 2014). The Jubilee Singers are also discussed in Paul Gilroy, "Sounds Authentic: Black Music, Ethnicity, and the Challenge of a *Changing* Same," *Black Music Research Journal* 11/2 (1991): 111–36.

70. "The Jubilee Singers," *Musical Standard*, 17 May 1873, 312.

71. "The Jubilee Singers." This opinion was echoed in a similarly titled article for the *Orchestra* (9 May 1873, 86).

72. "The Jubilee Singers," *Musical World* 10 May 1873, 303.

73. "The Jubilee Singers," *Tonic Sol-Fa Reporter*, 15 June 1875, 188. On the connection to Wales, see Sarah Hill, *"Blerwytirhwng?" The Place of Welsh Pop Music* (Abingdon, UK: Ashgate, 2007).

74. "The Jubilee Singers," *Tonic Sol-Fa Reporter*, 15 May 1873, 154.

75. W[illiam]. C[hambers]., "The Jubilee Singers," *Chambers's Journal of Popular Literature, Science, and Art*, 12 January 1878, 19.

76. W[illiam]. C[hambers]., 19. On the history of this distinction, see Lawrence W. Levine, *Highbrow / Lowbrow: The Emergence of Cultural Hierarchy in America* (Cambridge, MA: Harvard University Press, 1988).

77. "The Fisk Jubilee Singers," *Times of India* 3 January 1890, 3.

78. W. E. Burghardt Du Bois, *The Souls of Black Folk: Essays and Sketches* (Chicago: A. C. McClurg & Co., 1903), viii.

79. Du Bois, viii.

80. Du Bois, 250, 251.

81. Du Bois, 251.

82. Du Bois, 257, 258, 253, 261.

83. Du Bois., 261; Martin Luther King, Jr., "I Have a Dream" address delivered at the March on Washington for Jobs and Freedom, 28 August 1963, https://kinginstitute.stanford.edu/king-papers/documents/i-have-dream-address-delivered-march-washington-jobs-and-freedom, accessed 7 August 2019. The legacy of this moment is explored in Houston A. Baker, Jr., *Betrayal: How Black Intellectuals Have Abandoned the Ideals of the Civil Rights Era* (New York: Columbia University Press, 2008) and Houston A. Baker Jr. and K. Merinda Simmons, eds., *The Trouble with Post-Blackness* (New York: Columbia University Press, 2015).

84. King, "I Have a Dream."

85. King, "I Have a Dream."

86. See Edward J. Blum, *W. E. B. Du Bois: American Prophet* (Philadelphia: University of Pennsylvania Press, 2007), 211.

87. Du Bois, *The Souls of Black Folk*, 252.

88. Du Bois, 253.

89. Du Bois, 254, 257.

90. The classic text on this topic is Benedict Anderson, *Imagined Communities: Reflections on the Origins and Spread of Nationalism*, rev. ed. (London: Verso, 2006); see also Kay Kaufman Shelemay, "Musical Communities: Rethinking the Collective in Music," *Journal of the American Musicological Society* 64/2 (2011): 349–90.

91. Du Bois, *The Souls of Black Folk*, 256. On the idea of Black music as a "changing same," see Gilroy, "Sounds Authentic," who is drawing on Amiri Baraka [LeRoi Jones], *Black Music* (New York: William Morrow, 1968).

92. Du Bois, *The Souls of Black Folk*, 262–63.

93. W. E. Burghardt Du Bois, *The Gift of Black Folk: The Negroes in the Making of America* (Boston, MA: The Stratford Co., 1924), i.

94. Du Bois, i.

95. Du Bois, i.
96. Du Bois, i–ii.
97. Du Bois, ii–iii.
98. Hannah Arendt, *The Origins of Totalitarianism* (London: Penguin, 2017), 389.
99. Du Bois, *The Gift of Black Folk*, 33.
100. W. E. Burghardt Du Bois, "The Study of the Negro Problems," *Annals of the American Academy of Political and Social Science* 11 (1898): 20.
101. Du Bois, *The Gift of Black Folk*, 33.
102. Baker, *Modernism and the Harlem Renaissance*, 8, 91.
103. Baker, 91.
104. Houston A. Baker, Jr., "Modernism and the Harlem Renaissance," *American Quarterly* 39/1 (1987): 93.
105. Baker, *Modernism and the Harlem Renaissance*, 56.
106. Baker, 56.
107. Baker., 58, 73, 57.
108. Du Bois, "The Study of the Negro Problems," 20.
109. Baker, *Modernism and the Harlem Renaissance*, 61.
110. Baker, 63.
111. This racializing habit of thought would come to define the reception of Black music in terms of authenticity. See Simon Frith, "'The Magic That Can Set You Free': The Ideology of Folk and the Myth of the Rock Community," *Popular Music* 1 (1981): 159–68; Allan F. Moore, "Authenticity as Authentication," *Popular Music* 21/2 (2002): 209–23; and Emily I. Dolan, "'. . . This Little Ukulele Tells the Truth': Indie Pop and Kitsch Authenticity," *Popular Music* 29/3 (2010): 457–69.
112. See Gates, *The Signifying Monkey*; this "slave's trope" is discussed further in Ayana Smith, "Blues, Criticism, and the Signifying Trickster," *Popular Music* 24/2 (2005): 179–91.
113. Alongside Baker, a classic text on this era is Nathan Irvin Huggins, *Harlem Renaissance*, updated ed. (New York: Oxford University Press, 2007). See also George Hutchinson, *The Harlem Renaissance in Black and White* (Cambridge, MA: Belknap Press of Harvard University Press, 1995); Paul Allen Anderson, *Deep River: Music and Memory in Harlem Renaissance Thought* (Durham, NC: Duke University Press, 2001); George Hutchinson, ed., *The Cambridge Companion to the Harlem Renaissance* (Cambridge: Cambridge University Press, 2007); and Davarian L. Baldwin and Minkah Makalani, eds., *Escape from New York: The New Negro Renaissance beyond Harlem* (Minneapolis: University of Minnesota Press, 2013).
114. Du Bois, *The Gift of Black Folk*, 284–85. See also Houston A. Baker Jr., *Blues, Ideology, and Afro-American Literature: A Vernacular Theory* (Chicago: University of Chicago Press, 1984); Angela Y. Davis, *Blues Legacies and Black Feminism: Gertrude "Ma" Rainey, Bessie Smith and Billie Holiday* (New York: Vintage Books, 1999); Andy Fry, *Paris Blues: African American Music and French Popular Culture, 1920–1960* (Chicago: University of Chicago Press, 2014); and Charles A. Riley, *Free as Gods: How the Jazz Age Reinvented Modernism* (Hanover, NH: ForeEdge, An imprint of University Press of New England, 2017).

115. W. C. Handy, *Father of the Blues: An Autobiography*, ed. Arna Bontemps (New York: Macmillan, 1944), 76, 77, 120. With its emphasis on entertainment, Handy's notion of folk blues is radically different from that imagined and venerated by many white revivalists during the 1960s.

116. Handy, 77.

117. Handy, 78–79.

118. Handy, 79.

119. Handy, 79.

120. Baker, *Modernism and the Harlem Renaissance*, 92.

121. Baker, 92.

122. See Baker, 68 on Du Bois's *Souls* as a "singing book." On Toomer, see David G. Nicholls, *Conjuring the Folk: Forms of Modernity in African America* (Ann Arbor: University of Michigan Press, 2000); Karen Jackson Ford, *Split-Gut Song: Jean Toomer and the Poetics of Modernity* (Tuscaloosa: University of Alabama Press, 2005); and Geneviève Fabre and Michel Feith, eds., *Jean Toomer and the Harlem Renaissance* (New Brunswick, NJ: Rutgers University Press, 2001).

123. Jean Toomer, letter "To the Editors of the *Liberator*, August 19, 1922," reproduced in *Cane: A Norton Critical Edition*, 2nd ed., ed. Rudolph P. Byrd and Henry Louis Gates Jr. (New York: W. W. Norton & Company, 2011), 155. Thank you, CW, for introducing me to this novel.

124. Jean Toomer, "The *Cane* Years" reproduced in *Cane*, 130.

125. Toomer,, 130.

126. Jean Toomer, letter "To Waldo Frank, Early to mid-January 1923," in *Cane*, 166.

127. Toomer, 166.

128. Toomer, 166.

129. Toomer, 166.

130. Toomer, 166.

131. Jean Toomer, "The Negro Emergent" [1924?] in *A Jean Toomer Reader: Selected Unpublished Writings*, ed. Frederik L. Rusch (New York: Oxford University Press, 1993), 88.

132. Toomer, *Cane*, 83, 96. On this mosaic technique, see Rachel Farebrother, "'Adventuring through the Pieces of a Still Unorganized Mosaic': Reading Jean Toomer's Collage Aesthetic in *Cane*," *Journal of American Studies* 40/3 (2006): 503–21.

133. Toomer, *Cane*, 31.

134. Toomer, 103.

135. Toomer, 6.

136. Toomer, from "Song of the Son" (1922), in *Cane*, 16.

137. Toomer, from "Georgia Dusk" (1922), in *Cane*, 17.

138. Zora Hurston, "Hoodoo in America," *Journal of American Folklore* 44/174 (1931): 317–417.

139. See Andrew Peart, "'The Abstract Pathos of Song': Carl Sandburg, John Lomax, and the Modernist Revival of Folksong," *New Literary History* 46/4 (2015): 691–714.

140. William G. Roy, *Reds, Whites, and Blues: Social Movements, Folk Music, and Race in the United States* (Princeton, NJ: Princeton University Press, 2010), 57.

141. Roy, 57.

## CHAPTER 5. SOUL THROUGH THE SOIL

1. See Woody Guthrie, *Bound for Glory* (London: Penguin, 2004). See also Robbie Lieberman, *"My Song Is My Weapon": People's Songs, American Communism, and the Politics of Culture, 1930–50* (Urbana: University of Illinois Press, 1989) and John S. Partington, ed., *The Life, Music and Thought of Woody Guthrie: A Critical Appraisal* (Abingdon, UK: Routledge, 2011).

2. I deal with MacColl's politics at greater length in Ross Cole, "Industrial Balladry, Mass Culture, and the Politics of Realism in Cold War Britain," *Journal of Musicology* 34/3 (2017): 354–90. See also Ben Harker, *Class Act: The Cultural and Political Life of Ewan MacColl* (London: Pluto, 2007).

3. G. A. Borgese, "The Intellectual Origins of Fascism," *Social Research* 1/1 (1934): 466.

4. Benito Mussolini, "The Political and Social Doctrine of Fascism," trans. Jane Soames, *Political Quarterly* 4/3 (1933): 342, 346–47.

5. Mussolini, 353. For context, see A. James Gregor, *Mussolini's Intellectuals: Fascist Social and Political Thought* (Princeton, NJ: Princeton University Press, 2005).

6. Borgese, "The Intellectual Origins of Fascism," 467.

7. "Occasional Notes," *Musical Times* 46/748 (1905): 383. A selection of these songs were published by the Folk-Song Society with annotations by Frank Kidson, Lucy Broadwood, and J. A. Fuller Maitland: see Cecil Sharp, "Folk-Songs Noted in Somerset and North Devon," *Journal of the Folk-Song Society* 2/6 (1905): 1–60. See also Cecil J. Sharp and Charles L. Marson, eds., *Folk Songs from Somerset*, (London: Simpkin & Co., 1904).

8. See Frederick Keel, "The Folk Song Society 1898–1948," *Journal of the English Folk Dance and Song Society* 5/3 (1948): 111–26.

9. "Annual Report, June, 1904," *Journal of the Folk-Song Society* 2/6 (1905): ix.

10. "*A Book of British Song for Home and School*. Edited by Cecil J. Sharp," *Musical Times* 44/719 (1903): 28.

11. Sharp, "Folk-Songs Noted," 1.

12. Sharp, 1.

13. "Mr. Cecil Sharp on Folk-Songs," *Musical Times* 47/755 (1906): 43.

14. Letter from Cecil J. Sharp published as a debate under the title "A Folk-Song Book Wanted," *Musical Opinion and Music Trade Review* 32/327 (1904): 190.

15. "English Folk-Song," *Musical Herald* 694 (1906): 10.

16. See "A Folk-Song Discussion," *Musical Times* 47/766 (1906): 806–9. These debates initially occurred in the correspondence pages of the *Morning Post* but were reported elsewhere.

17. Cecil J. Sharp, *English Folk-Song: Some Conclusions* (London: Simpkin & Co., 1907), x.

18. Sharp, x.

19. Sharp, 44; Cecil J. Sharp, "Some Characteristics of English Folk-Music," *Folklore* 19/2 (1908): 140.

20. Sharp, *English Folk-Song*, 3–4.

21. Sharp, "Folk-Songs Noted," 2–3; Sharp, *English Folk-Song*, 8.

22. Cecil J. Sharp, "Folk-Song Collecting," *Musical Times* 48/767 (1907): 16; "The Stratford-On-Avon Festival," *Musical Times* 51/811 (1910): 596.

23. Sharp, *English Folk-Song*, 127.

24. Sharp, 130.

25. Sharp, 135–36.

26. Sharp, 135.

27. Sharp, 136. Emphasis added.

28. Sharp, 137. See Hubert Parry, "Inaugural Address," *Journal of the Folk-Song Society* 1/1 (1899): 1–3. See also John Carey, *The Intellectuals and the Masses: Pride and Prejudice among the Literary Intelligentsia, 1880–1939* (London: Faber and Faber, 1992) and Andreas Huyssen, *After the Great Divide: Modernism, Mass Culture and Postmodernism* (Basingstoke: Macmillan, 1988). I discuss this further in Ross Cole, "Notes on Troubling 'the Popular,'" *Popular Music* 37/3 (2018): 392–414.

29. R. Murray Schafer, *The Soundscape: Our Sonic Environment and the Tuning of the World* (Rochester, VT: Destiny Books, 1994), 3, 7, 12.

30. Sharp, *English Folk-Song*, 132.

31. Sharp, 134, 132, 136.

32. Sharp, 133. On this theme, see Maureen N. McLane, *Balladeering, Minstrelsy, and the Making of British Romantic Poetry* (Cambridge: Cambridge University Press, 2008) and Nick Groom, *The Making of Percy's "Reliques"* (Oxford: Oxford University Press, 1999).

33. Sharp believed that the last English folk singers had been born around 1840.

34. *Peasant* was a term regularly used by folk song enthusiasts: see Arthur Knevett and Vic Gammon, "English Folk Song Collectors and the Idea of the Peasant," *Folk Music Journal* 11/1 (2016): 42–64.

35. See Roy Palmer, "Kitchen, (William) Frederick [1890–1969]," *Oxford Dictionary of National Biography*, Oxford University Press, http://www.oxforddnb.com/view/article/71087, accessed 1 July 2017.

36. Fred Kitchen, *Brother to the Ox: The Autobiography of a Farm Labourer* (Harmondsworth, UK: Penguin, 1983), 11, 151.

37. Kitchen, 59–60. Kitchen's book holds a particular appeal for me personally, as my great grandfather George Powell, also a farm laborer, lived with his family in Ollerton, just two miles to the east of Edwinstowe on the edge of Sherwood Forest. I like to imagine they knew each other.

38. These latter two ballads are accessible via the online collection of Oxford's Bodleian Library: http://ballads.bodleian.ox.ac.uk/view/edition/5431; http://ballads.bodleian.ox.ac.uk/view/edition/4508, accessed 27 March 2017.

On this history, see: Adam Fox, *Oral and Literate Culture in England 1500–1700* (Oxford: Oxford University Press, 2000); Christopher Marsh, *Music and Society in Early Modern England* (Cambridge: Cambridge University Press, 2010); Paula McDowell, *The Invention of the Oral: Print Commerce and Fugitive Voices in Eighteenth-Century Britain* (Chicago: University of Chicago Press, 2017); and Paul Watt, Derek B. Scott, and Patrick Spedding, eds., *Cheap Print and Popular Song in the Nineteenth Century: A Cultural History of the Songster* (Cambridge: Cambridge University Press, 2017).

39. Kitchen, *Brother to the Ox*, 149.

40. Kitchen, 125.

41. Folk-Song Society, "Hints to Collectors of Folk Music," *Folklore* 19/2 (1908): 149. This document was published as an appendix to Sharp's paper "Some Characteristics of English Folk-Music," along with a prospectus and sample "Leaflet to Clergy" written by Lucy Broadwood.

42. Lucy E. Broadwood, "On the Collecting of English Folk-Song," *Proceedings of the Musical Association* 31 (1904–5): 90.

43. Frank Kidson, "English Folk-Song," *Musical Times* 49/779 (1908): 23.

44. Kidson, 23. On this point, see also John Francmanis, "National Music to National Redeemer: The Consolidation of a 'Folk-Song' Construct in Edwardian England," *Popular Music* 21/1 (2002): 1–25.

45. "A Folk-Song Discussion," 807.

46. "A Folk-Song Discussion," 807.

47. C. S. Myers, "*English Folk-Song: Some Conclusions*. By Cecil J. Sharp," *Folklore* 20/1 (1909): 98.

48. Myers, 99.

49. J. A. Fuller Maitland, "English Folk-Song," *Times Literary Supplement*, 23 January 1908, 26.

50. Maitland, 26.

51. Maitland, 26.

52. Edward W. Said, *Culture and Imperialism* (London: Vintage,1994), 1. See also Paul Gilroy, *The Black Atlantic: Modernity and Double Consciousness* (London: Verso, 1993) and Homi K. Bhabha, *The Location of Culture* (London: Routledge, 2004).

53. Edward Baughan, "A Plea for Cosmopolitanism," *Monthly Musical Record* 28/326 (1898): 25.

54. Baughan, 25.

55. Baughan, 25.

56. Baughan, 26.

57. "The Folk-Song Obsession," *Observer*, 26 May 1912, 5.

58. Ernest Newman, "The Folk-Song Fallacy," *English Review* 11 (1912): 266.

59. Newman, 257–58.

60. Newman, 266–67.

61. Newman, 264. For illustrations of this point, see Adam Fox, "The Emergence of the Scottish Broadside Ballad in the Late Seventeenth and Early Eighteenth Centuries," *Journal of Scottish Historical Studies* 31/2 (2011): 169–94,

and Matthew Gelbart, "Allan Ramsay, The Idea of 'Scottish Music' and the Beginnings of 'National Music' in Europe," *Eighteenth-Century Music* 9/1 (2012): 81–108.

62. Newman, "The Folk-Song Fallacy," 261, 263. On the convoluted history of the noble savage, see Ter Ellingson, *The Myth of the Noble Savage* (Berkeley: University of California Press, 2001).

63. Cecil J. Sharp, "'The Folk-Song Fallacy': A Reply," *English Review* 12 (1912): 542.

64. Sharp, 543.

65. Sharp, 545.

66. Sharp, 545–46.

67. Ernest Newman, "The Folk-Song Fallacy: A Rejoinder," *English Review* 12 (1912): 66.

68. Sharp, "'The Folk-Song Fallacy,'" 550.

69. Board of Education, *Suggestions for the Consideration of Teachers and Others Concerned in the Work of Public Elementary Schools* (London: Darling & Son., 1905), 70.

70. Sabine Baring-Gould and Cecil J. Sharp, eds., *English Folk-Songs for Schools* (London: J. Curwen & Sons., 1906), iii.

71. Board of Education, *Suggestions for the Consideration of Teachers*, 71; Baring-Gould and Sharp, *English Folk-Songs*, iii.

72. G. C., "English Folk-Songs for Schools," *Musical Standard* 26/658 (1906): 93.

73. The Folk-Song Society's Annual Report of 1908–09, for example, listed the areas covered by collectors: "BERKS: Mr. C. Sharp. DEVONSHIRE: Mr. C. Sharp. ESSEX: Dr. Vaughan Williams. GLOUCESTERSHIRE: Mr. C. Sharp, Mr. Percy Grainger. HEREFORDSHIRE: Mrs. Leather, Dr. V. Williams. HAMPSHIRE: Dr. G. B. Gardiner. KENT: Mr. C. Sharp, Mr. Percy Grainger. LANCASHIRE (North): Miss Gilchrist. LONDON: Mr. C. Sharp. OXFORDSHIRE: Mr. C. Sharp. RUTLANDSHIRE: Mr. C. Sharp. SURREY: Dr. G. B. Gardiner, Mr. C. Sharp. SOMERSET: Mr. C. Sharp. SUSSEX: Mr. G. S. Kaye Butterworth. WESTMORLAND: Miss Gilchrist. WARWICKSHIRE: Mr. C. Sharp. Wiltshire: Dr. G. B. Gardiner. YORKSHIRE: Miss Gilchrist." In addition, it continues: "the work of Mr. Cecil Sharp and Mr. MacIlwaine in collecting and recording Morris Dances and Tunes also deserves to be chronicled, especially in view of the interesting announcement from the Board of Education that these are now to be included in the curriculum of the Elementary Schools." See "Annual Report, June, 1908–09," *Journal of the Folk-Song Society* 4/14 (1910): iv. See also Cecil J. Sharp, "Folk-Dancing in Elementary and Secondary Schools," *School Music Review* 1 (December 1912): 162–65; Vic Gammon, "'Many Useful Lessons': Cecil Sharp, Education and the Folk Dance Revival, 1899–1924," *Cultural and Social History* 5/1 (2008): 75–97; and Daniel J. Walkowitz, *City Folk: English Country Dance and the Politics of the Folk in Modern America* (New York: New York University Press, 2010).

74. Percy A. Scholes, "Cecil Sharp," *Observer*, 29 June 1924, 10.

75. Scholes, 10.

76. Sharp, *English Folk-Song*, 140.

77. Frank Kidson and Mary Neal, *English Folk-Song and Dance* (Cambridge: Cambridge University Press, 1915), 47.

78. Lucy E. Broadwood, Letter to Bertha Broadwood from 41 Drayton Court, 22 July 1924 (Surrey History Centre, Ref.2297/9).

79. "Mr. Cecil Sharp," *Musical Times* 53/836 (1912): 639; W. G. McN., "The Cult of Folk-Song and Dance," *Musical Times* 53/835 (1912): 602.

80. Phillips Barry, for instance, cites *English Folk-Song* during the article in which he first uses the phrase "communal re-creation." See Phillips Barry, "Folk-Music in America," *Journal of American Folk-lore* 22/83 (1909): 77.

81. Maud Karpeles, *Cecil Sharp: His Life and Work* (London: Faber & Faber, 2008), 146–47. On this topic, see Max Nordau, *Entartung* [Degeneration], ed. Karin Tebben (Berlin: De Gruyter, 2013).

82. Cecil J. Sharp, unpublished diary (8 December 1918), 342, Vaughan Williams Memorial Library, https://www.vwml.org/vwml-projects/vwml-cecil-sharp-diaries, accessed 28 November 2017.

83. Sharp (31 August 1918), 243.

84. Sharp (2 May 1918), 122.

85. Evelyn K. Wells, "Cecil Sharp in America," *Journal of the English Folk Dance and Song Society* 8/4 (1959): 182–84.

86. Charles Peabody, "The English Folk-Dance Society and Its Work," *Journal of American Folk-Lore* 28/109 (1915): 316.

87. "Resolutions: Definition of Folk Music and Folk Music in Education," *Journal of the International Folk Music Council* 7 (1955): 23.

88. "Resolutions," 23.

89. "Resolutions," 23.

90. "Folk-Songs from Somerset," *Academy*, 17 August 1907, 801.

91. John Masefield, "On Folk Songs," *The Speaker*, 23 December 1905, 302, 301.

92. Myers, "English Folk-Song," 99.

93. Sharp, "Folk-Dancing," 164.

94. Karpeles, *Cecil Sharp*, 19.

95. "Basis of the Fabian Society," in *The Fabian Society Report for the Year Ended March 1891* (London: Fabian Society, 1891), 3. Fabian Tracts were published anonymously; many, however, were by George Bernard Shaw or Sidney Webb (partner of Beatrice Webb). Webb would later draft "clause 4" of the British Labour Party's constitution. For an overview of the Society's views, see George Bernard Shaw, ed., *Fabian Essays in Socialism* (London: Fabian Society 1889).

96. *Facts for Socialists from the Political Economists & Statisticians* [Fabian Tract No. 5] (London: Fabian Society, 1890), 16.

97. *What Socialism Is* [Fabian Tract No. 13] (London: Fabian Society, 1890), 3.

98. See *A Manifesto* [Fabian Tract No. 2] (London: Fabian Society, 1884) and Karpeles, *Cecil Sharp*, 20.

99. Letter to Charles Sharp, 31 January 1918, quoted in Karpeles, 19.

100. Mussolini, "The Political and Social Doctrine of Fascism," 347.

101. Letter dated 26 June 1893, quoted in Karpeles, *Cecil Sharp*, 19.

102. John Clifford, *Socialism and the Teaching of Christ* [Fabian Tract No. 78] (London: Fabian Society, 1897), 10.

103. Clifford, 11.

104. Karpeles, *Cecil Sharp*, 19.

105. Matthew Johnson, "The Liberal Party and the Navy League in Britain before the Great War," *Twentieth Century British History* 22/2 (2011): 140.

106. See Karpeles, *Cecil Sharp*, 18–19.

107. Zeev Sternhell, *Neither Right nor Left: Fascist Ideology in France*, trans. David Maisel (Princeton, NJ: Princeton University Press, 1986), xviii; Zeev Sternhell with Mario Sznajder and Maia Asheri, *The Birth of Fascist Ideology: From Cultural Rebellion to Political Revolution*, trans. David Maisel (Princeton, NJ: Princeton University Press, 1994), 3.

108. Sharp, unpublished diary (1 January 1918), 1.

109. Sharp, unpublished diary (5 March 1918), 64. The official transcription on the VWML website is unfortunately incorrect on the spelling of names in this passage.

110. Sternhell, *Neither Right nor Left*, 272.

111. Sternhell, 27.

112. Sternhell, 27.

113. Sternhell, 303, 271.

114. Sternhell, 271. On the Edwardian revival's misogyny, see Georgina Boyes, *The Imagined Village: Culture, Ideology and the English Folk Revival* (Manchester: Manchester University Press, 1993).

115. See Matthew Jefferies and Mike Tyldesley, ed., *Rolf Gardiner: Folk, Nature and Culture in Interwar Britain* (Farnham, UK: Ashgate, 2011).

116. Sharp, *English Folk-Song*, 89–90.

117. Fuller Maitland, "English Folk-Song."

118. "Arian" in *Cyclopædia of India and of Eastern and Southern Asia*, 2nd ed., ed. Edward Balfour, Vol. 1 (Madras: Scottish and Adelphi Presses, 1871): 179.

119. "Arian," 183. This theme is explored at greater length in Michael G. Hanchard, *The Spectre of Race: How Discrimination Haunts Western Democracy* (Princeton, NJ: Princeton University Press, 2018).

120. See, for instance, "The Arian Race," *Calcutta Review*, June 1856: 479. Many thanks to Peter Asimov for his generosity in helping me to understand this aspect of Sharp's work.

121. Sharp, *English Folk-Song*, 36.

122. Sharp, unpublished diary (19 February 1916), unpaged; see also unpublished diary (7 November 1918), 311. Sharp knew Ananda and Alice Coomaraswamy (who performed Hindu songs under the stage name Ratan Devī) through his travels to the United States, and met them on several occasions.

123. *Des recueils nombreux de mélodies populaires de ces différents pays permettent de constater chez toutes, au point de vue* modal *et* rythmique, *un air de famille évident. Il parait aujourd'hui démontré que des caractères identiques se retrouvent dans la musique primitive de tous les peuples qui composent le groupe indo-européen, c'est-à-dire de race âryenne. . . . Aujourd'hui, l'étude des*

*chants populaires apporte à la conscience de l'unité âryenne un argument nouveau: l'argument musical.*

Louis-Albert Bourgault-Ducoudray, *Trente Mélodies Populaires de Basse-Bretagne* (Paris: Henry Lemoine, 1885), 14–16. Author's translation.

124. Bourgault-Ducoudray, 11.

125. Hannah Arendt, *The Origins of Totalitarianism* (London: Penguin, 2017), 294. See also Michael Wildt, *Hitler's* Volksgemeinschaft *and the Dynamics of Racial Exclusion: Violence against Jews in Provincial Germany, 1919–1939*, trans. Bernard Heise (New York: Berghahn Books, 2014).

126. Miriam Beard, "The Tune Hitlerism Beats for Germany: It Sets the Street Vibrating to Wotan and Valhalla and Stirs the 'Unknown Folk' of Village and Countryside," *New York Times*, 7 June 1931, 7 and 21.

127. Beard, 7.

128. Beard, 7.

129. Beard, 7. For an extended critique of racialized nationalism, see Paul Gilroy, *Against Race: Imagining Political Culture Beyond the Color Line* (Cambridge, MA: Belknap Press, 2000).

130. Rolf Gardiner, "D. H. Lawrence and the Youth Movements of the Twenties" (privately printed and circulated by Gardiner, 1959), cited in Walter Z. Laqueur, *Young Germany: A History of the German Youth Movement* (New York: Basic Books, 1962), 241.

131. Rolf Gardiner and Heinz Rocholl, eds., *Britain and Germany: A Frank Discussion Instigated by Members of the Younger Generation* (London: Williams and Norgate, 1928), 130. There are a number of revealing parallels between Sharp's ideas and the discourse surrounding music in Oswald Mosley's British Union of Fascists: see Graham Macklin, "'Onward Blackshirts!' Music and the British Union of Fascists," *Patterns of Prejudice* 47/4–5 (2013): 430–57. See also Julie V. Gottlieb and Thomas P. Linehan, eds., *The Culture of Fascism: Visions of the Far Right in Britain*, (London: I.B. Tauris, 2004).

132. Beard, "The Tune Hitlerism Beats for Germany," 7. See Michael H. Kater, *Hitler Youth* (Cambridge, MA: Harvard University Press, 2004). On this period, see also Richard J. Evans, *The Coming of the Third Reich* (New York: Penguin, 2003) and Ian Kershaw, *Hitler, The Germans, and the Final Solution* (New Haven, CT: Yale University Press, 2008).

133. Beard, "The Tune Hitlerism Beats for Germany," 7.

134. Beard, 7.

135. Beard, 21.

136. Beard, 21.

137. Mussolini, "The Political and Social Doctrine of Fascism," 353.

138. Mussolini, 346. On this topic, see Eden K. McLean, *Mussolini's Children: Race and Elementary Education in Fascist Italy* (Lincoln: University of Nebraska Press, 2018).

139. Zeev Sternhell, *The Anti-Enlightenment Tradition*, trans. David Maisel (New Haven, CT: Yale University Press, 2010), 16.

140. Raymond Williams, *The Country and the City* (London: Chatto & Windus, 1973), 35–36.

141. Sharp, *English Folk-Song*, viii.

142. Robert O. Paxton, *The Anatomy of Fascism* (London: Penguin, 2005), 17. Roger Griffin has termed this form of rebirth "palingenesis"; Roger Griffin, *The Nature of Fascism* (London: Routledge, 1993).

143. Sharp, "'The Folk-Song Fallacy,'" 544.

144. Sharp, *English Folk-Song*, 1.

145. Sharp, 1.

146. Sharp, 2–3, 32.

147. T. S. Eliot, "The Ballet," *The Criterion* 3/11 (April 1925): 441. See Cecil J. Sharp and A. P. Oppé, *The Dance: An Historical Survey of Dancing in Europe* (London: Halton and Truscott Smith Ltd., 1924).

148. Eliot, "The Ballet," 442.

149. Eliot, 442.

150. Eliot, 442.

151. Eliot, 442.

152. Eliot, 442.

153. Eliot, 442.

154. Eliot, 443.

155. On the intersection of fascism and the petty bourgeoisie, see Leon Trotsky, "The Political Programs of the Petty Bourgeoisie," *The Militant* 5/36 (3 September 1932): 1 and 4 and Wilhelm Reich, *The Mass Psychology of Fascism*, trans. Vincent R. Carfagno (New York: The Noonday Press, 1970).

156. Sternhell, *Neither Right nor Left*, 213

157. Sternhell, 214.

158. Sternhell, 214.

159. Sharp, *English Folk-Song*, 134, 140.

160. Robert H. Hull, "The Folk-Song Movement," *Musical Times* 70/1038 (1929): 712.

## CODA

1. Bob Dylan, *The Nobel Lecture* (London: Simon & Schuster, 2017), 3. There are echoes here of John Lomax's attitude to Lead Belly, aka Huddie Ledbetter, during the 1930s: see, for instance, John A. Lomax and Alan Lomax, *Negro Folk Songs as Sung by Lead Belly* (New York: Macmillan, 1936). See also Nolan Porterfield, *Last Cavalier: The Life and Times of John A. Lomax, 1867–1948* (Urbana: University of Illinois Press, 1996) and Benjamin Filene, *Romancing the Folk: Public Memory and American Roots Music* (Chapel Hill: University of North Carolina Press, 2000).

2. Dylan, *The Nobel Lecture*, 4.

3. Dylan, 5.

4. Marcel Proust, *In Search of Lost Time, V: The Captive; The Fugitive*, trans. C. K. Scott Moncrieff and Terence Kilmartin, rev. D. J. Enright (London: Vintage Books, 2000), 29–30. I borrow the term *retrotopian* from Zygmunt Bauman, *Retrotopia* (Cambridge: Polity Press, 2017).

5. Proust, *In Search of Lost Time, V*, 30. See, of course, Benedict Anderson, *Imagined Communities: Reflections on the Origins and Spread of Nationalism*, rev. ed. (London: Verso, 2006).

6. Katharine Ellis, *Interpreting the Musical Past: Early Music in Nineteenth-Century France* (New York: Oxford University Press, 2005), 163–64.

7. Proust, *In Search of Lost Time, V*, 31.

8. Proust, 33.

9. Proust, 39. More broadly, see Jane F. Fulcher, *French Cultural Politics and Music: From the Dreyfus Affair to the First World War* (New York: Oxford University Press, 1999).

10. On this history, see Zeev Sternhell, *Neither Right nor Left: Fascist Ideology in France*, trans. David Maisel (Princeton, NJ: Princeton University Press, 1986) and Hannah Arendt, *The Origins of Totalitarianism* (London: Penguin, 2017).

11. Brendan Joel Kelley, "The Alt-Right's New Soundtrack of Hate," *Hatewatch*, 9 October 2017, https://www.splcenter.org/hatewatch/2017/10/09/alt-right's-new-soundtrack-hate, accessed 25 October 2019.

12. Trey Knickerbocker, "An Interview with Paddy Tarleton: The Volkish Folk Singer," Culture section of altright.com, 2017, https://altright.com/2017/06/28/an-interview-with-paddy-tarleton-the-volkish-folk-singer, accessed 25 October 2019. On whiteness, see Richard Dyer, *White* (London: Routledge, 1997).

13. Knickerbocker, "An Interview with Paddy Tarleton."

14. Knickerbocker.

15. Knickerbocker. Sharp's views are discussed in chapter 5; see also Cecil J. Sharp, *English Folk-Song: Some Conclusions* (London: Simpkin & Co., 1907).

16. On these different species of nationalism, see James G. Kellas, *The Politics of Nationalism and Ethnicity*, 2nd ed. (Basingstoke, UK: Macmillan, 1998), 65–88.

17. https://theorthodoxnationalist.wordpress.com, https://www.rusjournal.org, accessed 28 October 2019.

18. "Author Spotlight: About Matthew Raphael Johnson," http://www.lulu.com/spotlight/DeiparaFrRaphael, accessed 28 October 2019; https://www.rusjournal.org.

19. See Arendt, *The Origins of Totalitarianism*, 36.

20. https://www.rusjournal.org.

21. See Sternhell, *Neither Right nor Left*, 272.

22. Knickerbocker, "An Interview with Paddy Tarleton."

23. Knickerbocker. For a point of comparison, see Hubert Parry, "Inaugural Address," *Journal of the Folk-Song Society* 1/1 (1899): 1–3, discussed in chapter 2.

24. See Ben Harker, *Class Act: The Cultural and Political Life of Ewan MacColl* (London: Pluto Press, 2007) and Allan F. Moore and Giovanni Vacca, eds., *Legacies of Ewan MacColl: The Last Interview* (Farnham, UK: Ashgate, 2014).

25. Ewan MacColl, *Journeyman: An Autobiography* (London: Sidgwick and Jackson, 1990), 337.

26. MacColl, 340–41, 338.

27. On this point in relation to MacColl, see Ross Cole, "Industrial Balladry, Mass Culture, and the Politics of Realism in Cold War Britain," *Journal of Musicology* 34/3 (2017): 354–90.

28. Knickerbocker, "An Interview with Paddy Tarleton."

29. Knickerbocker.

30. Arendt, *The Origins of Totalitarianism*, 296.

31. Arendt, 296; see also 303.

32. Benito Mussolini, "The Political and Social Doctrine of Fascism," trans. Jane Soames, *Political Quarterly* 4/3 (1933): 346.

33. Kellas, *The Politics of Nationalism and Ethnicity*, 66.

34. Knickerbocker, "An Interview with Paddy Tarleton." For Sharp's views on this subject, see Maud Karpeles, *Cecil Sharp: His Life and Work* (London: Faber & Faber, 2008), 140–71.

35. Knickerbocker, "An Interview With Paddy Tarleton."

36. Knickerbocker.

37. See, for instance, Max Nordau, *Entartung* [Degeneration], ed. Karin Tebben (Berlin: De Gruyter, 2013) and Richard Soloway, *Demography and Degeneration: Eugenics and the Declining Birthrate in Twentieth-Century Britain* (Chapel Hill: University of North Carolina Press, 1995).

38. Knickerbocker, "An Interview with Paddy Tarleton."

39. Anderson, *Imagined Communities*, 5.

40. Eric Hobsbawm, "Mass-Producing Traditions: Europe, 1870–1914," in *The Invention of Tradition*, ed. Eric Hobsbawm and Terence Ranger (Cambridge: Cambridge University Press, 1983): 303, 263.

41. Jacques Derrida, *Specters of Marx: The State of the Debt, the Work of Mourning and the New International*, trans. Peggy Kamuf (New York: Routledge, 1994), 136.

42. Knickerbocker, "An Interview with Paddy Tarleton."

43. Knickerbocker.

44. https://twitter.com/realdonaldtrump/status/1150381395078000643, accessed 29 October 2019.

45. Andrew Anglin, "Trump Tells Brown Communist Democrats to Leave America, Return to Their Shitholes," *Daily Stormer*, 15 July 2019, https://dailystormer.name/trump-tells-brown-communist-democrats-to-leave-america-return-to-their-shitholes, accessed 29 October 2019. Thanks to Eliot Weinberger for this reference in "One Summer in America," *London Review of Books* 41/18 (2019): 11–18.

46. See Ashley Feinberg, "This Is the *Daily Stormer*'s Playbook," *Huffington Post*, 13 December 2017, https://www.huffingtonpost.co.uk/entry/daily-stormer-nazi-style-guide_n_5a2ece19e4b0ce3b344492f2, accessed 1 March 2020. All quotations in the paragraph are from this style guide (unpaged).

47. Slavoj Žižek, *For They Know Not What They Do: Enjoyment as a Political Factor* (London: Verso, 2008), 18.

48. Arendt, *The Origins of Totalitarianism*, 615.

49. Anglin suggests that the alt-right learn from 1960s activists by reading Saul Alinsky's *Rules for Radicals: A Practical Primer for Realistic Radicals* (New York: Random House, 1971), a book intended as a leftist manual for working-class "have-nots" to destabilize power from below.

50. https://www.bitchute.com/video/ImoVKAu2IMVb, accessed 29 October 2019.

51. Thanks to Adam Behan for pointing out this connection after a talk I gave in Cambridge in February 2020. For context, see D. M. Leeson, *The Black and Tans: British Police and Auxiliaries in the Irish War of Independence, 1920–1921* (Oxford: Oxford University Press, 2011).

52. On the nexus of ideas revived by this theory, see Soloway, *Demography and Degeneration*; Daniel J. Kevles, *In the Name of Eugenics: Genetics and the Uses of Human Heredity* (Cambridge, MA: Harvard University Press, 1995); and Alison Bashford and Philippa Levine, eds., *The Oxford Handbook of the History of Eugenics* (New York: Oxford University Press, 2010).

53. Susan Sontag, "What's Happening to America (A Symposium)," *Partisan Review* 34/1 (1967): 57–58. See also Theodore Roszak, *The Making of a Counter Culture: Reflections on the Technocratic Society and its Youthful Opposition* (Berkeley: University of California Press, 1995) and Peter Braunstein and Michael W. Doyle, eds., *Imagine Nation: The American Counterculture of the 1960s and '70s* (New York: Routledge, 2002).

54. See Renaud Camus, *Le Grand Remplacement* (Neuilly-sur-Seine: D. Reinharc, 2011) and Eric Kaufmann, *White Shift: Populism, Immigration and the Future of White Majorities* (London: Allen Lane, 2018).

55. A. Dirk Moses, "'White Genocide' and the Ethics of Public Analysis," *Journal of Genocide Research* 21/2 (2019): 212.

56. Matthew Raphael Johnson, "Open Letter to the Orthodox, Clerical Authors of the 'Statement Concerning the Sin of Racism'" (Revised, September 2019), accessed 28 October 2019. This revised version from which I am quoting here is no longer available online. The original document can be found at https://theorthodoxnationalist.files.wordpress.com/2018/06/race_orthodoxy.pdf.

57. Johnson.

58. On this point, see Bruno Latour, "Why Has Critique Run Out of Steam? From Matters of Fact to Matters of Concern," *Critical Inquiry* 30/2 (2004): 225–48 and Jacques Rancière, *The Emancipated Spectator*, trans. Gregory Elliott (London: Verso, 2009).

59. See https://www.bitchute.com/video/ImoVKAu2IMVb, accessed 29 October 2019. For an excellent definition of racism, see: "Declaration on Race and Racial Prejudice," Adopted and proclaimed by the General Conference of the United Nations Educational, Scientific and Cultural Organization at its twentieth session, on 27 November 1978, https://www.un.org/ruleoflaw/blog/document/declaration-on-race-and-racial-prejudice, accessed 29 October 2019.

60. Michael Wildt, *Hitler's* Volksgemeinschaft *and the Dynamics of Racial Exclusion: Violence against Jews in Provincial Germany, 1919–1939*, trans. Bernard Heise (New York: Berghahn Books, 2014), 9, 17.

61. See Stephen Jay Gould, *The Mismeasure of Man*, revised and expanded ed. (New York: W. W. Norton, 1996); Paul Gilroy, *Against Race: Imagining Political Culture beyond the Color Line* (Cambridge, MA: Belknap Press of Harvard University Press, 2000); and Michael Omi and Howard Winant, *Racial Formation in the United States*, 3rd ed. (New York: Routledge, 2015).

62. Gould, *The Mismeasure of Man*, 61.

63. Gilroy, *Against Race*, 37. See also Gregory Claeys, "The 'Survival of the Fittest' and the Origins of Social Darwinism," *Journal of the History of Ideas*

61/2 (2000): 223–40. Musicology is indebted to these discourses of difference: see Rachel Mundy, "Evolutionary Categories and Musical Style from Adler to America," *Journal of the American Musicological Society* 67/3 (2014): 735–67 and Bennett Zon, *Evolution and Victorian Musical Culture* (Cambridge: Cambridge University Press, 2017).

64. Arendt, *The Origins of Totalitarianism*, 241.

65. Arif Dirlik, "Race Talk, Race, and Contemporary Racism," *PMLA* 123/5 (2008): 1374.

66. Edward W. Said, *Culture and Imperialism* (London: Vintage, 1994), 1.

67. Knickerbocker, "An Interview with Paddy Tarleton."

68. Gerhard Kubik, *Africa and the Blues* (Jackson: University Press of Mississippi, 1999), 16.

69. See Katrina Dyonne Thompson, *Ring Shout, Wheel About: The Racial Politics of Music and Dance in North American Slavery* (Urbana: University of Illinois Press, 2014) and Karen Linn, *That Half-Barbaric Twang: The Banjo in American Popular Culture* (Urbana: University of Illinois Press, 1991).

70. On this southern history, see Ronald Radano, *Lying Up a Nation: Race and Black Music* (Chicago: University of Chicago Press, 2003) and Karl Hagstrom Miller, *Segregating Sound: Inventing Folk and Pop Music in the Age of Jim Crow* (Durham, NC: Duke University Press, 2010). More broadly, see Eric Lott, *Love and Theft: Blackface Minstrelsy and the American Working Class*, twentieth anniversary ed. (New York: Oxford University Press, 2013); Karen Sotiropoulos, *Staging Race: Black Performers in Turn of the Century America* (Cambridge, MA: Harvard University Press, 2006); and J. Griffith Rollefson, "'He's Calling His Flock Now': Black Music and Postcoloniality from Buddy Bolden's New Orleans to Sefyu's Paris," *American Music* 33/3 (2015): 375–97.

71. Knickerbocker, "An Interview with Paddy Tarleton."

72. Knickerbocker.

73. https://www.youtube.com/watch?v=CLuPE49zk2w, accessed 31 October 2019. See Robbie Lieberman, *"My Song Is My Weapon": People's Songs, American Communism, and the Politics of Culture, 1930–50* (Urbana: University of Illinois Press, 1989); Richard A. Reuss with JoAnne C. Reuss, *American Folk Music and Left-Wing Politics, 1927–57* (Lanham, MD: Scarecrow Press, 2000); and William G. Roy, *Reds, Whites, and Blues: Social Movements, Folk Music, and Race in the United States* (Princeton, NJ: Princeton University Press, 2010).

74. William Pierce, "Fashion for Genocide," *American Dissident Voices* radio program, 26 September 1998, https://natall.com/adv/98/092698.txt, accessed 31 October 2019.

75. https://www.youtube.com/watch?v=CLuPE49zk2w; see also https://www.adl.org/education/references/hate-symbols/14-words, accessed 31 October 2019.

76. https://www.youtube.com/watch?v=J7jRzGfZFUg, accessed 31 October 2019. "Wobbly" refers to members of the revolutionary labor union Industrial Workers of the World, founded in Chicago in 1905. See Melvyn Dubofsky, *We Shall Be All: A History of the Industrial Workers of the World*, ed. Joseph A. McCartin (Urbana: University of Illinois Press, 2000) and Peter Cole, David

Struthers, and Kenyon Zimmer, eds., *Wobblies of the World: A Global History of the IWW* (London: Pluto Press, 2017).

77. https://www.youtube.com/watch?v=J7jRzGfZFUg; https://www.youtube.com/watch?v=lFgJSJneihM, accessed 31 October 2019.

78. Dylan describes some of his early work as "finger-pointing" in Nat Hentoff, "Bob Dylan, the Wanderer," *New Yorker*, 16 October 1964, https://www.newyorker.com/magazine/1964/10/24/the-crackin-shakin-breakin-sounds, accessed 31 October 2019.

79. https://www.youtube.com/watch?v=lFgJSJneihM, accessed 31 October 2019.

80. https://www.youtube.com/watch?v=66gSYseg5jI, accessed 31 October 2019.

81. Phil Ochs, *Phil Ochs in Concert*, Elektra Records (1966). See Michael Schumacher, *There but for Fortune: The Life of Phil Ochs* (Minneapolis: University of Minnesota Press, 2018). More broadly, see Maurice Isserman and Michael Kazin, *America Divided: The Civil War of the 1960s*, 5th ed. (New York: Oxford University Press, 2015); Todd Gitlin, *The Sixties: Years of Hope, Days of Rage*, rev. ed. (New York: Bantam Press, 1993); and Phil Ford, "Hip Sensibility in an Age of Mass Counterculture," *Jazz Perspectives* 2/2 (2008): 121–63.

82. On systems in 1960s discourse, see Howard Brick, *Age of Contradiction: American Thought and Culture in the 1960s* (Ithaca, NY: Cornell University Press, 1998).

83. See Zeev Sternhell, *The Anti-Enlightenment Tradition*, trans. David Maisel (New Haven, CT: Yale University Press, 2010).

84. Anderson, *Imagined Communities*, 3.

85. This is a reference, of course, to Woody Guthrie's "This Land Is Your Land," a song originally penned in satirical response to Irving Berlin's "God Bless America." See Ed Cray, *Ramblin' Man: The Life and Times of Woody Guthrie* (New York: W. W. Norton, 2004).

86. Svetlana Boym, *The Future of Nostalgia* (New York: Basic Books, 2001), 43.

87. Boym, 43. Useful in this regard is https://rationalwiki.org/wiki/Alt-right_glossary, accessed 31 October 2019.

88. Boym, *The Future of Nostalgia*, 43.

89. Boym, 43. Folk music and the study of folk music were indeed used to support the Third Reich: see Pamela Potter, "Musicology under Hitler: New Sources in Context," *Journal of the American Musicological Society* 49/1 (1996): 70–113.

# Bibliography

Abrahams, Roger D. "Mr Lomax Meets Professor Kittredge." *Journal of Folklore Research* 37/2–3 (2000): 99–118.

Achinstein, Peter, ed. *Science Rules: A Historical Introduction to Scientific Methods*. Baltimore: Johns Hopkins University Press, 2004.

Adelt, Ulrich. *Blues Music in the Sixties: A Story in Black and White*. New Brunswick, NJ: Rutgers University Press, 2010.

Adler, Hans, and Wulf Koepke, eds. *A Companion to the Works of Johann Gottfried Herder*. Rochester, NY: Camden House, 2009.

Adorno, Theodor W. *Essays on Music*. Edited by Richard Leppert. Berkeley: University of California Press, 2002.

Adorno, Theodor W., and Max Horkheimer. *Dialectic of Enlightenment*. Translated by John Cumming. London: Verso, 1997.

Agawu, Kofi. *Representing African Music: Postcolonial Notes, Queries, Positions*. New York: Routledge, 2003.

Alinsky, Saul. *Rules for Radicals: A Practical Primer for Realistic Radicals*. New York: Random House, 1971.

Anderson, Benedict. *Imagined Communities: Reflections on the Origins and Spread of Nationalism*, rev. ed. London: Verso, 2006.

Anderson, Paul Allen. *Deep River: Music and Memory in Harlem Renaissance Thought*. Durham, NC: Duke University Press, 2001.

Anderson, Toni P. *"Tell Them We Are Singing for Jesus": The Original Fisk Jubilee Singers and Christian Reconstruction, 1871–1878*. Macon, GA: Mercer University Press, 2010.

Arendt, Hannah. *The Origins of Totalitarianism*. London: Penguin, 2017.

Arscott, Caroline. *William Morris and Edward Burne-Jones: Interlacings*. New Haven, CT: Yale University Press, 2008.

Atkinson, David. "The English Revival Canon: Child Ballads and the Invention of Tradition." *Journal of American Folklore* 114/453 (2001): 370–80.

———. "Folk Songs in Print: Text and Tradition." *Folk Music Journal* 8/4 (2004): 456–83.

Atkinson, David, and Steve Roud, eds. *Street Ballads in Nineteenth-Century Britain, Ireland, and North America: The Interface between Print and Oral Traditions*. London: Routledge, 2016.

Axon, William A. E. *Folk Song and Folk-Speech of Lancashire: On the Ballads and Songs of the County Palatine*. Manchester: Tubbs & Brook, 1870.

Bachelard, Gaston. *The Poetics of Space*. Translated by Maria Jolas. New York: Penguin, 2014.

Bailey, Peter. *Leisure and Class in Victorian England: Rational Recreation and the Contest for Control, 1830–1885*. London: Routledge & Kegan Paul, 1978.

———. *Popular Culture and Performance in the Victorian City*. Cambridge: Cambridge University Press, 1998.

Bailey, William Whitman. *Botanizing: A Guide to Field-Collecting and Herbarium Work*. Providence, RI: Preston and Rounds Co., 1899.

Baker, Houston A. Jr. *Betrayal: How Black Intellectuals Have Abandoned the Ideals of the Civil Rights Era*. New York: Columbia University Press, 2008.

———. *Blues, Ideology, and Afro-American Literature: A Vernacular Theory*. Chicago: University of Chicago Press, 1984.

———. "Modernism and the Harlem Renaissance." *American Quarterly* 39/1 (1987): 84–97.

———. *Modernism and the Harlem Renaissance*. Chicago: University of Chicago Press, 1987.

Baker, Houston A. Jr., and K. Merinda Simmons, eds. *The Trouble with Post-Blackness*. New York: Columbia University Press, 2015.

Bakunin, Mikhail. *Bakunin on Anarchy: Selected Works by the Activist-Founder of World Anarchism*. Edited by Sam Dolgoff. New York: Vintage, 1971.

Baldwin, Davarian L., and Minkah Makalani, eds. *Escape from New York: The New Negro Renaissance beyond Harlem*. Minneapolis: University of Minnesota Press, 2013.

Balfour, Edward, ed. *Cyclopædia of India and of Eastern and Southern Asia, Commercial, Industrial and Scientific: Products of the Mineral, Vegetable and Animal Kingdoms, Useful Arts and Manufactures*, 2nd ed. Madras: Scottish and Adelphi Presses, 1871.

Ball, Bentley. *The Song-A-Logue of America*. Detroit, MI: Geo. A. Drake & Co. Press, 1922.

Baraka, Amiri [LeRoi Jones]. *Black Music*. New York: William Morrow, 1968.

Baring-Gould, Sabine. *Strange Survivals: Some Chapters in the History of Man*. London: Methuen & Co., 1892.

Baring-Gould, Sabine, and Cecil J. Sharp, eds. *English Folk-Songs for Schools*. London: J. Curwen & Sons., 1906.

Barringer, Tim, and Tom Flynn, eds. *Colonialism and the Object: Empire, Material Culture and the Museum*. London: Routledge, 1998.

Barry, Phillips. "Folk-Music in America." *Journal of American Folk-lore* 22/83 (1909): 72–81.

Barthes, Roland. *Camera Lucida: Reflections on Photography*. Translated by Richard Howard. London: Vintage, 2000.

———. *Mythologies*. London: Vintage, 2009.

———. *Roland Barthes*. Translated by Richard Howard. New York: Hill and Wang, 2010.

Bashford, Alison, and Philippa Levine, eds. *The Oxford Handbook of the History of Eugenics*. New York: Oxford University Press, 2010.

Baudrillard, Jean. *The System of Objects*. Translated by James Benedict. London: Verso, 1996.

Baughan, Edward. "A Plea for Cosmopolitanism." *Monthly Musical Record* 28/326 (1898): 25–26.

Bauman, Zygmunt. *Retrotopia*. Cambridge: Polity Press, 2017.

Baxendale, John. "'. . . into another kind of life in which anything might happen. . .': Popular Music and Late Modernity, 1910–1930." *Popular Music* 14/2 (1995): 137–54.

Baycroft, Timothy, and David M. Hopkin, eds. *Folklore and Nationalism in Europe during the Long Nineteenth Century*. Leiden: Brill, 2012.

Beard, Miriam. "The Tune Hitlerism Beats for Germany: It Sets the Street Vibrating to Wotan and Valhalla and Stirs the 'Unknown Folk' of Village and Countryside." *New York Times*, 7 June 1931, 7 and 21.'

Bearman, C. J. "Cecil Sharp in Somerset: Some Reflections on the Work of David Harker." *Folklore* 113/1 (2002): 11–34.

———. "Kate Lee and the Foundation of the Folk-Song Society." *Folk Music Journal* 7/5 (1999): 627–43.

———. "Percy Grainger, the Phonograph, and the Folk Song Society." *Music & Letters* 84/3 (2003): 434–55.

Beaumont, Matthew, ed. *A Concise Companion to Realism*. Oxford: Wiley-Blackwell, 2010.

———. *Utopia Ltd.: Ideologies of Social Dreaming in England, 1870–1900*. Leiden: Brill, 2005.

Bellamy, Edward. *Looking Backward: 2000–1887*. Oxford: Oxford University Press, 2007.

Bendix, Regina. *In Search of Authenticity: The Formation of Folklore Studies*. Madison: University of Wisconsin Press, 1997.

Benjamin, Walter. *Illuminations*. Translated by Harry Zorn. London: Pimlico, 1999.

Berkowitz, Carin, and Bernard Lightman, eds. *Science Museums in Transition: Cultures of Display in Nineteenth-Century Britain and America*. Pittsburgh, PA: University of Pittsburgh Press, 2017.

Berlin, Edward A. *Ragtime: A Musical and Cultural History*. Berkeley: University of California Press, 1980.

Bevir, Mark. *The Making of British Socialism*. Princeton, NJ: Princeton University Press, 2011.

Bhabha, Homi K. *The Location of Culture*. London: Routledge, 2004.

Bird, John. *Percy Grainger*. Oxford: Oxford University Press, 1999.

Birdsall, Esther K. "Some Notes on the Role of George Lyman Kittredge in American Folklore Studies." *Journal of the Folklore Institute* 10/1–2 (1973): 57–66.

Bithell, Caroline, and Juniper Hill, eds. *The Oxford Handbook of Music Revival*. Oxford: Oxford University Press, 2014.

Blum, Edward J. *W. E. B. Du Bois: American Prophet*. Philadelphia: University of Pennsylvania Press, 2007.

Board of Education. *Suggestions for the Consideration of Teachers and Others Concerned in the Work of Public Elementary Schools*. London: Darling & Son., 1905.

Bohlman, Philip V. *Focus: Music, Nationalism, and the Making of the New Europe*, 2nd ed. New York: Routledge, 2011.

———. *The Study of Folk Music in the Modern World*. Bloomington: Indiana University Press, 1988.

Bonnett, Alastair. *Left in the Past: Radicalism and the Politics of Nostalgia*. New York: Continuum, 2010.

Borgese, G. A. "The Intellectual Origins of Fascism." *Social Research* 1/1 (1934): 458–85.

Born, Georgina, and David Hesmondhalgh, eds. *Western Music and Its Others: Difference, Representation, and Appropriation in Music*. Berkeley: University of California Press, 2000.

Bourgault-Ducoudray, Louis-Albert. *Trente mélodies populaires de Basse-Bretagne*. Paris: Henry Lemoine, 1885.

Boyes, Georgina. *The Imagined Village: Culture, Ideology and the English Folk Revival*, rev. ed. Leeds: No Masters Co-operative, 2010.

Boym, Svetlana. *The Future of Nostalgia*. New York: Basic Books, 2001.

Brady, Erika. *A Spiral Way: How the Phonograph Changed Ethnography*. Jackson: University Press of Mississippi, 1999.

Braunstein, Peter, and Michael W. Doyle, eds. *Imagine Nation: The American Counterculture of the 1960s and '70s*. New York: Routledge, 2002.

Brewer, John. "Microhistory and the Histories of Everyday Life." *Cultural and Social History* 7/1 (2010): 87–109.

Brick, Howard. *Age of Contradiction: American Thought and Culture in the 1960s*. Ithaca, NY: Cornell University Press, 1998.

Broadwood, Lucy E. "On the Collecting of English Folk-Song." *Proceedings of the Musical Association* 31 (1904–05): 89–109.

Broadwood, Lucy E., and J. A. Fuller Maitland, eds. *English County Songs*. London: The Leadenhall Press, 1893.

Brown, Mary Ellen. *Child's Unfinished Masterpiece: The English and Scottish Popular Ballads*. Urbana: University of Illinois Press, 2011.

———. "Placed, Replaced, or Misplaced? The Ballads' Progress." *The Eighteenth Century* 47/2 (2006): 115–29.

Bullivant, Joanna. *Alan Bush, Modern Music, and the Cold War: The Cultural Left in Britain and the Communist Bloc*. Cambridge: Cambridge University Press, 2017.

Burlin, Natalie Curtis. *Negro Folk-Songs, in Four Books*. New York: G. Schirmer, 1918.

Burstow, Henry. *Reminiscences of Horsham: Recollections of Henry Burstow, the Celebrated Bellringer and Songsinger*, edited by William Albery. Norwood, PA: Norwood Editions, 1975.

Camus, Renaud. *Le Grand Remplacement.* Neuilly-sur-Seine: D. Reinharc, 2011.

Cannadine, David. *Class in Britain.* London: Penguin, 2000.

Cantwell, Robert. *Ethnomimesis: Folklife and the Representation of Culture.* Chapel Hill: University of North Carolina Press, 1993.

———. *When We Were Good: The Folk Revival.* Cambridge, MA: Harvard University Press, 1996.

Carey, John. *The Intellectuals and the Masses: Pride and Prejudice Among the Literary Intelligentsia, 1880–1939.* London: Faber and Faber, 1992.

Certeau, Michel de. *Culture in the Plural.* Translated by Tom Conley. Minneapolis: University of Minnesota Press, 1994.

———. *Heterologies: Discourse on the Other.* Translated by Brian Massumi. Minneapolis: University of Minnesota Press, 1986.

———. *The Mystic Fable, Vol.1: The Sixteenth and Seventeenth Centuries.* Translated by Michael B. Smith. Chicago: University of Chicago Press, 1992.

———. *The Possession at Loudun.* Translated by Michael B. Smith. Chicago: University of Chicago Press, 2000.

———. *The Practice of Everyday Life.* Translated by Steven Rendall. Berkeley: University of California Press, 1984.

———. *The Writing of History.* Translated by Tom Conley. New York: Columbia University Press, 1988.

C[hambers]., W[illiam]. "The Jubilee Singers." *Chambers's Journal of Popular Literature, Science, and Art*, 12 January 1878, 17–20.

Chappell, William. *The Ballad Literature and Popular Music of the Olden Time: A History of the Ancient Songs, Ballads, and of the Dance Tunes of England, with Numerous Anecdotes and Entire Ballads.* London: Chappell and Co., 1855.

Charters, Samuel B. *The Country Blues.* New York: Rinehart, 1959.

Chomsky, Noam. *The Essential Chomsky.* Edited by Anthony Arnove. New York: The New Press, 2008.

Claeys, Gregory, ed. *The Cambridge Companion to Utopian Literature.* Cambridge: Cambridge University Press, 2010.

———. *Citizens and Saints: Politics and Anti-Politics in Early British Socialism.* Cambridge: Cambridge University Press, 1989.

———. *Dystopia: A Natural History.* Oxford: Oxford University Press, 2017.

———. "The 'Survival of the Fittest' and the Origins of Social Darwinism." *Journal of the History of Ideas* 61/2 (2000): 223–40.

Clifford, John. *Socialism and the Teaching of Christ* (Fabian Tract No. 78). London: Fabian Society, 1897.

Cochran, Robert. *Louise Pound: Scholar, Athlete, Feminist Pioneer.* Lincoln: University of Nebraska Press, 2009.

Cohen, Ronald D. *Rainbow Quest: The Folk Music Revival and American Society, 1940–1970.* Amherst: University of Massachusetts Press, 2002.

Cohen, Ronald D. and Rachel Clare Donaldson. *Roots of the Revival: American and British Folk Music in the 1950s*. Urbana: University of Illinois Press, 2014.

Cohen, Stuart. *The Likes of Us: Photography and the Farm Security Administration*. Boston, MA: David R. Godine, 2009.

Cole, Peter, David Struthers, and Kenyon Zimmer, eds. *Wobblies of the World: A Global History of the IWW*. London: Pluto Press, 2017.

Cole, Ross. "Industrial Balladry, Mass Culture, and the Politics of Realism in Cold War Britain." *Journal of Musicology* 34/3 (2017): 354–90.

———. "Mastery and Masquerade in the Transatlantic Blues Revival." *Journal of the Royal Musical Association* 143/1 (2018): 173–210.

———. "Notes on Troubling 'The Popular.'" *Popular Music* 37/3 (2018): 392–414.

———. "On the Politics of Folk Song Theory in Edwardian England." *Ethnomusicology* 63/1 (2019): 19–42.

———. "Towards an Ecological History of Music." In *Remixing Music Studies: Essays in Honour of Nicholas Cook*, edited by Ananay Aguilar, Ross Cole, Matthew Pritchard, and Eric Clarke, 194–209. Abingdon, UK: Routledge, 2020.

———. "Vernacular Song and the Folkloric Imagination at the *Fin de Siècle*." *19th-Century Music*, 42/2 (2018): 73–95.

Copper, Bob. *A Song for Every Season: A Hundred Years of a Sussex Farming Family*. London: Heinemann, 1971.

Cramer, Jeffrey S., ed. *I to Myself: An Annotated Selection from the Journal of Henry D. Thoreau*. New Haven, CT: Yale University Press, 2007.

Cray, Ed. *Ramblin' Man: The Life and Times of Woody Guthrie*. New York: W. W. Norton, 2004.

Curwen, J. Spencer. "The Progress of Popular Music." *Contemporary Review* 52 (1887): 236–48.

Czank, James M. "On the Origin of Species-Being: Marx Redefined." *Rethinking Marxism* 24/2 (2012): 316–23.

Davis, Angela Y. *Blues Legacies and Black Feminism: Gertrude "Ma" Rainey, Bessie Smith and Billie Holiday*. New York: Vintage, 1999.

Derrida, Jacques. *Of Grammatology*. Translated by Gayatri Chakravorty Spivak. Baltimore: Johns Hopkins University Press, 1997.

———. *Specters of Marx: The State of the Debt, the Work of Mourning and the New International*. Translated by Peggy Kamuf. New York: Routledge, 1994.

de Val, Dorothy. *In Search of Song: The Life and Times of Lucy Broadwood*. Farnham, UK: Ashgate, 2011.

Dibble, Jeremy. *C. Hubert H. Parry: His Life and Music*. Oxford: Clarendon Press, 1992.

Dirlik, Arif. "Race Talk, Race, and Contemporary Racism." *PMLA* 123/5 (2008): 1363–79.

Dobrenko, Evgeny. *Political Economy of Socialist Realism*. Translated by Jesse M. Savage. New Haven, CT: Yale University Press, 2007.

Dolan, Emily I. "'. . . This Little Ukulele Tells the Truth': Indie Pop and Kitsch Authenticity." *Popular Music* 29/3 (2010): 457–69.

Donald, Robert. "Housing the Poor: Experiments and Problems." *Contemporary Review* 77 (March 1900): 323–33.

Du Bois, W. E. Burghardt. *The Gift of Black Folk: The Negroes in the Making of America*. Boston, MA: The Stratford Co., 1924.

———. *The Souls of Black Folk: Essays and Sketches*. Chicago: A. C. McClurg & Co., 1903.

———. "The Study of the Negro Problems." *Annals of the American Academy of Political and Social Science* 11 (1898): 1–23.

Dubofsky, Melvyn. *We Shall Be All: A History of the Industrial Workers of the World*, edited by Joseph A. McCartin. Urbana: University of Illinois Press, 2000.

Dunlap, James. "Through the Eyes of Tom Joad: Patterns of American Idealism, Bob Dylan, and the Folk Protest Movement." *Popular Music and Society* 29/5 (2006): 549–73.

Dyer, Richard. *White*. London: Routledge, 1997.

Dylan, Bob. *Chronicles: Volume One*. London: Simon & Schuster, 2004.

———. *The Nobel Lecture*. London: Simon & Schuster, 2017.

Easterby-Smith, Sarah. *Cultivating Commerce: Cultures of Botany in Britain and France, 1760–1815*. Cambridge: Cambridge University Press, 2018.

Eliot, T. S. "The Ballet." *The Criterion* 3/11 (April 1925): 441–43.

Ellingson, Ter. *The Myth of the Noble Savage*. Berkeley: University of California Press, 2001.

Ellis, Katharine. *Interpreting the Musical Past: Early Music in Nineteenth-Century France*. New York: Oxford University Press, 2005.

Ellison, Ralph. *Invisible Man*. London: Penguin, 2001.

———. *Shadow and Act*. New York: Vintage International, 1995.

Elsner, John, and Roger Cardinal, eds. *The Cultures of Collecting*. London: Reaktion, 1994.

Emerson, Ken. *Doo-dah! Stephen Foster and the Rise of American Popular Culture*. New York: Simon & Schuster, 1997.

Emerson, Ralph Waldo. *Nature and Selected Essays*. Edited by Larzer Ziff. New York: Penguin, 2003.

Engels, Frederick. *Socialism: Utopian and Scientific*. Translated by Edward Aveling. London: Swan Sonnenschein & Co, 1892.

Epstein, Dena J. *Sinful Tunes and Spirituals: Black Folk Music to the Civil War*. Urbana: University of Illinois Press, 1977.

Evans, Dylan. *An Introductory Dictionary of Lacanian Psychoanalysis*. London: Routledge, 1996.

Evans, Richard J. *The Coming of the Third Reich*. New York: Penguin, 2003.

Fabian, Johannes. *Time and the Other: How Anthropology Makes Its Object*. New York: Columbia University Press, 2014.

Fabre, Geneviève, and Michel Feith, eds. *Jean Toomer and the Harlem Renaissance*. New Brunswick, NJ: Rutgers University Press, 2001.

Fanon, Frantz. *Black Skin, White Masks*. Translated by Charles Lam Markmann. London: Pluto Press, 2008.

Farebrother, Rachel. "'Adventuring through the Pieces of a Still Unorganized Mosaic": Reading Jean Toomer's Collage Aesthetic in *Cane*." *Journal of American Studies* 40/3 (2006): 503–21.

Faulk, Barry J. *Music Hall & Modernity: The Late-Victorian Discovery of Popular Culture*. Athens: Ohio University Press, 2004.

Feagin, Joe R. *The White Racial Frame: Centuries of Racial Framing and Counter-Framing*, 2nd ed. New York: Routledge, 2013.

Filene, Benjamin. *Romancing the Folk: Public Memory and American Roots Music*. Chapel Hill: University of North Carolina Press, 2000.

Fitzgerald, F. Scott. *The Great Gatsby*. London: Penguin, 2000.

Fitzgerald, Percy. *The Book Fancier; or, The Romance of Book Collecting*. Revised edition. London: Sampson Low, Marston, Searle, & Rivington, 1887.

Flannery, Tim. *Europe: The First 100 Million Years*. London: Penguin, 2019.

Floyd, Samuel A. Jr. *The Power of Black Music: Interpreting Its History from Africa to the United States*. New York: Oxford University Press, 1995.

Foard, Isabel. "The Power of Heredity." *Westminster Review* 151/5 (1899): 538–53.

Ford, Karen Jackson. *Split-Gut Song: Jean Toomer and the Poetics of Modernity*. Tuscaloosa: University of Alabama Press, 2005.

Ford, Phil. "Hip Sensibility in an Age of Mass Counterculture." *Jazz Perspectives* 2/2 (2008): 121–63.

Foucault, Michel. *Discipline and Punish: The Birth of the Prison*. Translated by Alan Sheridan. London: Penguin, 1991.

———. *The Will to Knowledge: The History of Sexuality Volume I*. Translated by Robert Hurley. London: Penguin, 1998.

Fox, Adam. "The Emergence of the Scottish Broadside Ballad in the Late Seventeenth and Early Eighteenth Centuries." *Journal of Scottish Historical Studies* 31/2 (2011): 169–94.

———. *Oral and Literate Culture in England, 1500–1700*. Oxford: Oxford University Press, 2000.

Francmanis, John. "National Music to National Redeemer: The Consolidation of a 'Folk-Song' Construct in Edwardian England." *Popular Music* 21/1 (2002): 1–25.

———. "The Roving Artist: Frank Kidson, Pioneer Song Collector." *Folk Music Journal* 8/1 (2001): 41–66.

Franks, Benjamin, Nathan Jun, and Leonard Williams, eds. *Anarchism: A Conceptual Approach*. New York: Routledge, 2018.

Frith, Simon. "'The Magic That Can Set You Free': The Ideology of Folk and the Myth of the Rock Community." *Popular Music* 1 (1981): 159–68.

Frogley, Alain, and Aiden J. Thompson, eds. *The Cambridge Companion to Vaughan Williams*. Cambridge: Cambridge University Press, 2013.

Frost, Mark. *The Lost Companions and John Ruskin's Guild of St George*. London: Anthem Press, 2014.

Fry, Andy. *Paris Blues: African American Music and French Popular Culture, 1920–1960*. Chicago: University of Chicago Press, 2014.

Fulcher, Jane F. *French Cultural Politics and Music: From the Dreyfus Affair to the First World War*. New York: Oxford University Press, 1999.

Fuller Maitland, J. A. "English Folk-Song." *Times Literary Supplement*, 23 January 1908, 26.

Gammon, Vic. "Folk Song Collecting in Sussex and Surry, 1843–1914." *History Workshop Journal* 10 (1980): 61–89.

———. "'Many Useful Lessons': Cecil Sharp, Education and the Folk Dance Revival, 1899–1924." *Cultural and Social History* 5/1 (2008): 75–97.

———. "'Not Appreciated in Worthing?' Class Expression and Popular Song Texts in Mid-Nineteenth-Century Britain." *Popular Music* 4 (1984): 5–24.

Gandhi, Leela. *Affective Communities: Anticolonial Thought, Fin-de-Siècle Radicalism, and the Politics of Friendship*. Durham, NC: Duke University Press, 2006.

Garabedian, Steven. "Reds, Whites, and the Blues: Lawrence Gellert, 'Negro Songs of Protest,' and the Left-Wing Folk-Song Revival of the 1930s and 1940s." *American Quarterly* 57/1 (2005): 179–206.

Gardiner, Rolf, and Heinz Rocholl, eds. *Britain and Germany: A Frank Discussion Instigated by Members of the Younger Generation*. London: Williams and Norgate, 1928.

Garratt, James. *Music, Culture and Social Reform in the Age of Wagner*. Cambridge: Cambridge University Press, 2010.

Gates, Henry Louis Jr. *The Signifying Monkey: A Theory of African-American Literary Criticism*, 25th anniversary ed. New York: Oxford University Press, 2014.

Gelbart, Matthew. "Allan Ramsay, The Idea of 'Scottish Music,' and the Beginnings of 'National Music' in Europe." *Eighteenth-Century Music* 9/1 (2012): 81–108.

———. *The Invention of "Folk Music" and "Art Music": Emerging Concepts from Ossian to Wagner*. Cambridge: Cambridge University Press, 2007.

Gibson, James J. *The Ecological Approach to Visual Perception*. Boston: Houghton Mifflin, 1979.

Gilroy, Paul. *Against Race: Imagining Political Culture beyond the Color Line*. Cambridge, MA: Belknap Press of Harvard University Press, 2000.

———. *The Black Atlantic: Modernity and Double Consciousness*. London: Verso, 1993.

———. "Sounds Authentic: Black Music, Ethnicity, and the Challenge of a *Changing* Same." *Black Music Research Journal* 11/2 (1991): 111–36.

Gitlin, Todd. *The Sixties: Years of Hope, Days of Rage*, rev. ed. New York: Bantam Press, 1993.

Glennie, J. S. Stuart. "The Principles of the Classification of Folk-Lore." *The Folk-Lore Journal* 4/1 (1886): 75–79.

Goffman, Erving. *Frame Analysis: An Essay on the Organization of Experience*. Cambridge, MA: Harvard University Press, 1974.

Gomme, G. L. "Folk-Lore Terminology." *The Folk-Lore Journal* 2/9 (1884): 285–86.

Gottlieb, Julie V., and Thomas P. Linehan, eds. *The Culture of Fascism: Visions of the Far Right in Britain*. London: I.B. Tauris, 2004.

Gould, Stephen Jay. *The Mismeasure of Man*, rev. and exp. ed. New York: W. W. Norton, 1996.

Graham, William. "*News from Nowhere* by William Morris." *The Economic Journal* 1/3 (1891): 590–94.

Grainger, Percy. "Collecting with the Phonograph." *Journal of the Folk-Song Society* 3/12 (1908): 147–62.

———. "The Impress of Personality in Traditional Singing." *Journal of the Folk-Song Society* 3/12 (1908): 163–66.

———. "Mrs. Burlin's Study of Negro Folk-Music." *New York Times* 14 April 1918, BR5.

Gregor, A. James. *Mussolini's Intellectuals: Fascist Social and Political Thought*. Princeton, NJ: Princeton University Press, 2005.

Gregory, David. "Before the Folk-Song Society: Lucy Broadwood and English Folk Song, 1884–97." *Folk Music Journal* 9/3 (2008): 372–414.

———. "Fakesong in an Imagined Village? A Critique of the Harker-Boyes Thesis." *Musique Folklorique Canadienne* 43/3 (2009): 18–26.

———. *The Late Victorian Folksong Revival: The Persistence of English Melody, 1878–1903*. Lanham, MD: Scarecrow Press, 2010.

———. "Lomax in London: Alan Lomax, the BBC and the Folk-Song Revival in England, 1950–58." *Folk Music Journal* 8/2 (2002): 136–69.

———. *Victorian Songhunters: The Recovery and Editing of English Vernacular Ballads and Folk Lyrics, 1820–1883*. Lanham, MD: Scarecrow Press, 2006.

Griffin, Roger. *The Nature of Fascism*. London: Routledge, 1993.

Grimm, Jacob. *Teutonic Mythology*. Translated by James Steven Stallybrass. Cambridge: Cambridge University Press, 2012.

Groom, Nick. *The Making of Percy's "Reliques."* Oxford: Oxford University Press, 1999.

Groys, Boris. *The Total Art of Stalinism: Avant-Garde, Aesthetic Dictatorship, and Beyond*. Translated by Charles Rougle. Princeton, NJ: Princeton University Press, 1992.

Gummere, Francis B., ed. *Old English Ballads*. Boston, MA: Ginn & Company, 1914.

Guthrie, Woody. *Bound for Glory*. London: Penguin, 2004.

Haines, Christian P. *A Desire Called America: Biopolitics, Utopia, and the Literary Commons*. New York: Fordham University Press, 2019.

Hamilton, Marybeth. *In Search of the Blues: Black Voices, White Visions*. London: Jonathan Cape, 2007.

Hampton, Timothy. *Bob Dylan's Poetics: How the Songs Work*. New York: Zone Books, 2019.

Hanchard, Michael G. *The Spectre of Race: How Discrimination Haunts Western Democracy*. Princeton, NJ: Princeton University Press, 2018.

Handy, W. C. *Father of the Blues: An Autobiography*. Edited by Arna Bontemps. New York: Macmillan, 1944.

Harker, Ben. *Class Act: The Cultural and Political Life of Ewan MacColl*. London: Pluto Press, 2007.

Harker, Dave. "Cecil Sharp in Somerset: Some Conclusions." *Folk Music Journal* 2/3 (1972): 220–40.

———. *Fakesong: The Manufacture of British "Folksong," 1700 to the Present Day*. Milton Keynes: Open University Press, 1985.

Harper-Scott, J. P. E. *The Quilting Points of Musical Modernism: Revolution, Reaction, and William Walton*. Cambridge: Cambridge University Press, 2012.

Harris, Joel Chandler. *Uncle Remus, His Songs and His Sayings: The Folk-Lore of the Old Plantation*. New York: D. Appleton and Company, 1881.

Harris, Jonathan. *Federal Art and National Culture: The Politics of Identity in New Deal America*. Cambridge: Cambridge University Press, 1995.

Harvey, David. *A Brief History of Neoliberalism*. Oxford: Oxford University Press, 2005.

Hawkins, Mike. *Social Darwinism in European and American Thought, 1860–1945: Nature as Model and Nature as Threat*. Cambridge: Cambridge University Press, 1997.

Heidegger, Martin. *Off the Beaten Track*. Translated by Julian Young and Kenneth Haynes. Cambridge: Cambridge University Press, 2002.

Helsinger, Elizabeth. "Poem into Song." *New Literary History* 46/4 (2015): 669–90.

Herder, Johann Gottfried, and Philip V. Bohlman. *Song Loves the Masses: Herder on Music and Nationalism*. Oakland: University of California Press, 2017.

Hight, Eleanor M., and Gary D. Sampson, eds. *Colonialist Photography: Imag(in)ing Race and Place*. New York: Routledge, 2002.

Hill, Sarah. *"Blerwytirhwng?" The Place of Welsh Pop Music*. Abingdon, UK: Ashgate, 2007.

Hirsch, Jerrold. "Modernity, Nostalgia, and Southern Folklore Studies: The Case of John Lomax." *Journal of American Folklore* 105/416 (1992): 183–207.

Hobsbawm, Eric, and Terence Ranger, eds. *The Invention of Tradition*. Cambridge: Cambridge University Press, 1983.

Holland, Owen. *William Morris's Utopianism: Propaganda, Politics, and Prefiguration*. Basingstoke: Palgrave Macmillan, 2017.

Hoppen, K. Theodore. *The Mid-Victorian Generation, 1846–1886*. Oxford: Oxford University Press, 1998.

Huggins, Nathan Irvin. *Harlem Renaissance*, updated ed. New York: Oxford University Press, 2007.

Hughes, Meirion and Robert Stradling. *The English Musical Renaissance, 1840–1940: Constructing a National Music*. Manchester: Manchester University Press, 2001.

Hull, Robert H. "The Folk-Song Movement." *Musical Times* 70/1038 (1929): 711–12.

Hurston, Zora. "Hoodoo in America." *Journal of American Folklore* 44/174 (1931): 317–417.

Hutchinson, George. ed. *The Cambridge Companion to the Harlem Renaissance*. Cambridge: Cambridge University Press, 2007.

———. *The Harlem Renaissance in Black and White*. Cambridge, MA: Belknap Press of Harvard University Press, 1995.

Huyssen, Andreas. *After the Great Divide: Modernism, Mass Culture and Postmodernism*. Basingstoke, UK: Macmillan, 1988.

Ingold, Tim. *Evolution and Social Life*, 2nd ed. Abingdon, UK: Routledge, 2016.

Isserman, Maurice, and Michael Kazin. *America Divided: The Civil War of the 1960s*, 5th ed. New York: Oxford University Press, 2015.

Jacobs, Joseph. "The Folk." *Folklore* 4/2 (1893): 233–38.

Jameson, Fredric. *Archaeologies of the Future: The Desire Called Utopia and Other Science Fictions*. London: Verso, 2005.

Jefferies, Matthew, and Mike Tyldesley, eds. *Rolf Gardiner: Folk, Nature and Culture in Interwar Britain*. Farnham, UK: Ashgate, 2011.

Jensen, Oskar Cox. "The *Travels* of John Magee: Tracing the Geographies of Britain's Itinerant Print-Sellers, 1789–1815." *Cultural and Social History* 11/2 (2014): 195–216.

Jensen, Oskar Cox, David Kennerley, and Ian Newman, eds. *Charles Dibdin and Late Georgian Culture*. Oxford: Oxford University Press, 2018.

Jevons, W. Stanley. "Methods of Social Reform: I—Amusements of the People." *Contemporary Review* 33 (1878): 498–513.

Johnson, Julian. *Out of Time: Music and the Making of Modernity*. New York: Oxford University Press, 2015.

Johnson, Lionel. "*News from Nowhere* by William Morris." *The Academy*, 23 May 1891, 483–84.

Johnson, Matthew. "The Liberal Party and the Navy League in Britain before the Great War." *Twentieth Century British History* 22/2 (2011): 137–63.

Johnson, Walter. *Folk-Memory; or The Continuity of British Archaeology*. Oxford: Clarendon Press, 1908.

Kandiyali, Jan, ed. *Reassessing Marx's Social and Political Philosophy: Freedom, Recognition, and Human Flourishing*. New York: Routledge, 2018.

Karpeles, Maud. *Cecil Sharp: His Life and Work*. London: Faber & Faber, 2008.

———. "The International Folk Music Council." *Journal of the Folklore Institute* 2/3 (1965): 308–13.

Kater, Michael H. *Hitler Youth*. Cambridge, MA: Harvard University Press, 2004.

Katz, Mark. *Capturing Sound: How Technology Has Changed Music*. Berkeley: University of California Press, 2010.

Kaufmann, Eric. *White Shift: Populism, Immigration and the Future of White Majorities*. London: Allen Lane, 2018.

Keel, Frederick. "The Folk Song Society 1898–1948." *Journal of the English Folk Dance and Song Society* 5/3 (1948): 111–26.

Keightley, Keir. "Tin Pan Allegory." *Modernism/modernity* 19/4 (2012): 717–36.

Keil, Charles. *Urban Blues*. Chicago: University of Chicago Press, 1966.

———. "Who Needs 'the Folk'?" *Journal of the Folklore Institute* 15/3 (1978): 263–65

Kellas, James G. *The Politics of Nationalism and Ethnicity*, 2nd ed. Basingstoke, UK: Macmillan, 1998.

Keller, Lisa. *Triumph of Order: Democracy and Public Space in New York and London*. New York: Columbia University Press, 2009.

Kellerer, Sidonie. "Rewording the Past: The Postwar Publication of a 1938 Lecture by Martin Heidegger." *Modern Intellectual History*, 11/3 (2014): 575–602.

Kelley, Robin D. G. "Notes on Deconstructing 'The Folk.'" *American Historical Review* 97/5 (1992): 1400–1408.

Kemp-Welch, A. *Poland under Communism: A Cold War History*. Cambridge: Cambridge University Press, 2008.

Kenney, William Howland. *Recorded Music in American Life: The Phonograph and Popular Memory, 1890–1945*. Oxford: Oxford University Press, 1999.

Kershaw, Ian. *Hitler, The Germans, and the Final Solution*. New Haven, CT: Yale University Press, 2008.

Kevles, Daniel J. *In the Name of Eugenics: Genetics and the Uses of Human Heredity*. Cambridge, MA: Harvard University Press, 1995.

Kidson, Frank. "English Folk-Song." *Musical Times* 49/779 (1908): 23–24.

———. *Traditional Tunes: A Collection of Ballad Airs, Chiefly Obtained in Yorkshire and the South of Scotland; Together with Their Appropriate Words from Broadsides and from Oral Tradition*. Oxford: Chas. Taphouse & Son, 1891.

Kidson, Frank, and Mary Neal. *English Folk-Song and Dance*. Cambridge: Cambridge University Press, 1915.

Kitchen, Fred. *Brother to the Ox: The Autobiography of a Farm Labourer*. Harmondsworth, UK: Penguin, 1983.

Kittredge, George Lyman, and Helen Child Sargent, eds. *English and Scottish Popular Ballads*. London: Harrap, 1904.

Knevett, Arthur, and Vic Gammon. "English Folk Song Collectors and the Idea of the Peasant." *Folk Music Journal* 11/1 (2016): 42–64.

Kramer, Lawrence. *Interpreting Music*. Berkeley: University of California Press, 2011.

———. *Music as Cultural Practice, 1800–1900*. Berkeley: University of California Press, 1990.

Krehbiel, Henry Edward. *Afro-American Folksongs: A Study in Racial and National Music*. New York: G. Schirmer, 1914.

Kripke, Saul A. *Naming and Necessity*. Cambridge, MA: Harvard University Press, 1980.

Kubik, Gerhard. *Africa and the Blues*. Jackson: University Press of Mississippi, 1999.

Kundera, Milan. *The Joke*. Translated by Michael Henry Heim. London: Faber and Faber, 1992.

Kuper, Adam. *The Reinvention of Primitive Society: Transformations of a Myth*, 3rd ed. Abingdon, UK: Routledge, 2017.

Lambert, Constant. *Music Ho! A Study of Music in Decline*. New York: Charles Scribner's Sons, 1934.

Lang, Andrew. "The Folk-Lore of France." *The Folk-Lore Record* 1 (1878): 99–117.

Laqueur, Walter Z. *Young Germany: A History of the German Youth Movement*. New York: Basic Books, 1962.

Latour, Bruno. *We Have Never Been Modern*. Translated by Catherine Porter. Cambridge, MA: Harvard University Press, 1993.

———. "Why Has Critique Run Out of Steam? From Matters of Fact to Matters of Concern." *Critical Inquiry* 30/2 (2004): 225–48.

Lawrence, Jon. "Popular Radicalism and the Socialist Revival in Britain." *Journal of British Studies* 31/2 (1992): 163–86.

———. *Speaking for the People: Party, Language, and Popular Politics in England, 1867–1914*. Cambridge: Cambridge University Press, 1998.

Lebow, Katherine. *Unfinished Utopia: Nowa Huta, Stalinism, and Polish Society, 1949–56*. Ithaca, NY: Cornell University Press, 2013.

Lee, Kate. "Some Experiences of a Folk-Song Collector." *Journal of the Folk-Song Society* 1/1 (1899): 7–12.

Leeson, D. M. *The Black and Tans: British Police and Auxiliaries in the Irish War of Independence, 1920–1921*. Oxford: Oxford University Press, 2011.

Lévi-Strauss, Claude. *The Savage Mind*. Translated by Sybil Wolfram. London: Weidenfeld and Nicolson, 1966.

Levine, Lawrence W. *Black Culture and Black Consciousness: Afro-American Folk Thought from Slavery to Freedom*, 30th anniversary ed. New York: Oxford University Press, 2007.

———. *Highbrow / Lowbrow: The Emergence of Cultural Hierarchy in America*. Cambridge, MA: Harvard University Press, 1988.

Levitas, Ruth. *The Concept of Utopia*. Hemel Hempstead, UK: Philip Allan, 1990.

Lhamon, W. T. Jr. *Raising Cain: Blackface Performance from Jim Crow to Hip Hop*. Cambridge, MA: Harvard University Press, 1998.

Lieberman, Robbie. *"My Song Is My Weapon": People's Songs, American Communism, and the Politics of Culture, 1930–50*. Urbana: University of Illinois Press, 1989.

Lightman, Bernard, and Bennett Zon, eds. *Evolution and Victorian Culture*. Cambridge: Cambridge University Press, 2014.

Linn, Karen. *That Half-Barbaric Twang: The Banjo in American Popular Culture*. Urbana: University of Illinois Press, 1991.

Livingstone, David N., and Charles W. J. Withers, eds. *Geographies of Nineteenth-Century Science*. Chicago: University of Chicago Press, 2011.

Livingston, Tamara E. "Music Revivals: Toward a General Theory." *Ethnomusicology* 43/1 (1999): 66–85.

Lloyd, A. L. *The Singing Englishman: An Introduction to Folksong*. London: Workers' Music Association, 1944.

Lomax, John A. *Adventures of a Ballad Hunter*. New York: Macmillan, 1947.

———. *Cowboy Songs and Other Frontier Ballads*. New York: Sturgis & Walton Company, 1910.

———. "Cowboy Songs of the Mexican Border." *The Sewanee Review* 19/1 (1911): 1–18.

———. "A Quest for American Ballads." *New York Times* 14 May 1910, BR12.

———. "'Sinful Songs' of the Southern Negro." *Musical Quarterly* 20/2 (1934): 177–87.

———. "Some Types of American Folk-Song." *Journal of American Folklore* 28/107 (1915): 1–17.

Lomax, John A., and Alan Lomax. *Negro Folk Songs as Sung by Lead Belly.* New York: Macmillan, 1936.

Lott, Eric. *Love and Theft: Blackface Minstrelsy and the American Working Class*, 20th anniversary ed. New York: Oxford University Press, 2013.

Low, Sidney J. "The Rise of the Suburbs: A Lesson of the Census." *Contemporary Review* 60 (October 1891): 545–58.

Lowenthal, David. *The Heritage Crusade and the Spoils of History*. Cambridge: Cambridge University Press, 1998.

Lyotard, Jean-François. *The Postmodern Condition: A Report on Knowledge.* Translated by Geoff Bennington and Brian Massumi. Minneapolis: University of Minnesota Press, 1984.

MacColl, Ewan. *Journeyman: An Autobiography*. London: Sidgwick and Jackson, 1990.

Macklin, Graham. "'Onward Blackshirts!' Music and the British Union of Fascists." *Patterns of Prejudice* 47/4–5 (2013): 430–57.

Marsh, Christopher. *Music and Society in Early Modern England.* Cambridge: Cambridge University Press, 2010.

Marsh, J. B. T. *The Story of the Jubilee Singers; with Their Songs*, rev. ed. Boston, MA: Houghton, Mifflin and Company, 1880.

Marx, Karl. *Capital: A Critique of Political Economy*. Edited by Frederick Engels. New York: The Modern Library, 1906.

———. *Early Writings*. Translated by Rodney Livingstone and Gregor Benton. London: Penguin, 1992.

Marx, Karl, and Frederick Engels. *The Communist Manifesto*. London: Penguin, 2002.

———. *The German Ideology*. Edited by C. J. Arthur. New York: International Publishers, 1970.

Masefield, John. "On Folk Songs." *The Speaker*, 23 December 1905, 301–2.

McDowell, Paula. *The Invention of the Oral: Print Commerce and Fugitive Voices in Eighteenth-Century Britain*. Chicago: University of Chicago Press, 2017.

McGinley, Paige A. *Staging the Blues: From Tent Shows to Tourism*. Durham, NC: Duke University Press, 2014.

McLane, Maureen N. *Balladeering, Minstrelsy, and the Making of British Romantic Poetry*. Cambridge: Cambridge University Press, 2008.

McLean, Eden K. *Mussolini's Children: Race and Elementary Education in Fascist Italy*. Lincoln: University of Nebraska Press, 2018.

Merton, Ambrose [William Thoms]. "Folk-Lore." *The Athenaeum*, 22 August 1846, 862–63.

Middleton, Richard. *Studying Popular Music*. Milton Keynes, UK: Open University Press, 1990.

———. *Voicing the Popular: On the Subjects of Popular Music*. London: Routledge, 2006.

Miele, Chris, ed. *From William Morris: Building Conservation and the Arts and Crafts Cult of Authenticity, 1877–1939*. New Haven, CT: Yale University Press, 2005.

Miller, Karl Hagstrom. *Segregating Sound: Inventing Folk and Pop Music in the Age of Jim Crow*. Durham, NC: Duke University Press, 2010.

Moore, Allan F. "Authenticity as Authentication"." *Popular Music* 21/2 (2002): 209–23.

Moore, Allan F., and Giovanni Vacca, eds. *Legacies of Ewan MacColl: The Last Interview*. Farnham, UK: Ashgate, 2014.

Morgan, Mary S., ed. *Charles Booth's London Poverty Maps*. London: Thames & Hudson, 2019.

Morris, William. *The Collected Works of William Morris, Volume 12: The Story of Sigurd the Volsung and the Fall of the Niblungs*. Cambridge: Cambridge University Press, 2012.

———. *How I Became a Socialist*. London: Twentieth Century Press, 1896.

———. *News from Nowhere and Other Writings*. Edited by. Clive Wilmer. London: Penguin, 2004.

Morrison, Matthew D. "Race, Blacksound, and the (Re)Making of Musicological Discourse." *Journal of the American Musicological Society* 72/3 (2019): 781–823.

Morton, A. L. *A People's History of England*. London: Victor Gollancz, 1938.

Moses, A. Dirk. "'White Genocide' and the Ethics of Public Analysis." *Journal of Genocide Research* 21/2 (2019): 201–13.

Mullen, Patrick B. "The Dilemma of Representation in Folklore Studies: The Case of Henry Truvillion and John Lomax." *Journal of Folklore Research* 37/2–3 (2000): 155–74.

Mundy, Rachel. "Evolutionary Categories and Musical Style from Adler to America." *Journal of the American Musicological Society* 67/3 (2014): 735–67.

Munslow, Alun. 'Why Should Historians Write about the Nature of History (Rather Than Just Do It)?' *Rethinking History* 11/4 (2007): 613–25.

Mussolini, Benito. "The Political and Social Doctrine of Fascism." Translated by Jane Soames. *Political Quarterly* 4/3 (1933): 341–56.

Myers, Charles S. "*English Folk-Song: Some Conclusions*. By Cecil J. Sharp." *Folklore* 20/1 (1909): 97–101.

———. "A Study of Rhythm in Primitive Music." *British Journal of Psychology* 1/4 (1905): 397–406.

Nagel, Thomas. *The View From Nowhere*. New York: Oxford University Press, 1986.

Napier, James. "Old Ballad Folk-Lore." *The Folk-Lore Record* 2 (1879): 92–126.

Nelson, Cary, and Lawrence Grossberg, eds. *Marxism and the Interpretation of Culture*. Urbana: University of Illinois Press, 1988.

Newman, Ernest. "The Folk-Song Fallacy." *English Review* 11 (1912): 255–68.

———. "The Folk-Song Fallacy: A Rejoinder." *English Review* 12 (1912): 65–70.

Nicholls, David G. *Conjuring the Folk: Forms of Modernity in African America*. Ann Arbor: University of Michigan Press, 2000.

Nietzsche, Friedrich. *Beyond Good and Evil: Prelude to a Philosophy of the Future.* Translated by Judith Norman. Cambridge: Cambridge University Press, 2002.

Nordau, Max. *Entartung.* Edited by Karin Tebben. Berlin: De Gruyter, 2013.

Novak, David, and Matt Sakakeeny, ed. *Keywords in Sound.* Durham, NC: Duke University Press.

O'Gorman, Francis, ed. *The Cambridge Companion to John Ruskin.* Cambridge: Cambridge University Press, 2015.

O'Neill, Michael, and Charles Mahoney, eds. *Romantic Poetry: An Annotated Anthology.* Malden, MA: Blackwell, 2008.

Oliver, Paul. *Blues Fell This Morning: The Meaning of the Blues.* London: Cassell, 1960.

Ollman, Bertell. *Alienation: Marx's Conception of Man in a Capitalist Society,* 2nd ed. Cambridge: Cambridge University Press, 1976.

Omi, Michael, and Howard Winant, *Racial Formation in the United States,* 3rd ed. New York: Routledge, 2015.

Paddison, Max. *Adorno's Aesthetics of Music.* Cambridge: Cambridge University Press, 1993.

Palmer, Roy. "'Veritable Dunghills': Professor Child and the Broadside." *Folk Music Journal* 7/2 (1996): 155–66.

Pamuk, Orhan. *The Innocence of Objects: The Museum of Innocence, Istanbul.* Translated by Ekin Oklap. New York: Abrams, 2012.

———. *The Museum of Innocence.* Translated by Maureen Freely. London: Faber and Faber, 2009.

Parry, Hubert. *The Evolution of the Art of Music.* London: K. Paul, Trench, Trübner, 1896.

———. "Inaugural Address." *Journal of the Folk-Song Society* 1/1 (1899): 1–3.

———. "The Present Condition of English Song-Writing." *The Century Guild Hobby Horse* 2/10 (1888): 69–70.

———. *Style in Musical Art.* London: Macmillan, 1911.

Partington, John S., ed. *The Life, Music and Thought of Woody Guthrie: A Critical Appraisal.* Abingdon, UK: Routledge, 2011.

Paxton, Robert O. *The Anatomy of Fascism.* London: Penguin, 2005.

Peabody, Charles. "The English Folk-Dance Society and Its Work." *Journal of American Folk-Lore* 28/109 (1915): 316–17.

Pearce, Susan M. *On Collecting: An Investigation into Collecting in the European Tradition.* London: Routledge, 1995.

Peart, Andrew. "'The Abstract Pathos of Song': Carl Sandburg, John Lomax, and the Modernist Revival of Folksong." *New Literary History* 46/4 (2015): 691–714.

Perren, Richard. *Agriculture in Depression, 1870–1940.* Cambridge: Cambridge University Press, 1995.

Petrov, Petre. "The Industry of Truing: Socialist Realism, Reality, Realization." *Slavic Review* 70 (2011): 873–92.

Pickering, Michael. *Blackface Minstrelsy in Britain.* Aldershot, UK: Ashgate, 2008.

Pinny, Christopher, and Nicolas Peterson, eds. *Photography's Other Histories*. Durham, NC: Duke University Press, 2003.

Ponsonby, Dorothea. "Hubert Parry." *Musical Times* 97/1359 (1956): 263.

Porterfield, Nolan. *Last Cavalier: The Life and Times of John A. Lomax, 1867–1948*. Urbana: University of Illinois Press, 1996.

Potter, Pamela. "Musicology under Hitler: New Sources in Context." *Journal of the American Musicological Society* 49/1 (1996): 70–113.

Pound, Louise. "The Pedigree of a 'Western' Song." *Modern Language Notes* 29/1 (1914): 30–31.

———. *Poetic Origins and the Ballad*. New York: Macmillan, 1921.

———. "The Southwestern Cowboy Songs and the English and Scottish Popular Ballads." *Modern Philology* 11/2 (1913): 195–207.

———. "The Term 'Communal.'" *PMLA* 39/2 (1924): 440–54.

Prince, K. Stephen. *Stories of the South: Race and the Reconstruction of Southern Identity, 1865–1915*. Chapel Hill: University of North Carolina Press, 2014.

Proust, Marcel. *In Search of Lost Time, V: The Captive; The Fugitive*. Translated by C. K. Scott Moncrieff and Terence Kilmartin, rev. D. J. Enright. London: Vintage, 2000.

Radano, Ronald. *Lying up a Nation: Race and Black Music*. Chicago: University of Chicago Press, 2003.

Radano, Ronald, and Philip V. Bohlman, eds. *Music and the Racial Imagination*. Chicago: University of Chicago Press, 2000.

Radano, Ronald, and Tejumola Olaniyan, eds. *Audible Empire: Music, Global Politics, Critique*. Durham, NC: Duke University Press, 2015.

Rancière, Jacques. *The Emancipated Spectator*. Translated by Gregory Elliott. London: Verso, 2009.

———. *The Future of the Image*. Translated by Gregory Elliott. London: Verso, 2007.

Rehding, Alexander. "The Quest for the Origins of Music in Germany Circa 1900." *Journal of the American Musicological Society* 53/2 (2000): 345–85.

Reich, Wilhelm. *The Mass Psychology of Fascism*. Translated by Vincent R. Carfagno. New York: The Noonday Press, 1970.

Reuss, Richard A., with JoAnne C. Reuss. *American Folk Music and Left-Wing Politics, 1927–57*. Lanham, MD: Scarecrow Press, 2000.

Riley, Charles A. *Free as Gods: How the Jazz Age Reinvented Modernism*. Hanover, NH: ForeEdge, An imprint of University Press of New England, 2017.

Roach, Joseph. *Cities of the Dead: Circum-Atlantic Performance*. New York: Columbia University Press, 1996.

Robertson, Michael. *The Last Utopians: Four Late 19th-Century Visionaries and their Legacy*. Princeton, NJ: Princeton University Press, 2018.

Robinson, Suzanne, and Kay Dreyfus, eds. *Grainger the Modernist*. Abingdon, UK: Routledge, 2016.

Roe, Nicholas. *Wordsworth and Coleridge: The Radical Years*, 2nd ed. Oxford: Oxford University Press, 2018.

Rollefson, J. Griffith. "'He's Calling His Flock Now': Black Music and Postcoloniality from Buddy Bolden's New Orleans to Sefyu's Paris." *American Music* 33/3 (2015): 375–97.

Rosenberg, Neil V., ed. *Transforming Tradition: Folk Music Revivals Examined*. Urbana: University of Illinois Press, 1993.

Roszak, Theodore. *The Making of a Counter Culture: Reflections on the Technocratic Society and Its Youthful Opposition*. Berkeley: University of California Press, 1995.

Roud, Steve. *Folk Song in England*. London: Faber & Faber, 2017.

Roy, William G. *Reds, Whites, and Blues: Social Movements, Folk Music, and Race in the United States*. Princeton, NJ: Princeton University Press, 2010.

Rudy, Jill Terry. "American Folklore Scholarship, Tales of the North American Indians, and Relational Communities." *Journal of American Folklore* 126/499 (2013): 3–30.

Rummel, R. J. *Death by Government*. New Brunswick, NJ: Transaction Publishers, 1994.

Rusch, Frederik L., ed. *A Jean Toomer Reader: Selected Unpublished Writings*. New York: Oxford University Press, 1993.

Ruskin, John. *Praeterita: Outlines of Scenes and Thoughts Perhaps Worthy of Memory in My Past Life*, Volume 1. London: George Allen, 1907.

———. *Selected Writings*. Edited by Dinah Birch. Oxford: Oxford University Press, 2004.

———. *The Seven Lamps of Architecture*. 6th ed. Sunnyside, Orpington: George Allen, 1889.

———. *The Stones of Venice, Volume the Second: The Sea-Stories*. London: Smith, Elder and Co., 1867.

Russell, Dave. *Popular Music in England, 1840–1914*, 2nd ed. Manchester: Manchester University Press, 1997.

Russell, Ian, and David Atkinson, eds. *Folk Song: Tradition, Revival, and Re-Creation*. Aberdeen: University of Aberdeen Press, 2004.

Said, Edward W. *Culture and Imperialism*. London: Vintage, 1994.

———. *Orientalism*. London: Penguin, 2003.

Samuel, Raphael, ed. *People's History and Socialist Theory*. London: Routledge & Kegan Paul, 1981.

Saylor, Eric. *English Pastoral Music: From Arcadia to Utopia, 1900–1955*. Urbana: University of Illinois Press, 2017.

Scarborough, Dorothy. "American Ballads and Folksongs: The Lomax Collection Brings Together Chanteys, Spirituals, Mountain 'Lonesomes' and Desperado Ballads." *New York Times*, 11 November 1934, 2.

Schafer, R. Murray. *The Soundscape: Our Sonic Environment and the Tuning of the World*. Rochester, VT: Destiny Books, 1994.

Schenbeck, Lawrence. *Racial Uplift and American Music, 1878–1943*. Jackson: University Press of Mississippi, 2012.

Schneer, Jonathan. *London 1900: The Imperial Metropolis*. New Haven, CT: Yale University Press, 1999.

Schofield, Derek. "Sowing the Seeds: Cecil Sharp and Charles Marson in Somerset in 1903." *Folk Music Journal* 8/4 (2004): 484–512.

Scholes, Percy A. "Cecil Sharp." *Observer*, 29 June 1924, 10.

Schroeder, Patricia R. "Passing for Black: Coon Songs and the Performance of Race." *Journal of American Culture* 33/2 (2010): 139–53.

Schumacher, Michael. *There But for Fortune: The Life of Phil Ochs*. Minneapolis: University of Minnesota Press, 2018.

Scott, Derek B. *From the Erotic to the Demonic: On Critical Musicology*. Oxford: Oxford University Press, 2003.

———. *Sounds of the Metropolis: The Nineteenth-Century Popular Music Revolution in London, New York, Paris, and Vienna*. New York: Oxford University Press, 2008.

Searle, G. R. *A New England? Peace and War, 1886–1918*. Oxford: Oxford University Press, 2004.

Seery, John E., ed. *A Political Companion to Walt Whitman*. Lexington: University Press of Kentucky, 2011.

Service, Hugo. *Germans to Poles: Communism, Nationalism and Ethnic Cleansing after the Second World War*. Cambridge: Cambridge University Press, 2013.

Sharp, Cecil J. *English Folk-Song: Some Conclusions*. London: Simpkin & Co., 1907.

———. "Folk-Dancing in Elementary and Secondary Schools." *School Music Review* 1 (December 1912): 162–65.

———. "Folk-Song Collecting." *Musical Times* 48/767 (1907): 16–18.

———. "'The Folk-Song Fallacy': A Reply." *English Review* 12 (1912): 542–50.

———. "Folk-Songs Noted in Somerset and North Devon." *Journal of the Folk-Song Society* 2/6 (1905): 1–60.

———. "Some Characteristics of English Folk-Music." *Folklore* 19/2 (1908): 132–52.

Sharp, Cecil J., and Charles L. Marson, eds. *Folk Songs from Somerset*. London: Simpkin & Co., 1904.

Sharp, Cecil J., and A. P. Oppé. *The Dance: An Historical Survey of Dancing in Europe*. London: Halton and Truscott Smith Ltd., 1924.

Shaw, George Bernard. "Belloc and Chesterton." *The New Age*, 15 February 1908, 309–11.

———, ed. *Fabian Essays in Socialism*. London: Fabian Society 1889.

Shelemay, Kay Kaufman. "Musical Communities: Rethinking the Collective in Music." *Journal of the American Musicological Society* 64/2 (2011): 349–90.

Slater, J. H. *The Romance of Book-Collecting*. London: Elliot Stock, 1898.

Smith, Ayana. "Blues, Criticism, and the Signifying Trickster." *Popular Music* 24/2 (2005): 179–91.

Smith, Justin E. H. *Irrationality: A History of the Dark Side of Reason*. Princeton, NJ: Princeton University Press, 2019.

Soloway, Richard. *Demography and Degeneration: Eugenics and the Declining Birthrate in Twentieth-Century Britain*. Chapel Hill: University of North Carolina Press, 1995.

Sontag, Susan. *On Photography*. London: Penguin, 1977.

———. "What's Happening to America (A Symposium)." *Partisan Review* 34/1 (1967): 51–58.

Sotiropoulos, Karen. *Staging Race: Black Performers in Turn of the Century America*. Cambridge, MA: Harvard University Press, 2006.

Spencer, Herbert. "The Origin of Music." *Mind* 15/60 (1890): 449–68.

Sternhell, Zeev. *The Anti-Enlightenment Tradition*. Translated by David Maisel. New Haven, CT: Yale University Press, 2010.

———. *Neither Right nor Left: Fascist Ideology in France*. Translated by David Maisel. Princeton, NJ: Princeton University Press, 1986.

Sternhell, Zeev, with Mario Sznajder and Maia Asheri. *The Birth of Fascist Ideology: From Cultural Rebellion to Political Revolution*. Translated by David Maisel. Princeton, NJ: Princeton University Press, 1994.

Stumpf, Carl. *The Origins of Music*. Translated by David Trippett. Oxford: Oxford University Press, 2012.

Sutherland, Gillian. *In Search of the New Woman: Middle-Class Women and Work in Britain 1870–1914*. Cambridge: Cambridge University Press, 2015.

Tackley, Catherine. *The Evolution of Jazz in Britain, 1880–1935*. Aldershot, UK: Ashgate, 2005.

Taussig, Charles William, and Theodore Arthur Meyer. *The Book of Hobbies, or A Guide to Happiness*. New York: A. L. Burt Company, 1924.

Taussig, Michael. *Mimesis and Alterity: A Particular History of the Senses*. Abingdon, UK: Routledge, 2018.

Thompson, E. P. *The Making of the English Working Class*. London: Gollancz, 1963.

———. *William Morris: Romantic to Revolutionary*. Oakland: PM Press, 2011.

Thompson, Katrina Dyonne. *Ring Shout, Wheel About: The Racial Politics of Music and Dance in North American Slavery*. Urbana: University of Illinois Press, 2014.

Thoreau, Henry David. *Walden; or, Life in the Woods*. Edited by Jeffry S. Cramer. New Haven, CT: Yale University Press, 2004.

———. *A Week on the Concord and Merrimack Rivers*. New York: Penguin, 1998.

Toomer, Jean. *Cane: A Norton Critical Edition*, 2nd ed. Edited by Rudolph P. Byrd and Henry Louis Gates Jr. New York: W. W. Norton & Company, 2011.

Trotsky, Leon. "The Political Programs of the Petty Bourgeoisie." *The Militant* 5/36 (3 September 1932): 1, 4.

Tylor, E. B. "On the Survival of Savage Thought in Modern Civilization." *Appletons' Journal of Literature, Science and Art* 18–19 (1869): 566, 598.

Vermes, Geza. *Jesus: Nativity—Passion—Resurrection*. London: Penguin, 2010.

Wald, Elijah. *Escaping the Delta: Robert Johnson and the Invention of the Blues*. New York: Amistad, 2004.

Walkowitz, Daniel J. *City Folk: English Country Dance and the Politics of the Folk in Modern America*. New York: New York University Press, 2010.

Wallaschek, Richard. *Primitive Music: An Inquiry into the Origin and Development of Music, Songs, Instruments, Dances, and Pantomimes of Savage Races*. London: Longmans, Green, and Co., 1893.

Wartenberg, Thomas E. "'Species-Being' and 'Human Nature' in Marx." *Human Studies* 5/2 (1982): 77–95.

Washington, Booker T. *Up from Slavery: An Autobiography*. New York: Doubleday & Company, 1901.

Watt, Paul, Derek B. Scott, and Patrick Spedding, eds. *Cheap Print and Popular Song in the Nineteenth Century: A Cultural History of the Songster*. Cambridge: Cambridge University Press, 2017.

Wells, Evelyn K. "Cecil Sharp in America." *Journal of the English Folk Dance and Song Society* 8/4 (1959): 182–85.

Wells, H. G. *A Modern Utopia*. London: Penguin, 2005.

Wendling, Amy E. *Karl Marx on Technology and Alienation*. Basingstoke, UK: Palgrave Macmillan, 2009.

Western, Tom. "'The Age of the Golden Ear': *The Columbia World Library* and Sounding out Post-war Field Recording." *Twentieth-Century Music* 11/2 (2014): 275–300.

Whelan, Lara Baker. *Class, Culture and Suburban Anxieties in the Victorian Era*. New York: Routledge, 2010.

Whewell, William. *The Philosophy of the Inductive Sciences, Founded upon Their History*. New edition. London: John W. Parker, 1847.

White, Hayden. *The Content of the Form: Narrative Discourse and Historical Representation*. Baltimore: Johns Hopkins University Press, 1987.

Whitman, Walt. *Leaves of Grass*. Brooklyn, NY: 1855.

———. *Leaves of Grass*. New York: Wm. E. Chapin & Co, 1867.

Wilde, Oscar. *The Soul of Man Under Socialism and Selected Critical Prose*. Edited by Linda Dowling. London: Penguin, 2001.

Wildt, Michael. *Hitler's* Volksgemeinschaft *and the Dynamics of Racial Exclusion: Violence against Jews in Provincial Germany, 1919–1939*. Translated by Bernard Heise. New York: Berghahn, 2014.

Williams, Christian. *Bob Dylan: In His Own Words*. London: Omnibus Press, 1993.

Williams, Raymond. *The Country and the City*. London: Chatto & Windus, 1973.

———. *Culture and Society, 1780–1950*. London: Chatto & Windus, 1958.

———. *Keywords: A Vocabulary of Culture and Society*. London: Fourth Estate, 2014.

Wordsworth, William. *The Major Works*. Edited by Stephen Gill. Oxford: Oxford University Press, 2008.

Work, John Wesley. *Folk Song of the American Negro*. Nashville, TN: Press of Fisk University, 1915.

Yanni, Carla. *Nature's Museums: Victorian Science and the Architecture of Display*. Baltimore, MD: Johns Hopkins University Press, 1999.

Yates, Michael. "Percy Grainger and the Impact of the Phonograph." *Folk Music Journal* 4/3 (1982): 265–75.

Yeo, Richard. *Defining Science: William Whewell, Natural Knowledge, and Public Debate in Early Victorian Britain*. Cambridge: Cambridge University Press, 1993.

Yoxall, J. H. *The ABC about Collecting*. London: London Opinion Curio Club, 1908.

Žižek, Slavoj. *For They Know Not What They Do: Enjoyment as a Political Factor*. London: Verso, 2008.

———. *The Sublime Object of Ideology*. London: Verso, 2008.

Zon, Bennett. *Evolution and Victorian Musical Culture*. Cambridge: Cambridge University Press, 2017.

———. *Representing Non-Western Music in Nineteenth-Century Britain*. Rochester, NY: University of Rochester Press, 2007.

Zumwalt, Rosemary L. *American Folklore Scholarship: A Dialogue of Dissent*. Bloomington: Indiana University Press, 1988.

# Index

Founded in 1893,
UNIVERSITY OF CALIFORNIA PRESS
publishes bold, progressive books and journals on topics in the arts, humanities, social sciences, and natural sciences—with a focus on social justice issues—that inspire thought and action among readers worldwide.

The UC PRESS FOUNDATION
raises funds to uphold the press's vital role as an independent, nonprofit publisher, and receives philanthropic support from a wide range of individuals and institutions—and from committed readers like you. To learn more, visit ucpress.edu/supportus.